Finnigans, Slaters
—·and
Stonepeggers

A History of the Irish in Vermont

Finnigans, Slaters
and
Stonepeggers

A History of the Irish in Vermont

Vincent E. Feeney

IMAGES FROM THE PAST

Bennington, Vermont

Front cover: Burlington waterfront, c.1870. (Courtesy of Special Collections, University of Vermont.)

Back cover: Honora McCarthy on a Bennington County road in the 1890s. (Courtesy of Images from the Past.)

Library of Congress Cataloging-in-Publication Data

Feeney, Vincent.
  Finnigans, slaters, and stonepeggers : a history of the Irish in Vermont/
Vincent E. Feeney. — 1st ed.
    p. cm.
  Includes bibliographical references and index.
  ISBN 978-1-884592-52-2
  1. Irish—Vermont—History. 2. Irish Americans—Vermont—History.
  I. Title. II. Title: History of the Irish in Vermont.
  F60.I6F44 2009
  974.3'0049162—dc22
                                        2009032260

ISBN 9781884592522 paperback

First edition, First printing

Published by Images from the Past, Inc.
www.imagesfromthepast.com
PO Box 137, Bennington VT 05201
Tordis Ilg Isselhardt, Publisher

Printed in the USA
Design and Production: Toelke Associates, Chatham, NY
Printer: Versa Press, Inc., East Peoria, IL

For Carlen,

an Irish Vermonter

The Constitution of the United States was only three years old when Honora McCarthy was born in Drimoleague, County Cork, Ireland, in 1790. A well-known resident of Shaftsbury, Vermont, McCarthy emigrated to America shortly before the Great Famine of 1845–48 and was over a hundred years old when she posed for this photograph in the 1890s on a Bennington County road. She died in 1905.

CONTENTS

Preface and Acknowledgments

This book came about because of two interests of mine—Ireland and Vermont. The first came naturally enough: all four of my grandparents left Ireland in the first decade of the twentieth century and settled in San Francisco. Growing up in a large Irish family, I was surrounded with reminders of the old country, from some of the odd words and phrases used by family members—leather shoes were always "brogues"—to summer picnics of the Rebel Cork Benevolent Association, to the annual pilgrimage to Holy Cross Cemetery to visit the grave of Father Peter Yorke, San Francisco's popular Irish labor leader. The arrival of the occasional letter with its Eire stamp in Celtic script further reminded me that our family had connections to a land far away. How could one not wonder about that almost mythical place across the broad Atlantic?

My interest in Vermont is less direct. In 1966 I began working toward a master's degree in history at the University of Vermont. Why UVM?—almost pure chance. As a native Californian with limited experience outside the state—it is, after all, a big state—I wanted to see more of the country. And it was New England that topped my list of places to spend some time in. For an American interested in history, New England has a particular appeal: America was virtually born there; there the Pilgrims first landed; the American Revolution took root in Boston; and New England was home to the transcendentalist movement. When I asked a college friend who had been raised in Massachusetts where he would recommend I go in New England, he unhesitatingly replied "Vermont." Thus, in 1966, with little knowledge of the Northeast—I thought Vermont had beachfront on the Atlantic

Ocean—I landed in the Green Mountains. Except for a two-year tour in the Army and further graduate study in the West, I have been here ever since.

Though I was aware of the well-known Irish presence in Massachusetts, I initially thought of Vermont as quintessentially Yankee land, an image that organizations involved in promoting Green Mountain tourism, like *Vermont Life* magazine, had made every effort to maintain. But while I was teaching a course in modern Irish history at the University of Vermont over the years, my impression of "Yankee" Vermont began to change. There were too many Irish Vermonters in my classes—Howrigans, Leahys, Donovans, O'Rourkes, Eustaces, and others—for there not to be a large Irish community in the state. I was curious. Who were they, and what were they doing here?

Histories of Vermont were of little help. Until recently historians have overlooked the ethnic history of the Green Mountain State. Assessing the status of Vermont historiography in 1981, historian Tom Bassett wrote that "Immigrants who were refugees from the rural poverty of Quebec or Ireland . . . found nothing written in Vermont history to say that they counted." Indeed, in the numerous town histories written in the 1880s and 1890s, long after the Irish had settled in the state in large numbers, there is barely a mention of an Irish man or woman. They were invisible, living their lives amid Yankee neighbors, but unseen by them.

Until recently all that was written about the Vermont Irish was contained in two books about early Vermont's most famous Irishman, Matthew Lyon, and four brief articles on scattered Irish topics. Michael O'Brien of New York wrote two of the articles back in the early 1900s, but he barely scratched the surface of his subject. Then, for fifty years there was nothing, until in 1960 James O'Beirne, a professor of history at St. Michael's College in Colchester, published an article in *Vermont History* titled "Some Early Irish in Vermont," which at least recognized that there were Irish men and women living in Vermont in the early 1800s. This was followed in 1966 by Tom Bassett's "Irish Migration to Vermont before the Famine," which added to O'Beirne's findings. Unfortunately, Bassett's paper was published in the *Chittenden County Historical Society's Bulletin*, a newsletter with limited distribution. Following Bassett's work there was an almost thirty-year period in which again nothing appeared on the Irish in Vermont.

Beginning in the early 1990s, things began to change. In 1993 Brian Walsh, a social studies teacher in Essex Junction, making use of U.S. census records, wrote a UVM master's thesis on the Irish in nineteenth-century Burlington—"Dreams Realized? Irish-Americans and Progress, Burlington, Vermont, 1830–1910." Walsh's work documented the large numbers of Irish living in the Queen City in the 1800s. Then in 2003 retired Johnson State College professor John Duffy, working with Irishman Eugene Coyle, brought to light the little-known career of Irish land speculator and Loyalist Crean Brush in a *Vermont History* article, "Crean Brush vs. Ethan Allen: A Winner's Tale." In 2006 my "Pre-Famine Irish in Vermont, 1815–1844" appeared in *Vermont History*. In slightly altered form it is chapter two in this volume. Finally, in 2008 appeared *Ballykilcline Rising*, Mary Lee Dunn's study of evicted tenants from a village in County Roscommon who eventually settled in Rutland, Vermont.

In this book I have tried to catch the broad spectrum of the Irish experience in Vermont, touching on various aspects of the story from the colonial period down to 1950. At times I relate simple historical "facts," and at others I delve into folklore, music, and even linguistics. In all cases the story has been shaped by the information available. Where the sources are rich, the story is detailed and colorful; where information is scarce, the narrative is necessarily thin. Sadly, all too often the sources are mute, and we are left to speculate on what that silence is concealing.

Because there has been so little written on the subject, my research had to rely principally on primary sources: U.S. census reports, memoirs, family documents, newspapers, and personal interviews. Many of my findings came from close scrutiny of the U.S. census manuscript schedules—that is, copies of the actual tally sheets used by census enumerators as they went door to door collecting information. They are an invaluable source of information, although my experience is that they tend to underreport, particularly in the earlier years. For convenience I used the manuscript schedules available online from Heritage Quest rather than traveling back and forth to the Bailey/Howe Library at UVM, a distance of fifty miles from my home. Thus my census information is as good as the enumerators' diligence and Heritage Quest's completeness.

In the course of my research, many people provided information and encouragement. Chief among them was Peter Patten, a lifelong Fair Haven resident with a wealth of stories and anecdotes about the Irish of Rutland County. When he's not preparing to run marathons, he can be found doing research on his area's colorful past. Thanks, Peter. Farther north, in Fairfield, Tom Howrigan, a retired country physician who likes to say he was a doctor much of his life but a farmer all of his life, introduced me to the many Irish families still living in that beautiful part of the state. Mary Collins, the descendant of early Irish settlers in northern Vermont, provided me much information about her family's history. Gerald Heffernan filled me in on the colorful story of the Little Ireland community in Starksboro. John Leddy, the keeper of much information about his large Burlington family, provided me with documents shedding light on his ancestors.

John Duffy, professor emeritus at Johnson State College, read early drafts of a number of chapters and provided sound advice and fruitful research leads. Jeff Marshall's staff in Special Collections at the University of Vermont's Bailey/Howe

Library helped greatly, as did Paul Carnahan and Marjorie Strong at the Vermont Historical Society Library in Barre.

Tordis Isselhardt and her team at Images from the Past took my rough manuscript and vastly improved it. Editor Glenn Novak spent hours correcting my numerous grammatical mistakes and making suggestions that enhanced the narrative. Researcher Jill Hays tracked down a number of obscure images that now grace these pages, and Ron Toelke through his design and computer skills made the book visually appealing. I thank you all. Lastly, but certainly not least, Carlen Finn offered good counsel as I struggled with matters of composition, advised me on technical matters when the mystifying workings of a computer stumped me, and offered a seasoned ear to the flow of the manuscript. Happily, she also has the patience to be my wife.

Of course, even with the help of all these good people, whatever errors are contained herein are exclusively my own.

Because Vermont townships are constantly referred to in this study, perhaps a note explaining what a New England township is would be useful, particularly to those unfamiliar with the history of the region. A township is a geographic unit, roughly six miles on a side, for a total of thirty-six square miles. It need not be, as we might think of a town, a densely inhabited area with main streets, side streets, churches, schools, and shops. In fact, many townships in Vermont consist primarily of farm or forest land, with most of the inhabitants residing in one or two small villages within the township. Thus in the nineteenth century, for example, most of the town of Colchester was farmland, while the great majority of inhabitants lived in Winooski village. This led to a two-tier system of government, village and town, the two often at odds with each other because of different priorities.

Now, on to the story. Let's begin with Michael O'Brien, the researcher who first tried to bring to the attention of the American historical community the large number of Irish who resided in New England in its earliest days.

Vincent E. Feeney
Marshfield, Vermont

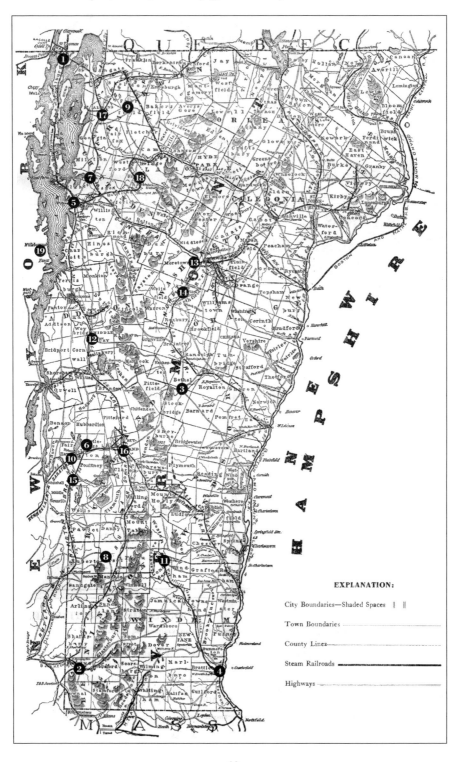

EXPLANATION:

City Boundaries—Shaded Spaces ‖ ‖

Town Boundaries

County Lines

Steam Railroads

Highways

Selected Towns

1. Alburg
2. Bennington
3. Bethel
4. Brattleboro
5. Burlington
6. Castleton
7. Colchester
8. Dorset
9. Fairfield
10. Fair Haven
11. Londonderry
12. Middlebury
13. Moretown
14. Northfield
15. Poultney
16. Rutland
17. St. Albans
18. Underhill
19. Willsboro (New York)

The Irish in Frontier Vermont: 1760–1815

I n many respects Michael J. O'Brien was a typical Irish immigrant living in New York City. He had been born in Fermoy, County Cork, in 1870, received the equivalent of a high school education, and emigrated to the United States while still a teenager. In 1889 he took a job in the accounting section of the Western Union Company. Steady and persevering, he worked for Western Union for the next forty-seven years, retiring in 1936. Along the way he married and raised two daughters. If these few facts had been the summation of his life's accomplishments, his biography would be of little interest to us; but early in life Michael J. O'Brien determined to revise American history.[1]

In his spare time—in the evenings, weekends, and on vacations—O'Brien researched and wrote about the Irish who settled in America in the colonial period. What drove him was the knowledge that the then widely held belief that few Irishmen lived in America in the seventeenth and eighteenth centuries was wrong. Perhaps "drove" is too tame a word—"enraged" might be better. He expressed his frustration with the historical establishment in a talk to the American Irish Historical Society in New York in 1919. Criticizing American historians for failing to acknowledge the role played by the Irish in helping to found the United States, he charged that "whatever evasive references are made to the Irish pioneers in America have been written mainly by persons whose minds were warped by religious or perhaps racial prejudices, and some of them, to my certain knowledge, suppressed the truth when they found it." To set the record straight, O'Brien traveled the eastern seaboard studying land documents, marriage and birth records, muster rolls—anything that might shed light on the ethnicity of British America's early settlers. The results of O'Brien's research appeared in dozens of articles and in a handful of books. Much to the chagrin of some academic historians, he showed, on the one hand, that there was a large Irish presence in colonial America and, on the other, that the Irish played a significant role in the fight for American independence.[2]

In the main, O'Brien left Vermont out of his research. Most of his work concentrated on New York, Massachusetts, Connecticut, New Jersey, Pennsylvania, and Maryland—old established British colonies. He devoted only two short articles to Vermont.[3] Together they totaled just ten pages in the *Journal of the American Irish Historical Society* and the *Recorder*. His lack of attention to Vermont is understandable. Prior to 1777 there was no Vermont: there was simply a heavily forested mountainous region claimed by both New York and New Hampshire—land that until 1763 formed a contested buffer zone between New France and New England. Only bands of Abenaki Indians and a few hardy settlers scattered near the Massachusetts line or along the Connecticut River resided in the Green Mountain wilderness. Perhaps because Vermont joined the United States late—in 1791 as the fourteenth state—O'Brien may simply not have thought of it as old New England and therefore paid it little attention. Or logistics may have played a part. In the opening decades of the twentieth century, when O'Brien did his research, traveling from New York City to Vermont required more than a weekend trip. Whatever the reasons, O'Brien's omission helped perpetuate the myth that only people of Yankee stock settled in Vermont.

Had O'Brien looked deeper into Vermont's past, he would have come across numerous Irish. Their names are found on old deeds, engraved on gray, crumbling tombstones, or mentioned in long-forgotten leather-covered town histories. A history of Rutland, for example, notes that the town's first landowner was Irishman John Murray, a resident of Rutland, Massachusetts, who bought land in this Green Mountain township in 1761 and probably gave the town its name. Abby Hemenway, a nineteenth-century chronicler of Vermont's past, noted that in 1783 the Baptist church in Ira, just west of Rutland, counted a Thomas O'Brien among its members. In the papers of the Allen family—a family made famous by the exploits of its eldest son, Ethan—is a deed from one Patrick Obrion to Ira Allen dated July 27, 1785, selling the latter two shares of land in the town of Irasburg. During the War of 1812, when the U.S. government required that all residents of the United States born abroad be registered, Burney McMeecham of Pownal in the southwest corner of the state signed up, listing his place of birth as Ireland and noting that he came to this country in 1784. Clearly, not all pioneer Vermonters were Yankees. [4]

This chapter looks at Vermont's formative years, that period from the French and Indian War down to the conclusion of the War of 1812—a span that goes beyond the time that interested O'Brien in his researches but in terms of Vermont's history forms a unified whole that can be described as its frontier phase. This was a time when settlers flooded into the Green Mountains, cut back the forests, laid out farms, established the first settlements, and created local and state governments. And because of the strategic importance of Lake Champlain, it was also a time when the region played a role in three wars: the French and Indian War, the American Revolution, and the War of 1812.

Londonderry's Scots-Irish

The earliest Irish found in Vermont generally came alone, as isolated individuals, part of the Irish flotsam and jetsam that was found everywhere in the English-speaking world beginning in the seventeenth century. But there was one exception to the story of isolated Irishmen finding their way into the Green Mountains: the town of Londonderry, Vermont. There, in 1770, a number of second- and third-generation New Hampshire families from Scots-Irish backgrounds bought, with a New York grant, an unsettled township in the eastern foothills of the Green Mountains named Kent, and quickly renamed it Londonderry, a choice that reflected their origins. Their Presbyterian ancestors, tired of disabilities imposed on them as Dissenters by the Church of Ireland (the Anglican Church in Ireland), and by the ongoing hostility of the dispossessed Catholic Irish, had sailed from Derry to Boston in 1718. But Massachusetts Puritans, making little distinction between Catholic and Protestant Irish—and particularly hostile to Presbyterians for their hierarchical church structure and their acceptance of individuals not considered of the "elect"—shunned them as "Irish vermin." In casting about for a safe haven, sixteen of the Presbyterian Irish families chose a location in what then were the wilds of southern New Hampshire and named their new home Londonderry. [5]

These pioneering families thrived in Londonderry. Drawing on skills honed in Ireland, they planted flax and produced fine-quality linen. Some authorities believe it was this community that introduced the potato to the Northeast. With economic success, the settlement grew and spawned satellite communities: Windham, Peterborough, Bedford, and Antrim in New Hampshire; Cherry Valley in New York; Truro in Nova Scotia; and, most important for our story, Londonderry in Vermont. [6]

When enumerators went door to door to take the first U.S. census in 1790, tiny Londonderry, Vermont, had a population of 362, and most residents had surnames that harked back to the land by Lough Foyle: names like Aiken, Cary, Cochran, Cummins, Montgomery, Patterson, and Taggart. How much of their Old World heritage they retained when they moved to Vermont is unknown. After generations in New Hampshire, they were old Americans, Yankees. In the middle of the twentieth century, one of the descendants of the Londonderry Scots-Irish, George Aiken, served Vermont as a popular governor and senator.[7]

The Impact of War

The Londonderry Scots-Irish were but one exception to the generalization that the Irish who came to Vermont in its early days arrived through happenstance. Many others, in fact, came as a result of war. Take the case of John Donaldson from Ulster. Because of Ireland's extreme poverty, British recruiters beginning in the eighteenth century viewed it as fertile soil for enlisting new soldiers. Donaldson joined the British army at age sixteen and found himself fighting in North America in the French and Indian War.[8] One can only speculate as to his motivation for taking the king's shilling: poor prospects at home, the pull of adventure, the chance to gain free passage to the New World, or a bit of all three. Whatever the motivation, when the war ended he chose to stay in the colonies, initially settling in northeastern Vermont but ending his days in Highgate in the northwest.

One ex-Irish soldier we know a little more about is William Gilliland. His story sheds light on the role war played in bringing Irishmen into the Northeast. His journey to the New World began with a failed romance. Growing up near the ecclesiastical capital of Armagh in the north of Ireland, Gilliland fell in love with a woman from a prominent local family. His suit, however, was rejected. Disappointed, in 1754 he enlisted in a British infantry regiment founded in Ireland in the 1690s. It was a decidedly Protestant unit, known initially as the Earl of Donegal's Regiment and later as the Prince of Orange's Own. With the outbreak of the French and Indian War the regiment sailed to America. There it suffered one of the greatest outrages of the conflict when, after the British surrendered Fort William Henry on Lake George to the French, General Montcalm's Indian allies attacked the evacuating garrison, slaughtering scores of British and Irish soldiers. As a member of the Prince of Orange's Own, Gilliland probably witnessed the horrors of that incident, although there is no definitive evidence that he was present. Rather than returning to Ireland when he was mustered out in 1758, he chose to remain in America. Moving to New York City, the young Irishman went into the mercantile business with a man named Phagen, eventually married his partner's daughter and acquired a significant dowry. With money and a driving ambition, Gilliland embarked on a new venture.[9]

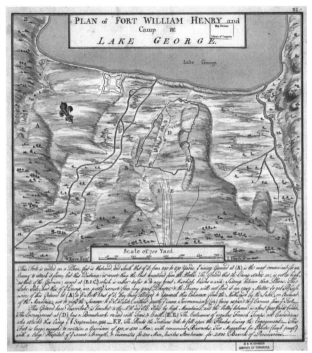

Many Irishmen like William Gilliland came to America as soldiers in Great Britain's Thirty-fifth Regiment of Foot, first raised in Ireland as the Belfast Regiment (Earl of Donegal's Regiment) and for a time known as the Prince of Orange's Own. They served at the 1757 siege of Fort William Henry on Lake George, as shown in this map (Courtesy Library of Congress). At right is a woodcut of a British soldier ca. 1750.

With his knowledge of northern New York gleaned from his days of military service, Gilliland developed a plan to create a settlement on the largely uninhabited western shore of Lake Champlain north of the British fortress at Crown Point. To populate his settlement he planned to bring in "a great number of Families of the Protestant Religion" from Ireland. To advance his project he petitioned the governor of New York for a grant of 60,000 acres. New York, however, was not interested in the Irishman's scheme. Undaunted, Gilliland simply changed tack: using his own money he proceeded to buy up land grants on the western shore of Champlain that had been made to other British army veterans—most of whom were also Irish but who were uninterested in pioneer life. In this way Gilliland acquired 12,000 acres with six miles of lakefront in New York, and lands on the Champlain islands of Grand Isle and North Hero, which later became part of Vermont.[10]

Gilliland was not the only one interested in settling Irishmen on the shores of Lake Champlain. On June 3, 1766, at about the same time Gilliland launched his

An early developer of the Lake Champlain region, William Gilliland suffered serious financial losses as a result of the American Revolution. (Painting by Ralph Earl, 1798, collection of the Fort Ticonderoga Museum, in memory of Peter S. Paine.)

settlement scheme, an ad appeared in Ireland's *Belfast Newsletter*. It called for Irish willing to go to "Grand Isle on Lake Champlain" to work as "redemptioners"—indentured laborers—on the land of Hutcheson Crozier.[11] Who was Crozier? Was he working in league with Gilliland, or was he another Ulster veteran of the Prince of Orange's Own who, like Gilliland, had acquired land on Lake Champlain? Whatever his role, his plan of settlement went nowhere, as no development took place on the Champlain islands until after the American Revolution.

In 1765 Gilliland and eight workmen, four women, and a minister journeyed north and staked out their small community. Putting up a sawmill on the Bouquet River just south of present-day Plattsburg, they called their new home Milltown, although early in the nineteenth century it was renamed Willsboro, after its founder. Over the next ten years Milltown prospered and grew. On the eve of the American Revolution the community contained fifty dwellings and ninety-eight residents. Were many of those residents Irish immigrants brought over by Gilliland? We do know that living with Gilliland were his mother, two brothers, a sister, and a cousin. Perhaps there were others from Ireland.

Gilliland's outpost, for that is what it was in this vast wilderness, was one of the few links in an emerging lake commerce that connected New York, the as-yet-unnamed Vermont, and Lower Canada (Quebec). From Milltown Gilliland conducted business with Philip Skene at Skenesboro (modern-day Whitehall) at the southern end of the lake, with the garrisons at Ticonderoga and Crown Point, with settlers at Otter Creek, Onion River, and Shelburne Point on the Vermont side, and with merchants at St. John (St-Jean) on the Richelieu River in Quebec. One of his contacts in Montreal was a Mr. McCord, who like himself hailed from the north of Ireland.[12]

But for the American Revolution, Gilliland might have become a wealthy man. The war left him in ruins. In 1777 Burgoyne's invading army occupied Milltown and left it a shambles. Financially, Gilliland never recovered from this loss. Moreover, his actions during the war tainted his reputation. Caught between the British to the north and the rebels to his east and south, Gilliland initially supported the rebellion but later may have tried to hedge his bet by remaining neutral. Branded a traitor and financially bankrupt after the war, he spent five years in debtor's prison, was released in 1791, and died insolvent a few years later.[13] Only the name Willsboro remains today to remind us that an Irishman named William Gilliland once played a key role in developments on Lake Champlain.

Irish Loyalists

The American Revolution brought more Irish to Vermont, not all of them patriots. In this regard the township of Alburgh, or Alburg, which juts into Lake

Champlain just south of the Quebec border, has an interesting story. During the Revolution British authorities frequently compensated loyalist refugees from the rebellious colonies with grants of land in the Eastern Townships, a swath of land in Quebec that today is situated along the Vermont and New Hampshire borders. One who accepted a grant of land there was Peter Carrigan, a loyalist from New York whose property had been confiscated at the onset of hostilities. There he was joined by his brothers, Patrick and Paul. By the time of the 1790 census, two other individuals with Irish surnames, Patrick Conroy and Thomas Kelly, had settled near the Carrigans. Another neighbor was William Bell, who had been born in Ireland, immigrated to Canada, and at age sixteen joined the British army and fought against the American rebels. Sometime after that conflict ended he settled near his fellow Irishmen.[14]

The twist in this story is that the land they settled on, while claimed by Lower Canada, was also claimed by the fledgling independent state of Vermont, the confusion created by vague wording in the Treaty of 1763, which ended the French and Indian War. In 1781 the Vermont legislature granted the land to a group of investors led by Ira Allen, Ethan's youngest brother. He called his new township Alburgh, a contraction of Allenburgh. The discrepancy over the border and the various claims to land titles led to years of litigation that was only finally settled in the 1840s. Alburgh was in Vermont. In the meantime, the Carrigans and other Irish loyalists had apparently made their peace with the United States and accepted their new status as Americans.[15]

Irish Deserters

Desertion may also have been a factor in Irish immigration to Vermont. This was a particularly troublesome problem in British army units stationed just north of Vermont in Quebec. Well into the nineteenth century, mounted police patrolled the borderlands between British North America and the American Northeast to prevent Irish deserters from British army units from crossing into the United States. Upper Canada's lieutenant governor in the late 1830s once remarked on this problem, noting that Irishmen all have "friends or relatives in the States and what will bind an Irish soldier if he has the opportunity of seeing his cousin." Conversely, during the War of 1812 the American Northern Army garrisoned in Burlington suffered numerous desertions from among its Irish recruits. On more than one occasion military authorities placed notices in Burlington's weekly newspaper, the *Northern Sentinel*, warning residents to be on the lookout for Irishmen who had left their posts. It would not be too much of an imaginative stretch to conclude that some Irish deserters ended up settling in Vermont.[16]

In only one case, that of Michael Madden, do we have any details of a deserter making his way to Vermont. Madden's case may be exceptional, because he did not willingly join the British military but was impressed into the navy. In the 1790s, while Britain fought revolutionary France, Madden was living in Cork, Ireland. Exactly where in Cork is unknown, but it was probably near Cork City, for Cork harbor is a large natural anchorage, and at that time it was a favorite port of the Royal Navy. Unhappily for Madden, in 1794, when he was about twelve years old, a press gang abducted him and put him to service on a British man-of-war. For the next three and a half years the young Irish boy sailed before the mast, probably plotting the whole while how to make his escape. His chance came when his ship put in to a Canadian port. There he jumped ship — free at last, but still in an out-post of the British Empire. Probably desirous of putting as much distance as he could between himself and the clutches of British authorities, he made his way to Vermont, settling in Sherburne, where he eventually married and where he farmed the rest of his life. He died there in 1875.[17]

The foregoing is not to imply that desertion from military service was a char-acteristic of Irishmen living in Vermont, only that for some it led to eventual resi-dence in the Green Mountains. The careers of men like William Gilliland, John Donaldson, and William Bell attest to their fealty to the forces of the British Crown; and as we shall see, Irishmen and Irish Americans like Matthew Lyon, John Fas-sett, and Michael Flynn loyally served in the War of Independence against Britain. One Vermont Irishman was even specifically lauded for his service. In 1781 Ver-mont's Council of Safety voted ten pounds to be paid to Hugh McCarty of Arlington "on account of his being a prisoner among the British in Canada the year past."[18] War, military service, and at times desertion were simply the back story for many people, not just the Irish, in frontier Vermont.

Lure of the Land

Whether British army veterans, loyalists, deserters, or Scots-Irish transplants, what brought the Irish to Vermont was the availability of land. In this they were no differ-ent from their Yankee neighbors. Since the middle of the 1700s, land speculation in the American colonies was rampant. As the old colonial communities along the Atlantic seaboard grew in population, people looked to the western and northern frontiers for unoccupied land. Even before the French and Indian War ended, spec-ulators and potential settlers alike bought land in what was to become Vermont, but the process was confused—confused because both the Province of New York and the Province of New Hampshire claimed title to the region, and both governments sold shares to townships there. It was this ambiguity that prompted Ethan Allen and others who held title under New Hampshire grants to form the Green Mountain Boys to resist the claims of "Yorkers."

Two of the most prominent Irish speculators to buy land under New York titles were John Kelly and Crean Brush. Kelly was a New York lawyer whose father had emigrated from Ireland around 1715. Kelly was a shrewd businessman, described by Ira Allen—who often owed him money—as a "Damned . . . Rascal." Like many of his generation, Kelly invested heavily in land. At the time of the American Revolution he owned thousands of acres in the Green Mountains, all under New York titles. His fortunes declined, however, as the claimants under the New Hampshire titles, led by the Allens and Thomas Chittenden, declared Vermont an independent republic. The new Vermont government, apparently suspicious of Kelly's loyalties and certainly rejecting his right of ownership, confiscated his lands. But the setback was only temporary. During the war Vermont reversed its policy of confiscating the holdings of alleged loyalists and returned Kelly's lands to him. Following the cessation of hostilities, Kelly continued to acquire real estate in Vermont and by the late 1780s owned almost 200,000 acres. One town owned by Kelly was named Kellyvale by the Vermont legislature in 1791. Early in the nineteenth century, however, it was renamed Lowell, by which it is known to this day.[19]

Unlike Kelly, Crean Brush lost everything as a result of the American Revolution, including his life. Brush himself was an Irish immigrant, having left Ireland for America in the early 1760s, but he was not the typically poor Irish immigrant. As Vermont historian John Duffy has noted, Brush's family was part of the minor landed gentry. His great-grandfather had settled in Ireland after serving in the Williamite armies that suppressed the Jacobite Rebellion in the 1690s. The Brushes were Church of Ireland in religion and loyalists in politics. Probably due to family connections, once Brush was in America he quickly obtained a position as a functionary of the New York provincial assembly, followed by licensure to practice law. Along the way he met fellow attorney and first-generation Irish American John Kelly. In the mid 1770s they formed a law firm, and Brush adopted Kelly's passion for land speculation. He acquired land in Westminster, a town chartered by New York on the Connecticut River in what would later become southeastern Vermont, and moved there in 1770. More land and government appointments followed. When the American Revolution erupted, Brush owned over 20,000 acres mainly in what was to become Vermont, and was clerk of what the Province of New York called Cumberland County. He was at the apex of his career.

For Brush, all went awry after 1775. An uncompromising loyalist, he actively supported the British military. On a number of occasions he tried to interest the British in authorizing him to organize loyalist militia units, and even went so far as to outline strategies to wrest back control of Vermont from the pro-rebel Green Mountain Boys. For his treasonous activities Vermont confiscated his properties. The British, on the other hand, while they did not adopt any of his military proposals, in 1775 put him in charge of sequestering the personal belongings looted from the homes of prominent Boston rebels. Unfortunately for Brush, following the British evacuation of Boston in 1776, an American privateer captured him as he fled to Halifax. Imprisoned in Boston, he made a daring escape in his wife's clothing and sought refuge in British-controlled New York City. There he died in 1778—according to one source, a suicide.[20]

Mad Matt the Democrat

One Irish land speculator whose fortunes rose with the American Revolution was Matthew Lyon, who would later gain some fame, or infamy, as the "Spitting Lyon." From the few facts known of his early life, Lyon seems to have been born in County Wicklow, Ireland, in 1749, received a basic education, and then apprenticed to a printer and bookbinder in Dublin. Apparently unsatisfied with his lot, in 1764 he sailed for America as a "redemptioner," like so many of his fellow Irishmen. Once he landed in New York, his services were acquired by a merchant of Litchfield County, in northwestern Connecticut. A hard worker, within a few years he had purchased his freedom, married Mary Horsford, a relative of the Allen family, and by 1773 owned land in the Litchfield town of Cornwall.

Lyon's residency in Litchfield was crucial in establishing the course of the young Irishman's future. Almost daily in the 1760s and 1770s, salesmen commissioned by the governor of New Hampshire set up shop in the inns and taverns of Litchfield County and extolled the virtues of the land between Lake Champlain and the Connecticut River. There, they said, good land was cheap. There a young man could make his fortune. Lyon saw his neighbors catch the fever. The Allen boys, Ethan, Heman, Heber, Zimri, and Ira, and their cousin Remember Baker bought. So too did a sagacious middle-aged farmer, "One-Eyed" Tom Chittenden, who eventually became the first governor of Vermont. In 1773 Lyon joined his neighbors in the rush to buy Green Mountain land and acquired "rights" in Wallingford, just south of Rutland.

Once settled in the New Hampshire Grants, Lyon became embroiled in the fight against "Yorkers" who held title under New York claims. To this end he joined the Green Mountain Boys formed by his Connecticut friends as a sort of vigilante militia pledged to defend the rights of New Hampshire titleholders. This suited Lyon well, for by his nature he was combative. He was an Irish Ethan Allen— loud, opinionated, frequently tactless, and quick to anger. The historian Richard B.

Matthew Lyon arrived in America as an indentured servant but, along with Thomas Chittenden and the Allen brothers, became part of the inner circle that dominated Vermont politics. (Courtesy of the Vermont Historical Society.)

Morris put it more strongly when he described Lyon as "rough-hewn, cantankerous, duplicitous, and withal a transparent opportunist." In short, he was the perfect frontiersman.[21]

When hostilities broke out between the British and the colonists, the Green Mountain Boys quickly took up the American cause, and Matthew Lyon was with them when they captured Fort Ticonderoga in May 1775. Despite his honorable service in the opening days of the conflict, one incident that took place during the Revolution marred his record and was used against him in later years by his political enemies. This occurred in 1776. That year he was a lieutenant in the Continental Army and second-in-command of a small garrison situated in Jericho on the Onion River (Winooski River) in north-central Vermont. The commanding officer, Captain John Fassett, a Bennington innkeeper who later represented Arlington for many years in the state legislature, also had an Irish background, although many generations removed: an ancestor, probably a great-grandfather, Patrick Mackfassy or Fassett, and his wife, Sarah Reilly, resided in Charlestown, Massachusetts, in 1670.[22]

Fassett's and Lyon's mission was to stop the British and their Indian allies from moving along the river. Hearing reports that a band of hostile Indians were approaching, the frightened militiamen mutinied and withdrew. Fassett's and Lyon's role in the affair is disputed. Their military superiors contended that they either failed to control their men or actively joined them in retreating. Fassett and Lyon countered that with their men refusing to stand and fight, they had little choice but to withdraw. Whatever the truth of the case, the military found against the two officers and cashiered them. This setback was not permanent, however, as within a year Lyon was back in uniform and fought at Saratoga. Fassett, like Lyon, later became a leading political figure in Vermont.

It was not his military career, however, that determined Lyon's future, but politics. In 1777, the same year as the battle of Saratoga, Vermont organized as an independent republic. Its key leaders were Lyon's old Litchfield neighbors, Thomas Chittenden and the Allen boys. They were the core of a small junta that dominated Green Mountain politics into the 1790s. Lyon's long connection with the junta was strengthened in 1784, when, following his wife's early death, he married Beulah, the daughter of Thomas Chittenden, then Vermont's governor.

Allied to the Chittenden-Allen clique, Lyon found his star rising. He was appointed assistant state treasurer under Ira Allen in the 1780s, and between 1778 and 1796 he was elected fourteen times to one-year terms in the General Assembly. As his political career progressed, he also engaged in numerous business ventures: these were concentrated in Fair Haven on the Castleton River, just a few miles east of Whitehall, New York. Chartered by Vermont in 1779, Fair Haven was the virtual fiefdom of Matthew Lyon. There he built and operated a commercial and industrial complex that included an iron forge, grist and saw mills, a general store, and a tavern. Significantly, he appears to have attracted a number of his fellow Irishmen to Fair Haven. In 1793 Lyon interested Irish-born Jeremiah Dwyer, who was then living in Pomfret, Vermont, to move to Fair Haven, and by the end of the decade there were families of Boyles, McCarters, McCarthys, a William Hennessy, and an Irish-born Dunahue family residing there. The small settlement of Fair Haven, with its Irish founder, may have had a community of about 60 Irishmen out of 545 inhabitants.[23]

The high point in Lyon's political career came in 1797, when Vermonters elected him to the United States House of Representatives. But it was a high point not without its trial—possibly the greatest of Lyon's career. Lyon was an ardent Jeffersonian Republican; he abhorred what he perceived as aristocratic government. Even the "trappings" of aristocracy disgusted him. He detested the Federalists as "a set of gentry . . . who consider the science of government to belong to only a few families."[24] One wonders whether Lyon's Irish upbringing, in a country where an oligarchy of landowners controlled government, might have molded his political ideology. Whatever the source, Lyon's strong views, coupled with his short temper, triggered an incident that epitomized the Federalist–Jeffersonian Republican feud of the 1790s. On January 30, 1798, during a recess on the floor of the House of Representatives, Lyon, in a voice calculated to be overheard, criticized Federalists as corrupt scoundrels. He particularly singled out the delegation from Connecticut. Roger Griswold, a Connecticut Federalist standing nearby, bristled at the remark and asked Lyon if he would march into Connecticut wearing his "wooden sword"—

The Matthew Lyon–Roger Griswold scuffle on the floor of Congress reflected the intense partisanship of the 1790s.

a clear reference to the charge of cowardice stemming from the events in Jericho so many years before. Now it was Lyon's turn to be angry. Enraged by Griswold's attack on his honor, Lyon spit in his face. Restrained by a few friends, Griswold withdrew, but two weeks later, on February 15, again on the floor of the House, he approached Lyon with a heavy cane and began beating him. In defense, Lyon grabbed a fireplace tong and fought off the attack. Onlookers quickly restrained the two combatants, but feeling between the two sides ran so high that Federalists later tried to have Lyon expelled for "indecorous" behavior but failed to obtain the necessary two-thirds vote.[25]

The Lyon-Griswold fracas was a cause célèbre. Federalists vilified the "wild Irishman from Vermont" as the "Spitting Lyon," or "Mad Matt, the Democrat," while Jeffersonians—even those who might abhor his behavior—applauded his politics. Lyon, refusing to retreat, kept up his attack on the Federalists, and found himself in serious trouble. Vermont Federalists, who saw him as their most vocal critic, castigated him as a "Jacobin" and used the recently enacted Sedition Act to charge him with defaming the president. A Vermont court convicted him in the summer of 1798 and sentenced him to four months imprisonment in Rutland jail. Vermonters, incensed over the way Lyon had been treated under the unpopular Sedition Act, reelected him to Congress in December 1798—while he was still in jail.

With the completion of his second term in 1801, Lyon dropped out of Vermont history, but not the history books. He and his family moved to Kentucky, where he was again active in politics. He represented his new state in Congress from 1803 to 1811. Ironically, as he grew older he became more conservative in his politics and found himself frequently voting with his old nemesis Roger Griswold. He died in 1822, in the Arkansas territory.

Religious Makeup of Early Vermont Irish

So far in this discussion of the Irish in early Vermont, little has been said about religion. This has been intentional. The subject is so big, so complex, that it could not be handled piecemeal and requires a specific focus.

One thing that can be fairly certain about these first Irishmen in Vermont is that in religion they were Protestant, primarily Congregationalist or Baptist, although many of them originally had Presbyterian connections. There were some—how many is unknowable—who had Catholic forebears but had lost that connection in America. This would have been the pattern almost anywhere in New England. Because of Puritan prejudices against Catholics, the Church of Rome came late to New England. As recently as 1688 the authorities in Boston hanged Irishwoman Ann "Goody" Glover, ostensibly for being a witch, although in reality her crime was a refusal to give up her Catholic beliefs. Not until the late 1780s did Boston's fledgling Catholic community feel secure enough to erect its first church, Holy Cross. The situation was similar in Vermont. Except for a temporary chapel built for a small garrison of French soldiers on Isle La Motte in Lake Champlain in the 1660s, and possibly some short-lived French missions to the Abenaki, no place of Catholic worship existed in Vermont until the 1830s. In fact, so strong was early Vermont's antipathy toward Catholics that its first constitution, adopted in 1777 and often cited for its enlightened stance prohibiting slavery, excluded Catholics from holding political office.[26]

In colonial New England an Irishman from a Catholic background who might have wished to remain faithful to the old religion would have found it impossible. In New England's early days, religion and community were one: for an individual not to belong to the local church invited ostracism. As late as 1800 in Vermont, a town resident who chose to belong to a church in a neighboring town had to obtain a signed certificate from that church's pastor in order to exempt himself from paying the local church tax in his own town. In essence the town church was an established church. In the seventeenth and through most of the eighteenth century, a Catholic Irishman just off the boat in Boston, or Portsmouth, New Hampshire, or New London, Connecticut, found of necessity that he had to become Congregationalist, Baptist, or member of some other Protestant denomination to be an accepted member of a community. The fact that there were no Catholic churches available to him only made the decision so much easier. An erstwhile Irish Catholic quickly metamorphosed into an American Protestant. The stories of two early Vermonters, Michael Flynn and Stephen Powers, help us to understand this process.

Michael Flynn

In 1791 Michael Flynn, thirty-seven, lived in Bethel, a town in east-central Vermont lying on the White River, a major tributary of the Connecticut. In that year the people of Bethel selected him to attend the convention in Bennington, which later voted to accept the Constitution of the United States, the last hurdle in Vermont's admittance to the union. He was one of Bethel's first settlers, having come up from his native Woodstock, Connecticut, about the year 1780, shortly after serving in the Revolutionary War. In Bethel he rose to a position of prominence. Almost continuously from 1784 to 1798 his neighbors elected him town clerk and on numerous occasions sent him to serve in the state legislature. Married with a growing family, a member of the Baptist church, he was known as "Squire" Flynn. He was a logical choice to send to the all-important Bennington convention.[27]

What is unusual about him is his name. Among those at the Bennington convention were men with names like Gideon Olin, Nathaniel Chipman, Ira Allen, Eleazor Claghorn—good Yankee names. In this company Michael Flynn's name stands out. It is clearly Irish — not Scots-Irish, but a name associated with pre-plantation Ireland, with Catholic Ireland. So who was he, or more important, what was his background? Fortunately, there is some information about his family, although not as much as one would like.

Michael Flynn was the grandson of Richard Flynn. Richard left Ireland sometime prior to 1723. How he came to America, or what his status was—was he an indentured servant, a demobilized soldier, did he come with a wife or was he single?—is unknown. Was he Catholic or Protestant? With an old Gaelic name like Flynn, one more associated with Catholic Ireland than with the Scots-Irish, the chances are great that he was of the old religion. That he left Ireland sometime in the late seventeenth or early eighteenth century is suggestive also, for this was a time when Irish Catholics were in full retreat under the repressive Penal Laws. The New World offered a dispossessed Catholic a chance to begin anew.

Our earliest information about Richard is that in 1723 in Billerica, a small town twenty miles north of Boston, his wife bore him a son, Richard Jr. Sometime later, along with other Billerica families, the Flynns moved to Woodstock, a town in northeastern Connecticut (although at the time considered a part of Massachu-setts), probably drawn by the availability of land. There, in 1742, Richard Jr. mar-ried Sarah Manning, in "the Congregational church." Interestingly, the Mannings were an old Billerica family, a branch of which probably moved to Woodstock about the time the Flynns did. Today the Manning home in Billerica is the oldest exist-ing house in town, built in 1696. That young Richard married a Manning in a Con-gregational church suggests that the Flynns were an accepted part of Protestant Yankee society. Over the years Richard Jr. plied his trade as a blacksmith, enthu-siastically participated in the proceedings of Woodstock's Congregational church, and raised a family of ten. His son Michael was born in 1754.

It would be interesting to know if Michael, grandson of an Irishman, had any sense of the family's Irish past: probably not, for his Irish grandfather died before Michael was born, drowned along with his wife one winter while trying to cross the frozen Charles River in Massachusetts. Thus there were no grandfatherly stories to remind a young boy of an older heritage. If Michael thought of himself as any-thing, it probably was as an American, that new breed of people that the French observer, J. Hector St. John de Crèvecoeur, so enthusiastically described in the 1780s. A second-generation American, Flynn had Irish blood, but he probably would have been surprised and possibly offended if anyone had referred to him as an Irishman.[28]

The 1770s saw young Michael swept up in the two great passions of the age: rebellion against England, and land speculation. When war broke out, Michael and one of his brothers joined the Connecticut militia. Michael served from 1776 through the late 1770s as an orderly sergeant in Captain Dixon's Company.[29] With his service ended when he returned to Woodstock, he found many of his neigh-bors speculating in Vermont land, particularly in the recently chartered township of Bethel. Michael joined them, bought land in Bethel, and moved to Vermont, where he married, raised a family, prospered, and entered politics. Grandson of an Irishman, Michael Flynn had become a Vermont "Yankee."

There is a curious twist in the religious evolution of Flynn's extended family. Michael's wife was Fannie Child. The Childs were an old Woodstock, Connecti-cut, family that saw many of its members move to Bethel. Michael and Fannie would have known each other growing up in Woodstock, although they did not marry until living in Vermont. Fannie's niece (or grandniece) Emily Child mar-ried a Richard Roche—an Irish surname—and they brought up their daughter, Joanna, born in 1833, in "the Church of Rome." As Joanna lived most of her early life in Bethel, this might suggest that there was little antipathy toward Catholics there, and possibly much tolerance borne from a dimly remembered Catholic connection. Whatever the genesis of her convictions, Joanna entered a convent as a young girl, became a Holy Names nun as Sister Mary Elizabeth, and in a long career founded convents and schools in Canada, Florida, Oregon, and California.[30]

Stephen Powers

Another Vermont "Yankee" with distant Irish, and probably Catholic, roots was Stephen Powers, born in Old Hardwick, Massachusetts, in 1735. A physician, Powers moved to the frontier town of Woodstock, Vermont, in the 1770s. There he raised a family, practiced medicine as *the* doctor in town, and stood as a pillar of the Congregational church. Both a son and grandson became doctors, although the grandson, Thomas, was more interested in politics than medicine: in the 1850s he represented Woodstock in the Vermont House and served one term as its Speaker. Another of Stephen's descendants, Hiram Powers, was a sculptor of note.[31]

Growing up as a "Yankee" in Massachusetts, it is quite possible that Powers knew little if anything of his Irish roots. It was only in the nineteenth century that some family members, interested in their ancestry, discovered a forgotten past. The great numbers of Irish immigrants coming into the United States in the second quarter of the century indirectly helped to spawn this interest. Heman Powers, a merchant in Boston who was interested in his family's genealogy, in 1856 wrote Nathaniel Powers, a cousin in Vermont, that in the last fifty years "many of the name [Powers] have come here, [and I] find many of <u>them</u> have come from Ireland. It has sometimes crossed my mind whether the family is not an Irish family."[32] Whether he was pleased or anguished over this epiphany he did not say.

Heman's genealogical work and that of other family members traced the American origins of the family to two brothers, Walter and Thomas Power—the *s* was added later—who arrived in Salem, Massachusetts, from Waterford, Ireland, in the 1650s.[33] Both the place of origin in Ireland and the date of immigration dovetail with contemporary events in Ireland. Power is a Norman-Irish name long associated with Waterford. During the rebellion against the Puritan-controlled English Parliament in the 1640s, the Catholic Powers sided with the rebels. When Cromwell's Roundheads put down the rebellion, they confiscated much Catholic-owned land and turned it over to English veterans of the Cromwellian army. Families like the Powers would have found their holdings greatly reduced, if not lost altogether. That at least two of the Power name made their way to Massachusetts is not surprising. For years British ships bound for North America often stopped in Waterford to take on provisions and add additional crew members before making the difficult journey across the Atlantic. Waterford men knew well the opportunities available in New England.

Because there is no definitive evidence that the Flynns and Powers came from Catholic backgrounds, this assumption is made on the basis of probability. But it is a reasonable assumption. The great migration of the Scots-Irish did not begin until about 1720. Most Irish emigration before that date consisted of Catholics, victims of the tumultuous English conquest of Ireland in the 1600s. Moreover, names like Flynn and Power are not Scots-Irish Presbyterian. If they were Protestants, they were more likely to be Church of Ireland, converts to the established church. But the fact that they fled to the New World suggests that they were outsiders, the dispossessed—in short, that they were Catholics. And once in Puritan New England, they had of necessity to become Protestants.

How Many Irish?

As we have seen, there were Irish in Vermont in its formative years—personalities like Crean Brush and Matthew Lyon, and obscure references to O'Briens, Conroys, Flynns, and others attest to that. But how many? Were there just a handful of scattered Irishmen, or were there a significant number? One answer came in the early 1930s—although it has been steeped in controversy ever since. That answer grew out of an intense interest in America's ethnic origins as a result of a series of immigration laws passed in the 1920s. Generally, these laws mandated that the admittance of future immigrants be related to the number of their fellow ethnics already living in America. Any attempt to determine the percentage of the population that came from a given background required that researchers go as far back as there were records. This meant reviewing the earliest U.S. census, that of 1790. That task was taken up by the American Council of Learned Societies, and its findings were published by the American Historical Association in 1931. The council concluded that 9.5 percent of the white population of the United States in 1790 was of Irish ancestry. For Vermont it put the figure at 10 percent of the state's 85,341 residents.[34]

In a general way, the findings of the research team confirmed the earlier claims of Michael J. O'Brien. He had always argued that there were more Irish in the colonies than had been recognized, and now he was vindicated. In recognition of his groundbreaking work, in 1932 the National University of Ireland awarded him the honorary degree of doctor of laws.[35]

While the Vermont figure cited above is impressive, it must be viewed with caution. The committee charged with studying the 1790 census had only surnames to go on: place of birth was not recorded until the 1850 census. There are, of course, problems with determining ethnicity solely through surnames: names like Smith, Clark, and Reynolds can be Irish or English or something else entirely, and differentiating between Irish and Scottish names is difficult at best.[36] Even with this bow to caution, however, the 10 percent figure may not be far off the mark. Somewhere between 300,000 and 500,000 Irish men, women, and children entered the American colonies in the seventeenth and eighteenth centuries, roughly one-fifth of all immigrants in that period, and not all of them went to the mid-Atlantic colonies.[37]

Clearly a significant number of Irish—or Americans of Irish descent—lived in Vermont in its frontier years. Some like Crean Brush and Matthew Lyon came as land speculators, others as discharged soldiers, some as dispossessed loyalists, and others as simple laborers. Except for the Scots-Irish of Londonderry, Vermont, and possibly those associated with William Gilliland, the Irish found in Vermont were not part of any large settlement schemes, but rather were solitary individuals who landed in the Green Mountains through happenstance. In religion they were to a man Protestant, with most coming from a Scots-Irish Presbyterian background, although some—had they wanted to in the face of unremitting disdain—could claim Catholic forebears. With many like Michael Flynn having deep roots in America, some of them were by the time of the American Revolution as much Yankee as any descendant of the Pilgrims. Only in the next century would the Irish in Vermont begin to constitute a people apart.

To the Eve of the
Great Famine: 1815–44

In the summer of 1832, Nathaniel Hawthorne, then an unknown writer, visited Burlington. At the time, the little village on the shore of Lake Champlain was experiencing unprecedented prosperity. Since its founding in the 1780s, merchants in Burlington had conducted a strong waterborne trade with middlemen in St-Jean-sur-Richelieu in Quebec, but the opening of the Champlain Canal in 1823, which connected the northern lake to the commercial centers of Albany and New York City, had made Burlington an important port. In warm weather, small sloops, double-masted schooners, narrow canal boats, and puffing steamboats daily moved people, goods, and produce in and out of the bustling harbor at Burlington.

In a short sketch published in 1835, Hawthorne recorded his impressions of Burlington. He remarked on the lofty outline of the Green Mountains to the east of the village, the curved, sandy beach at the bay, the wharves and warehouses at the water's edge, the "handsome and busy square" (now City Hall Park) at the center of the town, the presence of houses roofed in tin "in the fashion of Montreal," and the large brick customs house, which reminded him that "this inland port is a port of entry, largely concerned in foreign trade, and holding daily intercourse with the British Empire." In this international setting, Hawthorne noted, people from everywhere in North America could be found: "merchants from Montreal, British officers from the frontier garrisons, French Canadians . . . Scotchmen of a better class, gentlemen of the South on a pleasure-tour, country squires on business; and a great throng of Green Mountain Boys, with their horse-drawn wagons and ox-teams, true Yankees in aspect, and looking more superlatively so, by contrast with such a variety of foreigners."[1]

But nothing impressed Hawthorne more about Burlington "than the great number of Irish emigrants" to be found there. In his unflattering description they were everywhere: "lounging" around the wharves, "swarming in huts and mean dwellings near the lake," and "elbow[ing] the native citizens" out of work. If his words hinted of Yankee prejudice, they were at least on the mark in one respect: Burlington did have a large Irish population.

What had happened since Vermont's frontier days that suddenly there was a significant and highly visible Irish presence in the Green Mountains? The answer lies in a number of circumstances. Most important was a recession that followed the wars of the French Revolution. As long as Britain was mired in conflict with France, Irish agriculture prospered. Irish beef and Irish dairy products fed British soldiers and seamen. When the wars ended in 1815, Irish agriculture collapsed. Troubles in the farming sector coincided with the growing mechanization of the Irish textile industry, which undermined the once widespread activities of home spinning and weaving—occupations that had provided additional income for small tenant farmers whose livelihoods were marginal at best. To this desperate economic situation add recurring outbreaks of smallpox, typhus, and cholera, the periodic failure of the potato crop, and political tensions, and there was reason enough to leave.

In addition, the ills of home contrasted sharply with the perceived bounty of America. Irish veterans of the War of 1812 described North America as an "arcadian paradise," where a man with little means could "live like a prince." Letters home from those who had already made the crossing encouraged others to follow. In 1837 Bernard Brewin in Underhill wrote to his mother and father in County Leitrim: "I would be very [glad?] you would send Catharine to this Country for She would do well. Girls can get two Dollars per week where I was last Summer [Boston]." He went on to say, "I think that brother William would do well by coming here. I would encourage him to come for he will do well if he works well." To people long suffering under an oppressive political, social, and economic system, North America was an attractive alternative.[2]

A key factor in bringing Irishmen to Vermont was its proximity to Lower Canada (Quebec). To encourage immigration to the vastness of British North America, England made passage to the United States more expensive than to Canada by imposing tariffs on fares to the former colonies. Moreover, Canadian vessels that brought lumber to Britain, and formerly had returned with empty holds, now offered inexpensive travel back to British North America. The net result was that between 1816 and 1836 most immigrants from Ireland landed not in the United States but in the Maritime Provinces, Quebec City, and Montreal. Lower Canada saw a dramatic increase in its Irish inhabitants to an estimated 6.3 percent of the population in 1844—more than the province's English, Scots, and Welsh population combined. Small Irish communities dotted the length of the St. Lawrence River.[3]

After the opening of the Champlain Canal in 1823 created a navigable water route from Lake Champlain to the Hudson River, Burlington became an important port. (Courtesy of Special Collections, University of Vermont.)

But many Irish immigrants used their Canadian landfall as the first step on a journey to the United States. "Amerikay" was the land of liberty, while Canada was still part of the empire that they sought to escape. And the Canadian economy, only poorly developed, offered few jobs, while industry in the United States was booming. Irishmen recently landed in the New World streamed across the border into the American Northeast.

Vermont, particularly northwestern Vermont, was uniquely accessible to these wandering Irish. From La Prairie, just across the St. Lawrence from Montreal, a traveler could either take a coach or, beginning in 1836, a railroad car the fifteen miles to St-Jean-sur-Richelieu. St-Jean was the northern terminus of a maritime commerce that connected Canada to the Lake Champlain ports of Burlington, Plattsburg, and Whitehall. Every other day steamboats from the Lake Champlain Transportation Company carried passengers from the docks at St-Jean into the heart of the American Northeast. Burlington, because it was one of the largest ports on the lake—and also the center of a growing industrial and mercantile economy with plentiful jobs—became the objective of many of these backdoor Irish entrants into the United States. In the settling of the Irish in Vermont in the days before the Great Famine of 1845–48, it was not the southern part of the state, but the northwest, that first experienced large-scale Irish immigration.

Northeastern residents of the United States watched in disgust as Irish immigrants poured across the border. One American, a tavern keeper in upstate New York not far from Lake Champlain, expressed the thoughts of many:

> They [the Irish] will soon have five to one against us, Scotch and
> Englishmen. . . . They are very noisy people when they drink; they
> hitherto received from [the Canadian] government five pounds, with some
> rations, each family, as an encouragement to settle and clear the forest;
> when the allowance is consumed they almost invariably slip over into the
> United States; there is no stability in their loyalty to our government.[4]

Whatever the accuracy of the tavern keeper's comments on the character of the Irish, he was certainly correct in emphasizing their numbers.

From bits and scraps of information, a picture emerges of this waterborne migration. As early as 1822 Burlington's *Northern Sentinel* reported that "an unusual number of Irish emigrants have arrived [in Quebec City] the present season, in a distressed and starving condition"—and that many of them had come to the Burlington area. In 1827 Gideon Lathrop, captain of the steamboat *Congress* on Lake Champlain, wrote with dismay in his logbook that an Irishwoman "delivered of a son on deck." That same year an Englishman, traveling south on the lake, noted a large number of Irish on board and lamented how sad they looked in their homeless state, particularly one young woman "better dressed than the rest of the group of strangers, sitting apart from all the others, on a bundle containing her scanty store of worldly goods and gear, tied up in a thread bare handkerchief. Her face, covered with a much worn black lace veil, was sunk between her knees." A few years later the *Burlington Sentinel* reported on the trauma of an Irish family named Higgins. It said that the Higginses had lost their eleven-year-old son, Michael, while traveling from St-Jean. The parents did not know whether the boy had been left behind in Canada or had drowned along the way. Through the newspaper they pleaded for information, but whatever happened to Michael Higgins is unknown.[5]

In the summer of 1832 the American authorities put a halt to Irish immigration via Lake Champlain, not due to any political or social factors, but for health reasons. In that year cholera spread in Ireland, and immigrants carried the disease to the New World. Fearing an epidemic, the Canadian authorities established the infamous Grosse Île quarantine station on the St. Lawrence, just downriver from Quebec City. There health inspectors stopped ships and examined passengers. If disease was present, everyone was quarantined on the island. But some infected people slipped through, only to bring sickness to Quebec City and Montreal. In June, American steamboat companies operating on Lake Champlain curtailed trips to St-Jean. Not until late summer that year did passenger ships again ply the waters between Burlington and St-Jean, and the Irish pipeline resumed.[6]

The Journey

We have little or no detailed information on how most Irish immigrants to Vermont left Ireland, what their transatlantic voyage was like, or why they came to be in the Green Mountain State. But records and letters left by three families—the Shirlocks, O'Haras, and Donaghys—provide insights, if not total explanations.

William Shirlock's route to Vermont owed more to chance than design. He was born in County Kildare in 1809 to a Catholic family. His father, a veteran of the British navy, had served for many years on the flagship of Admiral Nelson. The Shirlocks must have struggled financially, for all four of the Shirlock children eventually emigrated to America. William left from Dublin in 1831, on board a ship bound for New Orleans. Along the way, however, he came down with "ship fever"—the common name for typhus—and when his ship made a stop at Quebec City, he was put ashore. Recovering from his sickness, the young Irishman made his way to Montreal. Though his motivation is unknown, his objective was Vermont.

Did he have a relative there, or a former neighbor? The answer is lost in time. From Montreal he traveled to St-Jean and caught a boat to Burlington. From Burlington Shirlock began walking. He traveled east along the Winooski River to Montpelier, then south following the Dog River. Fifty-five miles later, in the town of Royalton, he stopped, settled, and put down roots. He must have found the place congenial, for three years later his brother Francis joined him.[7]

Unlike Shirlock, the O'Haras traveled specifically to Vermont. Oliver and Mary O'Hara were Protestants from a Scottish background living in Bogue's Town, County Antrim, in the early 1840s. They had a small farm of twenty acres and some common grazing land on the hillside. But with eleven children, they just got by. They were, as one family member later wrote, "comfortably poor." When their sons Alexander and John announced they were going to America, mother and father decided they should all go, rather than see the family splintered. As Mary had a brother, Thomas McIver, living in Derby Line, Vermont, the Green Mountains became their destination. They sold their farm, packed some family possessions, and went to Belfast. There they hoped to take passage on the *Independence*, an American clipper, but it sailed before they arrived.

Instead of a fast clipper, the O'Haras found themselves aboard the *Exito*, a converted lumber ship. The family later described their seaborne home as "big and clumsy and a wretched sailor [*sic*]." The voyage was long. They left Belfast Lough, sailing past the old Norman fortress of Carrickfergus, on June 1, 1842. At one point they encountered a storm so fierce that it drove the old boat back 200 to 300 miles. Finally, forty-seven days after leaving Belfast, they arrived at Quebec City: July 17, 1842.

They did not tarry. The next day they caught a steamboat to Montreal, and at La Prairie took "the cars" to St-Jean. Once there they acquired a wagon, and with Oliver and son John walking, they traveled to Derby Line, just inside the Vermont border with Quebec. There Uncle Thomas met and sheltered them until they could support themselves. Eventually the family settled in the town of Holland, adjacent to Derby.[8]

The experience of the Donaghys, like that of the O'Haras, demonstrates the importance of family connections in bringing newcomers to Vermont. At the beginning of the 1830s, a young couple, Michael and Bridget "Biddy" Donaghy, decided to leave their home near Dungannon, County Tyrone, for America, possibly because Michael knew that a brother was slated to inherit the family farm. Their destination was Vermont, where a relative, Hugh Donaghy, either another brother or an uncle, had already settled in Brandon. What originally brought Hugh to Vermont can only be guessed at, but it is interesting to note that a William Donaghy is mentioned in the land records as buying and selling land in Middlebury as early as 1788, and a John and William Donaghy were among the original proprietors of Poultney in 1761. Could it be that the Donaghys of County Tyrone had a Vermont connection going back to colonial times? Whatever the antecedents, Michael and Biddy made their way to North America, stayed for a brief time in Montreal, and by 1834 were situated in Ferrisburg, a few miles south of Burlington.[9]

And they too continued the cycle of bringing over more family members. In August 1840 Michael's brother in Tyrone wrote him a letter:

> Dear Brother you wrote that you would take Hugh without any expense
> on me I am satisfied to let him go he is taller than you and is 12 weight
> and if you send for him he is determined to stay with you [?] he makes
> you a recompense.[10]

Apparently the brother was hard-pressed, for in the same letter he mentions to Michael that he now has three daughters and ten sons. The father's hopes for relief appear to have been met, however, for young Hugh left for America in 1843. Where he eventually settled is unrecorded.

The experiences of the Shirlocks, O'Haras, and Donaghys shared some similarities. First, all three families were from counties in the northern half of the country. Secondly, they came to Vermont via Canada. Finally, in two of the cases, that of the O'Haras and the Donaghys, there were already family ties to Vermont. Shirlock, while he does not appear to have had any previous connection to Vermont, and only fortuitously ended up in the Green Mountains, was responsible for bringing other family members to the area. Historians of the Irish diaspora, who have seen this pattern elsewhere, have called it "chain emigration."[11] Over and over again, we see that family ties played an important part in bringing the Irish to Vermont.

Six Irish Communities

Like the Shirlocks, O'Haras, and Donaghys, most Irish immigrants to Vermont scattered across the state, settling wherever jobs and opportunities presented themselves. By the early 1840s there were Lynches in St. Johnsbury, O'Gradys[12] in Shelburne, Hanleys in West Rutland, and Ennises in Marshfield. These Irish men and women lived solitary existences, strangers in a strange land. Frequently they had no old-country neighbors with whom to gossip or share memories of home. Moreover, unlike eighteenth-century Irish emigrants, the majority of the post-1815 Irish were Catholics—but as already noted, in Vermont there were no Catholic churches to give comfort and a sense of belonging. There were, however, a few places in the Green Mountains where the Irish clustered, maintained a separate identity, and eventually built vibrant Catholic communities: Burlington, Fairfield, Underhill, Moretown, Middlebury, and Castleton.

The largest Irish settlement in Vermont in the pre-famine years was Hawthorne's Burlington. Given Burlington's status as a port of entry, this is understandable. Many Irishmen first set foot in the United States when they walked off the gangplank onto the wharf in Burlington. Poor and desperate for work, they took what they could find. Fortunately, Burlington in the 1820s and 1830s was a boom town. The opening of the Champlain Canal led to unprecedented prosperity. Businessmen like Judge Timothy Follett built docks and warehouses on the lake, and shipbuilders turned out new vessels to carry the increased traffic. Retail establishments went up on Water and Church streets. Down at Winooski Falls on the northeastern edge of town a local business group operated one of Vermont's largest textile mills. Everywhere there was construction, on small tenements and hotels by the lake, to the large estates of the wealthy on Burlington's "hill." Unlimited employment was available for those willing to work. As a result population jumped from 2,111 in 1820 to 3,526 ten years later, a 60 percent increase.[13] Burlington was now Vermont's largest town. People began calling it the Queen City.

As suggested by Hawthorne's comments, many of those newcomers were Irish, constituting about 11 percent of the population. What Hawthorne perceived as overwhelming numbers, however, may have been an illusion, created by the fact that the Irish congregated along Water Street, the roadway closest to the lake. Water Street was an Irish enclave. It was as if once the Irish disembarked in Burlington, they dropped their bags, too poor or too tired to move farther, and settled in. By the early 1840s the Irish provided much of the labor on the waterfront and operated almost all the small businesses along Water Street. The two hotels on the street, Hart's and Soregan's, were Irish run, as were the three grocery stores—[Mc]Canna's, Killins', and Bradshaw's. On the waterfront an Irish person could find most of life's necessities supplied by his fellow countrymen. The area would remain an Irish neighborhood down to the end of the nineteenth century.[14]

Fairfield, the second-largest Irish community in the state, stood in stark contrast to Burlington: it was and is a rural farming community. It lies a dozen miles south of the Canadian border and ten miles east of Lake Champlain. Through the town's 200-year history it has never numbered more than 2,600 residents, most of whom have been small farmers scattered over a hilly terrain. At various times these hardy country people made their living raising sheep, dairying, and making maple syrup. Except for corn and hay for livestock, they raised few crops; pasturage was always more important than tillage. What was not produced or made on the farm was purchased or ordered at the few shops in the tiny villages of Fairfield and East

Fairfield or in nearby St. Albans. This was the rural community that drew unusual numbers of Irish in the 1820s and 1830s.

What attracted them? Other than a gristmill and an iron forge, there was no industry in Fairfield—no textile mills, no quarries, no canals: none of the usual works that one associates with the immigrant Irish. What Fairfield had was land. In the years following the War of 1812, Fairfield, like many rural Vermont towns, experienced a decline in population—from 1,618 in 1810 to 1,573 in 1820[15]—caused when Vermonters caught the Genesee or Ohio "fever" and gave up their hard-scrabble hillside farms for the flat, fertile soils of western New York, Ohio, Indiana, Michigan, and Illinois. What they left behind was inexpensive farmland that lay virtually in the path of the Irish entering Vermont from Canada.

The Irish craved land. Owing to various English colonization schemes in the sixteenth and seventeenth centuries, it was virtually impossible for a Catholic, and even members of dissenting Protestant religions, to own land in Ireland. One of the attractions of the New World was the possibility of acquiring land. In the 1837 letter of Bernard Brewin already cited, he proudly tells his parents that he owns his own farm "and got a deed for ever of it"—something they could not do in Ireland. In this same vein there is a well-known story in Rutland, perhaps apocryphal, about John Hanley of County Roscommon, who settled in the Rutland area in the 1830s. In 1843 he and his wife bought a small farm of twenty-one acres, and then a few years later bought a large parcel that was nothing more than a worthless, rocky mountain. His neighbors chided him that he only bought it so that he could tell his family back in Ireland that his land was so extensive it would take him all day to walk over it—as indeed it would. Even if just a story, it is a story that underlines the importance the Irish put on land ownership. Hanley's letters home had an impact, for in the famine years of the 1840s many of his County Roscommon neighbors followed him to Rutland. To this day, this rocky crag just west of Rutland is known as Hanley's Mountain.[16]

Exactly who were the first Irish to settle in Fairfield is open to dispute, but evidence suggests it was Peter and Lawrence Kirk, the McEnany brothers (Hugh, James, Patrick, and Matthew), and Patrick Deniver, all of whom hailed from County Louth and may have emigrated together. Although their names first appear on the U.S. census of 1830, there is some evidence that they arrived in Fairfield shortly after the War of 1812. They were soon joined by two unrelated Ryans (Thomas and James), Patrick King, James Carroll, and Peter Michael Connelly. In the 1830s a flood of others followed, and while most counties in Ireland were represented among the Fairfield Irish, the group had a decided orientation of people from Louth and nearby Meath and Cavan. Did those pioneer Irish, the Kirks, McEnanys, and Denivers, send word back home and encourage others to follow? Probably, for members of

Born in Fairfield, Vermont, Chester Alan Arthur, the twenty-first president of the United States, was the son of an Irish Protestant immigrant.

the McEnany family were still arriving in Fairfield in the mid-1830s.[17]

The Fairfield Irish were almost all Catholic, but there were a few exceptions, the most important being William Arthur, elder and pastor of North Fairfield's Red Brick Baptist Church in the early 1830s. Arthur had come from Ballymena in County Armagh, spent some time in Canada, come down to the United States, married, and settled in Vermont. In 1830 his wife gave birth to a son, Chester A. Arthur, a future president of the United States.

For the Catholics, Fairfield may have had another attraction besides land: its proximity to Catholic churches in southern Quebec. In the years between 1818 and 1854, Rev. Pierre-Marie Mignault, the priest at St. Joseph Church, Chambly, just outside Montreal, periodically made visits to Fairfield and other northwestern Vermont communities. In cases where a priest was needed immediately, Chambly was relatively close. A well-known story in Fairfield tells of Bridget Deniver, Patrick's wife, who in the 1820s gave birth to twins. Wanting her children to be baptized as soon as possible, she and her sister walked with the infants the fifty miles to Chambly and then back again.[18]

Unlike the experience of the seventeenth- and eighteenth-century New England Irish, the Fairfield Irish maintained their sense of identity through the sheer size of their community and ties to their church. As news of Fairfield's Irish community spread, it became a magnet for Irish immigrants who had settled elsewhere. Michael Connolly, who had been living in Hinesburg, Vermont, moved to Fairfield in the 1830s and bought one hundred acres. In 1840 Francis McMahon of nearby Highgate acquired land in Fairfield. Others gravitated to Fairfield after spending many years in Canada. Lawrence and Catherine Foley, for example, left Ireland for Canada in 1830, remained there twelve years, and then moved to Fairfield in the early 1840s. Patrick and Catherine Howrigan from Clonmel, County Tipperary, settled in Henryville, Quebec, not far from St-Jean-sur-Richelieu, in the 1830s, and in 1849 moved to Fairfield with their three Canadian-born children and bought a farm from another Irishman, Thomas Fitzgerald.[19]

By 1840 the Irish were a considerable presence in Fairfield—283 residents out of a total population of 2,448 (11.5 percent)—and were doing quite well. Many owned farms. Fairfield land records for the 1830s show Conleys, McEnanys, Sharkeys, Maloneys, O'Briens, Rooneys, Kirks, Tierneys, Ryans, and Malones constantly buying and selling land. Generally, the land they acquired lay along the high ridges, the Yankees being reluctant to sell off the more fertile lowlands. This was ironic, for the highlands had the best sugar bushes and in later years provided a good income from the annual run of maple sap. A number of the new arrivals did quite well. Patrick Houston, who had moved to Fairfield from Swanton in the 1830s, quickly became one of the richest men in town, owning real estate in 1850 valued at $5,000.[20]

Increasingly, the Irish were an accepted part of Fairfield life. Though an Irishman would not be elected a town selectman until 1859, as early as 1836 Thomas O'Brien became the first Irishman elected to local office in Fairfield when he was chosen one of the road surveyors at the annual town meeting.[21] When the great deluge of starving, diseased, and demoralized famine Irish poured into the United States in the late 1840s, the Irish of Fairfield were already a long-established, thriving community.

Twenty miles south of Fairfield and a dozen miles east of Burlington, Irishmen congregated in another rural town: Underhill. In the 1820s, Underhill, which lay just west of Mount Mansfield, was known primarily for lumbering, sheep raising, and farming. As loggers clear-cut stands of trees, the hillsides quickly became grazing lands. In 1840 there were more sheep than people in town—3,433 to 1,441. Certainly, raising sheep was an occupation Irishmen knew something about, but logging also attracted them. In 1841 a young Irishman named Daniel Wall who had initially settled in Shelburne went into partnership with a fellow countryman by the name of Patrick Green, bought forestland in Underhill, and logged there the rest of his life.[22]

Wall, however, was not the first Irishman in Underhill. That distinction goes to two brothers, John and Felix Doon, from County Armagh. They had come down from Canada in 1823, landing on St. Albans's Maquam Shore, and made their way to Underhill. There they took up residence on a ridge overlooking a fertile vale called Pleasant Valley. Through the 1820s and 1830s Underhill attracted other Irish people, with the earliest arrivals—as we saw with the Brewin letter—writing home and encouraging friends and relatives to follow. Soon there were Breens, Barretts, Shanleys, Flynns, and others scattered across the valleys and hills. By 1840 about 9 percent of Underhill's 1,441 residents were Irish. Locals called the track running along the ridge near the Doon place the Irish Settlement Road. Like Fairfield, the Underhill Irish community was well established before the famine Irish landed on America's shores.[23]

While logging and sheep husbandry brought in money to the early Irish in Underhill, it was often not enough. Frequently they had to find other work to supplement their incomes. One alternative was the Massachusetts textile industry, as some of the Underhill Irish had experience working in linen mills in Ireland. Each winter bands of Underhill men would put together a few belongings, kiss their loved ones goodbye, and trek down to Worcester, Massachusetts, not to return until spring. While they were gone, wives and older children maintained the household, saw to the livestock, and made preparations for spring. This cycle repeated itself well into the second half of the nineteenth century.[24]

A town further removed from Vermont's northwestern corner, but one that shared characteristics with Underhill, was Moretown. Situated thirty miles southeast of Burlington, Moretown is in a mountainous region with a long, narrow valley watered by the Mad River running through its center. Like Underhill, its extensive forests attracted loggers, and its fertile vale provided excellent farmland. Here a settler could manage a small farm and earn ready cash in lumbering. The only industrial works in the valley were the numerous sawmills along the river, although the nearby town of Northfield had textile mills, which also offered employment opportunities.

The name of the first Irish settler is unknown, but by the late 1830s a dozen or so Irish families lived in the town. They were Lees and Millers, Nicholses, Keltys, Devines, McCormicks, Cashmans, and Mahannas (Mahoneys?), about fifty people in all, constituting about 4–5 percent of the total population. Most of them congregated on South Hill, which in later days came to be called Paddy Hill. The Moretown Irish community would grow dramatically with the arrival of a railroad in Northfield in the late 1840s.[25]

Another area that had a significant Irish presence in the years prior to the Great Famine was Castleton, a town lying a short distance east of Fair Haven and twelve miles west of Rutland. In the 1830s Castleton was a bustling community, but it was also a bit unusual. Like most Vermonters at the time, the majority of Castleton's residents farmed, but in Castleton village economic activity centered on the Castleton Seminary, the Vermont Academy of Medicine—which for a time was the largest medical school in New England—and the headquarters of the stage line that connected New York to Montreal, and Boston to Saratoga and Buffalo. It was a college town and transportation center, with students and faculty mingling in their daily rounds with merchants, innkeepers, ostlers, stage drivers, and teamsters. Of its 1,700 townspeople in the 1830s, there were approximately 65 Irish men, women, and children. Their presence was probably related to the town's proximity to Whitehall, New York, and to Matthew Lyon's old Fair Haven community. Whitehall, only fifteen miles away, was the northern terminus of the Champlain Canal, and many of the workmen who built the canal were Irish. When the work was done, some simply settled in nearby communities. That was the case with Bryan McKean of Sligo, who settled in Castleton in the 1820s and was joined by two brothers, Michael and James. In addition to canal builders who settled in the area, a continual flood of Irish traveled the canal. One report in 1826 said that a hundred Irishmen a week were passing through Whitehall. Quite possibly some of them chose to put down roots near the route of the canal.[26]

One other Irish community worth mentioning was Middlebury. Today noted primarily for its college, in the first half of the nineteenth century Middlebury was an important industrial center. Besides the usual assortment of gristmills and sawmills, Middlebury was home to a number of large textile factories and a marble works. In the warm-weather months, goods produced in Middlebury were shipped via Otter Creek to Lake Champlain, and from there to Quebec to the north and New York City to the south. With so much economic activity, in the first three decades of the nineteenth century Middlebury's population expanded rapidly. In 1840 it stood at 3,161, making it one of the most populous towns in the state. Irish men found work as laborers in mills and marble quarries, while Irish girls could always find positions in the textile works. Five years before the Great Famine, 163 Irish men and women were living in Middlebury, over 5 percent of its total population.[27]

Reverend Jeremiah O'Callaghan

The presence of so many Irish Catholics in northern Vermont in 1829 prompted the Reverend Benedict Fenwick, the bishop of Boston, whose far-flung diocese then included all New England, to dispatch a priest to the Green Mountains to assess the situation. Exactly what his emissary, the Reverend James Fitton, reported to the bishop is unknown, but the broad outline is not hard to guess. Fitton would have confirmed that there were indeed many Catholics in Vermont, both Irish and French Canadian. And there were also problems. Without priests, too many Catholics were being married by justices of the peace, and many drifted away from the church. One had even become a prominent Protestant clergyman.

This was James Daugherty. From County Derry, Daugherty had been raised "a conscientious Catholic" and at about age twenty in 1819 emigrated with his two brothers to South Hero, Vermont. There, under the instruction of a Congregational minister, the Reverend Asa Lyon, he prepared to enter college. Lyon must have been a profound influence on young Daugherty, for when the Irishman eventually graduated from the University of Vermont in 1830, he entered the ministry. He spent the next thirty-five years first as the Congregational pastor in Milton, and later in Johnson. Clearly, from Boston's standpoint, something needed to be done.[28]

Apparently alarmed by Fitton's assessment, Fenwick himself visited Burlington in 1830, celebrating Mass at Howard's Hotel on Court House Square,[29] where only a few years before an aging Marquis de Lafayette had welcomed visitors. The bishop must have agreed with Fitton's assessment and begun looking for a priest to assign to Vermont. The problem was, there were no priests to spare in America. Quebec might have helped, but their priests were French speakers, and Fenwick's pressing need was for someone who could speak English, and, ideally, Irish. It was at this juncture that Fenwick met one of the most eccentric men ever to tread the roads and mountains of Vermont, and one destined to lead Vermont's Catholics for twenty-five years.

His name was Jeremiah O'Callaghan. Fifty years old when Bishop Fenwick met him in 1830, O'Callaghan had already lived a tumultuous life. He had been born into an Irish-speaking family near Macroom, County Cork, his parents poor, "of no large estates." With seventeen children to support, life for the O'Callaghans was a constant struggle. Those were the days when, owing to the Penal Laws, few Catholics owned land, and they could not sit in the Dublin parliament (or later the Westminster parliament) or hold political office. As a young man Jeremiah must have read with horror of the suppression of the United Irish Rebellion in Antrim and Wexford, although his native Cork was spared that catastrophe. Though later in life O'Callaghan became a prolific writer, he tells us little of his early days at home.

In 1805 he was ordained a priest. For fourteen years he ministered in Cork, but in 1819 O'Callaghan's theological ideas ran afoul of his bishop. This stemmed from O'Callaghan's view of money lending. As the Cork priest watched his countrymen suffer in the economic collapse that followed the Napoleonic wars, he concluded that their distress resulted from having borrowed money at interest. He came to believe that all money lending—even at what objective observers might call fair interest rates—was usury, and contrary to the teachings of Christian charity. Not content simply to argue his ideas, O'Callaghan turned his beliefs into actions. This put him at odds with his bishop. The climax to their dispute came when O'Callaghan refused the last rites to a dying man unless he promised to return his "ill-begotten" profits. This was too much; the bishop dismissed O'Callaghan from the diocese.

Then began a difficult ten-year period in O'Callaghan's life. An ordained priest, committed to serving his church, he was an exile, wandering from diocese to diocese, country to country, seeking a position. He spent time in France, returned to teach school in Cork, and in 1823 traveled to North America. There he applied to the Dioceses of New York and Baltimore, and the Archdiocese of Quebec. Everywhere he was turned down; no one wanted this combative and eccentric priest. That bishops who were in desperate need of priests rejected his offer of service underlines the low regard in which he was held. With North America shunning him, O'Callaghan returned to Ireland.

He did not stay long. In 1829 he learned that the Diocese of New York had received a new bishop, and that an old acquaintance and fellow Corkonian, Rev. John Power, had been appointed vicar general. Eager to return to the ministry, O'Callaghan made his second voyage to the New World, but when he approached the authorities in New York, the answer again was no. Here, however, fate stepped in. While in New York he chanced to meet Boston's Bishop Fenwick. Fenwick was desperately in need of priests to minister in his far-flung diocese, and here was O'Callaghan, ready to serve. That this energetic, middle-aged priest was bilingual, speaking English and Irish, was a bonus: many of the faithful in Vermont spoke only the language of the old country. The bishop decided to take a chance. After further discussions in Boston, Fenwick appointed O'Callaghan missionary to Vermont.

That summer O'Callaghan traveled to Burlington, the site chosen as the center of his mission. Along the way he stopped and celebrated Mass wherever he found groupings of Irish Catholics: Wallingford, Pittsford, Vergennes, and finally Burlington. Once settled in the lakeside village, the Irish priest assessed his charge:

> Catholics, principally Irish immigrants were as sheep without shepherds, scattered through the woods and villages, amidst the wolves in sheep's clothing—amidst fanatics of all creeds, or rather of no creed; all enticing them by bribery and menaces to protracted meetings, Sunday Schools and so forth. As I was the very first Catholic pastor sent to them, their joy seemed to know no bounds on my arrival. There were eight congregations, varying from 10 to 100 (in number), from 20 to 30 miles asunder. I was hardly able to visit them all in two months.

He reported back to Boston that in Burlington alone there were a thousand Catholics.

The difficulty of administering to his flock, rather than dampening his spirits, served to motivate him. After wandering so long in the desert, he described his work in Vermont as "the same thing as laboring in Paradise." O'Callaghan had found a home.[30]

Immediately upon arriving in Burlington, O'Callaghan undertook the task of building a church. In this he was helped by a local resident, Colonel Archibald

Hyde, who may have been as eccentric in his own right as O'Callaghan. Hyde was a prosperous Protestant lawyer known for his liberal religious beliefs and Democratic politics, and for the eccentric manner of his dress: he wore the old-fashioned "small clothes, wore knee and shoe-buckles or long boots, and withal a long cue hanging down his back."[31] Perhaps his backward-looking dress betrayed a romantic nostalgia for the past, and presaged the future, for, "much to the surprise of his acquaintances," in the mid-1830s he converted to Catholicism. Even before his conversion, however, he had given O'Callaghan five acres on the northern edge of Burlington for a church. With Hyde's donation, and the contributions of hundreds of Irish and French-Canadian Catholics, in 1832 Burlington had its first Catholic church: St. Mary.

While his church was under construction, and throughout his twenty-five-year Vermont ministry, O'Callaghan rode a circuit, bringing the sacraments to the scattered Irish. Traveling north he would visit St. Albans, say Mass, perform marriages, and hear confessions. While he was there, a rider would be sent out to the next stop on the itinerary to inform the faithful to get ready for the priest's upcoming visit. The next stop might be Fairfield, and then on to Bakersfield, Cambridge, Jeffersonville, and Underhill. For those Irishmen who spoke

Now hidden in the woods, a monument commemorates the stone on which Rev. Jeremiah O'Callaghan celebrated Mass in the church's early days.

Now part of a private residence, the building that was St. John the Baptist Church in Castleton is the oldest surviving structure that was once a Catholic church in Vermont.

little or no English, O'Callaghan resorted to his native Irish. On other trips he might visit Waterbury and Moretown, or move south to Vergennes, Rutland, Fair Haven, and Bennington. At times he ministered as far south as western Massachusetts.[32]

While on circuit in these early days before there were many church structures, O'Callaghan usually celebrated Mass in a private home. In Fairfield it was usually Thomas Ryan's place; in Underhill it was in Michael Barrett's homestead.[33] In fair weather O'Callaghan often said Mass in the open air, reminiscent of the practice during Penal Law times in Ireland of celebrating Mass clandestinely in some remote valley or woods. (In the 1920s Moretown Catholics placed a marker on a hillside stone adjacent to Paddy Hill Road where O'Callaghan said Mass in 1853.)

In 1837 Bishop Fenwick assigned another Irishman, Rev. John Daly, a Franciscan, to lighten O'Callaghan's load. Daly was made responsible for seeing to the needs of Catholics in the southern part of the state. While O'Callaghan based his ministry in Burlington, Daly made Middlebury and Castleton the center of his work. Already in 1835 the Irish in Castleton under the leadership of the McKean family and Francis Hoy, the Irish owner of a tavern, had purchased a building on the main street of the village formerly used to manufacture carriages and renovated it into a church: St. John the Baptist, the second Catholic church in Vermont after St. Mary. A third church came into being in 1836 when the small Irish community in Swanton built the Church of the Nativity of the Blessed Virgin Mary.[34] These three churches were followed in 1840 when the energetic Daly completed construction of the Church of the Assumption of the Blessed Virgin Mary in Middlebury. Through the efforts of Daly and O'Callaghan, the Catholic Church was firmly established in Vermont by the end of the 1830s.

But O'Callaghan was a firebrand, controversy and trouble his constant companions. His nature demanded confrontation. One bishop who worked with him in the 1840s and 1850s privately remarked that many churchmen "considered [O'Callaghan] crazy. In fact he was."[35] Not long after settling in Vermont, he began writing newspaper articles for the *Burlington Free Press* and the *Burlington Sentinel* and books attacking local customs and institutions. His favorite themes were opposition to usury (and therefore the local banks), the widespread practice of selling or renting church pews (which he considered simony), the failure of parents to give children the names of saints, the widespread practice of having marriages performed by justices of the peace, and what he called "store pay"—paying in kind rather than with cash. Those who challenged his views he considered not just misguided, but evildoers out to wreck the holy mission of his Catholic Church.

O'Callaghan was particularly sensitive to criticism from the Protestant clergy, who he was convinced were bent on converting Irish and French Catholics. He referred to them as "the clouds of false teachers rushing out of their lurking places [to] wage open warfare with the whole Christian Religion." Perhaps he had the case of James Daugherty in mind. There is no record that the two ever met, but certainly they knew of each other, and O'Callaghan must have lamented Daugherty's apostasy.

His first public foray against the Protestant establishment was a criticism of the Reverend John Converse, minister at Burlington's Congregational church. Converse, apparently in a sermon delivered in 1834, repeated the widely held belief that Catholicism, with its hierarchical structure, was inimical to republicanism. In a booklet published later in the year, *A Critical Review of Mr. J. K. Converse's Calvinistic Sermon*, O'Callaghan argued that contrary to the views expressed in that homily, there was no contradiction between Catholicism and democratic government. As evidence the Irish priest cited the republican governments that once existed in the city-states of Venice and Genoa. Not content to simply make his critique, O'Callaghan went one step further to castigate Converse's "Calvinistic system" as "dark [and] intolerant . . . tending to inflate and electrify his Calvinistic hearers into furious hatred towards all other Congregations."[36]

Dublin-born John Henry Hopkins became the first Episcopal bishop of Vermont.

Converse, however, was small potatoes in O'Callaghan's battle with Vermont Protestantism. The archenemy was the Right Reverend John Henry Hopkins, Episcopal bishop of Vermont. O'Callaghan's fight with Hopkins may have been as much personal as theological, for the bishop was a fellow Irishman, although from a different background. Hopkins was Anglo-Irish. His ancestors had come to Ireland from England on the heels of William III's victory over James II in the 1690s. They were adherents of the Church of Ireland (Anglican). John Henry Hopkins was born in Dublin in 1792 and came with his parents eight years later to America, where the family settled in Pittsburgh. In his early years the future bishop worked as an ironmaster, then turned to the law, and eventually became an Episcopal priest. In 1831 he was appointed rector of St. Paul's Church, Burlington, and the next year was named the first Episcopal bishop of Vermont.

Between these two Irishmen in Burlington, each representing traditions that had long been hostile to each other in Ireland, there was bound to be trouble. Hopkins was the first to open the battle. In two books, *Primitive Creed* (1834), and *Primitive Church* (1835), he argued that the idea that the bishop of Rome was the head of the Christian church was supported neither by scripture nor by the early church fathers.[37]

How O'Callaghan must have seethed at this challenge to his own deeply held beliefs! For the next two years he researched his response. In a letter that appeared in the *Burlington Sentinel* on February 10, 1837, O'Callaghan in his combative style announced that his book answering Hopkins's allegations would soon be out and that "Facts and truths which you did not expect shall meet your eye, in their innate and natural features, stript naked of all party colouring." When the 323-page book appeared in March with the uncompromising title *The Vagaries and Heresies of John Henry Hopkins, Protestant bishop*, it contained a lengthy defense of papal supremacy, mainly borrowed from the writings of European churchmen, and a critique of the views of Bishop Hopkins. For the doctrinaire O'Callaghan, Hopkins was a man who was all things to all people—"the Catholick, the 39 Article Protestant, the Methodist, the Calvinist, the Presbyterian, and even the Universalist"—because he believed nothing himself. For O'Callaghan, Hopkins's religious tolerance was evidence of theological muddiness and further proof of the necessity of having a church with one head.[38]

While O'Callaghan alienated many Protestant Vermonters with his critical religious writings, he created more enemies in the political arena. This stemmed from his beliefs about usury. The Bank of the United States, established in 1819, was up for congressional renewal in 1836. Rechartering became a principal issue in the presidential campaign of 1832: Andrew Jackson, the incumbent president, and his Democratic Party opposed it, and Henry Clay's Whigs favored renewal. Given his distaste for banks, it was no surprise that O'Callaghan was an avid Jacksonian. In subsequent years he became a Democratic spokesman, exhorting his fellow Irishmen to oppose the Whigs, and allied himself with the *Burlington Sentinel*, the local Jacksonian weekly.

O'Callaghan's efforts on behalf of the Democrats drew the ire of the Whig newspaper, the *Burlington Free Press*. In October 1837 the editor of the *Free Press* deplored the "incendiary political rantings" of "this Reverend Paddy" and pointed out that "according to his [O'Callaghan's] own showing, [he] has thrice been spewed from the Church and his native country as a shatter-brained disorganizer." Burlingtonians were aware of O'Callaghan's colorful past, as he had related it in a short autobiographical section in his 1834 book, *Usury, Funds and Banks*.[39]

Among his own people, the stubborn Irishman was popular. Like them he came from peasant stock, he knew their language, and he courageously took on the role of spokesman for the Irish community. But he had as many enemies as friends. Burlington's Protestant clergy viewed him with derision, and the *Free Press* dismissed him as an incompetent. Villagers on the streets probably thought him a crackpot, a classic exemplar of Irish loose thinking. Even French-Canadian members of his church found him difficult, for he had little empathy for their language or their culture. Few would have been surprised if a backlash developed to his aggressive ways.

And there may have been a backlash, but the facts are sparse. What is known is this: On the night of May 9, 1838, Burlington's little St. Mary Church burned to the ground. Many people, including O'Callaghan, believed it was arson. Even the *Burlington Free Press*, no great friend of O'Callaghan's, reported that "There is not a doubt but that it was the work of an incendiary as no fire had been used in the building for several weeks." Within a few days of the fire, Catholic and Protestant citizens of Burlington formed a committee to investigate; but if they ever found anything, it was never reported. O'Callaghan later charged that the committee did investigate "and in their inquiring found out more than they thought prudent to report." He maintained that the fire was started by a few students and "low" merchants, a "band of fanatics in hatred of the Catholic religion."[40]

Whatever the cause, the destruction of the church was promptly put right. O'Callaghan quickly raised money—relying only on contributions and studiously avoiding loans—much of it coming from liberal Protestant Burlingtonians, and construction was soon under way. His new St. Mary, located at the southeast corner of St. Paul and Cherry streets, close to the center of the village and a stone's throw from the Irish tenements at the waterfront, was completed in 1841. Once again the Reverend O'Callaghan had a church from which to lead northern Vermont's Irish community.

Vermonters' Attitudes toward the Irish

Did the burning of the original St. Mary Church, if indeed it was the work of an arsonist, symbolize widespread hostility toward Irish Catholics? There is no simple answer. On the one hand, Vermonters empathized with the Irish for the deplorable conditions under which the British had forced them to live. The *Northern Sentinel*, in an editorial on July 5, 1822, pointed at the distress in Ireland and said "strange has been the mismanagement and neglect evinced by the British government, ever since the conquest of that island." The same paper in 1825 commented that "the condition of the lower class of people there [Ireland], is to be lamented by every friend of humanity and by every patriot." To relieve

Irish distress, the *Sentinel* called on the British government to end absentee landlordism.[41]

Some Vermonters equated the plight of the Irish under English rule with their own history of rebellion against the Crown. A schoolteacher in Bennington put it this way:

> The American (though in full possession of his darling liberty) can never fail of commiserating the destiny of the Irish exiles, when he thinks of what would have been his fate, had the plans of our own Washington and the fortitude of our Revolutionary patriots failed. . . . We trust that she [England] will ere long listen to the dictates of justice, reason, her own honor, and the voice of the world, by emancipating the Irish Catholic from his present, degrading slavery.[42]

The second St. Mary Church, built in 1841, was converted to a school after the Burlington cathedral was completed in the late 1860s. The mansard roof was a later addition. (Courtesy of the Roman Catholic Diocese of Burlington.)

Burlingtonians went so far as to form a Repeal Group in 1843 to support Daniel O'Connell in his efforts to bring about legislative independence for Ireland.[43] The leaders of this organization were primarily Yankees, prominent members of Burlington society. They included Heman Lowry, formerly the longtime "high sheriff" of Chittenden County, and at this time United States marshal for the district of Vermont, and Nathan Haswell, grand master of the Grand Masonic Lodge of Vermont and Burlington's representative to the state legislature in 1836–37.

Empathy for the Irish abroad, however, did not always translate into sympathy for them at home. Except for the *Burlington Sentinel*, when the local press mentioned the Vermont Irish, it was usually in a negative way. Newspapers constantly depicted the Irish as a lawless people, prone to crime, drunkenness, and disease. When the steamer *Phoenix* burned and sank in Lake Champlain in 1819, and a large sum of money being transferred to a bank was reported missing, the press was quick to charge that the thief was an Irishman. In 1829 a report stated that $4,300 had been stolen in Montreal and that authorities were offering a reward of one hundred dollars for the capture of the suspect—an Irishman, John S. Barcomb, who "speaks the French language better than the English." And when an outbreak of smallpox occurred in Royalton in 1842, it was commonly believed that it had been introduced by "an Irishman who was riding in the stage with Mrs. Gibbs." The Irish were the scapegoats for whatever ills afflicted society.[44]

When the Vermont press did not portray the Irish as criminals, it cast them as either dull-witted and naive, or as the happy-go-lucky, not-a-care-in-the-world, stage Irishman. A play titled *Eskah*, written by a Burlingtonian and performed in the Queen City in 1830, included a character, Muckle O'Crie, who was described as "a fair picture of the jolly, unsuspecting and superstitious Paddy." Jokes in which the punch line depended on the simplemindedness attached to the Irish were a commonplace in the Vermont press beginning in the late 1820s. An example from the *Burlington Free Press*, April 14, 1843, is representative: "A man told his Irish servant to wake him at six-o'clock. Pat waked him at four observing that he came to tell him he had two hours yet to sleep." The depictions were not cruel but condescending.[45]

Religion was a sore point. Protestant New England had a long history of antipathy toward Roman Catholicism, exacerbated by long years of war with Catholic New France, and here now were large numbers of Irish Catholics coming to live in the midst of God-fearing Vermont Protestants. In general, like Bishop Hopkins, Vermonters thought Catholics reactionary and their religious beliefs incompatible with democracy. An editorial in the *Burlington Free Press* in 1835 expressed these sentiments. Quoting a Virginia paper, it said "All know the distinguishing trait of Catholics, among the unenlightened mass at least, to be blind and unqualifiedly submissive to their priest . . . which has kept Catholic Europe so far in the rear of modern enlightenment." John Stephen Michaud, born and raised in Burlington in the 1840s, and later a Catholic bishop, wrote that in the days before the Great Famine, "opposition to the Catholic Church [in Vermont] was bitter."[46]

The pope, because he embodied the hierarchical nature of the church, came in for particular scorn. When the editor of the *Rutland Herald* heard rumors in 1842 that the Catholics in Castleton were thinking of starting their own newspaper, he wrote, "They [the Catholics] have at Castleton, a meeting-house for jabbering mass, a priest to pardon sin and give tickets for a passage to Heaven, and now a Printing Press, with its immense power, to be added to the facilities for building up the Pope of Rome."

Theresa Viele, a Louisiana Catholic temporarily residing in Burlington with her soldier husband, commented that she was astonished at how Vermonters characterized the pope as "innately depraved."[47]

But this picture of intense anti-Catholic feeling in Vermont must be balanced, for there is much evidence of tolerance and even acceptance. Rev. James Fitton remarked that in his initial visit to Vermont the authorities in many localities invited him to say Mass in the schoolhouse or the town hall, and "occasionally, where liberality permitted, in the meeting house, and not infrequently where a Catholic had never been seen, much less a living Catholic priest." He went on to say, "The Green Mountain Boys ever seemed, from some cause or other, more open-hearted, courteous and obliging . . . than citizens of certain other states." Even Rev. O'Callaghan, himself an intolerant man, acknowledged that "the only open enemy" who ever came out against him in his twenty-four years labor in the Vermont mission was a man in Tinmouth who criticized the Catholic priest on the grounds that there was already enough religion in town—an attack aimed more at religion in general than Catholicism in particular. Interestingly, this comment by O'Callaghan was made a number of years after his church burned to the ground and could suggest that he had changed his mind as to the cause of the fire.[48]

Perhaps Vermont was more tolerant than other places in New England toward Catholicism. Certainly Vermonters were attracted to the new and unusual in religion. Joseph Smith, founder of Mormonism, was born in Sharon, Vermont, in 1805; and John Humphrey Noyes, who established the Oneida Community in New York with its unusual sexual practices, was born in Brattleboro in 1811. The Catholic Church itself appealed to the spiritual and romantic sensibilities of many Vermonters in the early nineteenth century. There were a number of prominent conversions. Chief among them were Fanny Allen, Ethan's daughter, who eventually became a nun; Orestes Brownson, editor of the *Boston Quarterly Review*; and DeWitt Clark, editor of the *Burlington Free Press* in the late 1840s.

Whatever the reason, Vermont seems to have been less antagonistic to the incoming Catholic Irish than elsewhere in New England.

Eve of Disaster

On the eve of the Great Famine of 1845–48, the Irish already had a significant presence in Vermont. Soon, hundreds of thousands of hapless immigrants fleeing the potato famine would pour into the Green Mountains, and they would find a network of earlier Irish settlers already in place: to welcome, to guide, and to advise. They would find their former countrymen tilling their own land, logging the forest, laboring on the docks, operating lathes and looms, working as clerks and as tailors.

They would also find an established Catholic Church. By 1840 Catholics could attend services in their own church structures in Burlington, Middlebury, Castleton, and Swanton, or, if living in an outlying area, await the periodic visit of one of the state's resident priests. Just as important, the priests—Jeremiah O'Callaghan and John Daly—were themselves from the old country and put an Irish stamp on the Catholic Church in Vermont.

Unlike the famine Irish, who arrived in the 1840s, most of those who arrived in Vermont in the 1820s and 1830s appear to have come from the north of Ireland, from above an imaginary line running from Dublin to Galway: not just the province of Ulster, from which so many Scots-Irish had emigrated in the eighteenth century, but from Counties Louth, Cavan, Meath, Westmeath, Leitrim, and Sligo. Theirs was probably a more calculated migration, one based more on existing family ties in America, rather than the desperate scrambling of half-starved famine emigrants.

These pre-famine emigrants found their way to Vermont primarily through Canada. They were part of what historians of the Irish diaspora came to call "two-boaters": immigrants who took one vessel to Canada and then, once landed in the New World, took another boat to the United States. In Vermont's case, the second boat was either one going up the St. Lawrence to Quebec City or Montreal—from whence they either walked or rode to Vermont—or one from St-Jean-sur-Richelieu to Lake Champlain.

Finally, Irish immigrants to Vermont in the first decades of the nineteenth century entered a region that was largely preindustrial. Except for textile mills, small quarries, and the humble grist and saw mills found in every town, the Green Mountain State was overwhelmingly agricultural. And it was an agriculture that the Irish understood: one based less on tillage than on animal husbandry—the raising of sheep and cattle. Within a few years of arrival, the hardworking, frugal Irishman, possibly with help from family and friends, and a little luck, owned his own farm.

His American experience was much different from what would confront most of the famine Irish.

In the decade of the 1840s a conjunction of factors—the most salient of which was the Great Famine itself—would change this earlier pattern of Irish life in Vermont.

The Famine Wave:
1845–60

I n late autumn 1847 Michael and Biddy Donaghy of Ferrisburg received a letter from Michael's brother in County Tyrone. It was dated August 16 and contained distressing news: Biddy's parents, Patrick and Polly Mann, had died that summer. There was no explanation and no details of their last days, only that they were gone. Perhaps the writer felt little need to paint a picture of the elderly couple's end, only to point out the catastrophe then engulfing Ireland, and thereby suggest the cause of death:

> [I want] to let you know the state of the Country at present was I to give
> you the statement of this neighborhood you would hardly credit me it was
> so visited with the severest calamity that ever was known to be in Ireland
> the people died with starvation and fever and the most of the people that
> is living you would think they were spirrits rising out of the grave for the
> want of food.[1]

The death of two parents in the same summer probably came as a surprise to the Donaghys, but the immensity of the disaster afflicting their home country would have been all too well known to them. American newspapers were full of accounts of Irish distress, and Michael and Biddy would have learned of the horrors in Ireland firsthand from the steadily increasing stream of haggard, disoriented, and sickly immigrants daily entering Vermont.

By the time the Donaghys received that sorrowful letter, the famine in Ireland was already in its third year. The blight that struck the Irish potato harvest first occurred in autumn 1845, affecting 30 to 40 percent of Ireland's potato crop.

The Emigrauts' Farewell.

The Great Famine of the 1840s forced thousands to flee Ireland, breaking up families and in many areas eradicating whole communities.

There was stress and hardship, but not yet disaster. With help from friends and relatives, plus using what meager money reserves they had been able to set aside, a family could survive one failure, but not two. Thus when the 1846 crop was again blighted, distress turned to panic. A bitterly cold winter in 1846–47, one of the worst in memory, added to the misery. Beginning in autumn 1846 and continuing through "Black '47," there was a rush to escape the country. In 1847 alone an estimated 214,000 Irish sailed for North America, approximately 117,000 going directly to the United States and another 98,000 to Canada. In the overall famine period, an estimated 2.1 million people fled Ireland.[2]

These new arrivals from the old country were different from their pre-famine predecessors. Before the famine, most emigrants had *chosen* to go to America to seek a better life; they often had some means, and even some skills, to stake their new beginnings. The famine Irish, almost all of whom had been tenant farmers, had few skills and had exhausted whatever money they had just to stay alive. Their decision to go to America was less a choice than an imperative.[3] Stay and starve, or leave and survive. They were more refugee than immigrant.

As before, many of those entering the Green Mountain State came through Canada. Almost daily in the warm-weather months of 1846 and 1847, emaciated, weak, human scarecrows tumbled down gangplanks onto Burlington's wharves. Most had been months in travel: from their inland home in Ireland to a nearby seaport, then two months in an ill-fitted, barely habitable sailing ship, and finally more days and weeks from a Canadian port to Lake Champlain.

Disease and death stalked them the whole way. Inadequate rations, dirty water, and poor sanitary conditions led to rampant disease. The infamous "ship fever," typhus, that killed thousands at sea earned transatlantic vessels the sobriquet "coffin ships." In the spring and summer of 1847 alone, over 5,000 people died on Grosse Île, the Canadian quarantine station in the St. Lawrence River established in the 1830s as a first defense against the spread of infectious diseases. The scenes there were horrific. One overwhelmed observer at the station remembered watching a crane hoist a netted sling filled with bodies from the hold of one ship, the golden hair of a young girl twisting in the breeze.[4] But Grosse Île could not stem the flow of typhus. Disease moved along the river. Thousands more died on the docks at Quebec City and Montreal.

News of what was happening in Canada quickly spread in Vermont. In July the *Vermont Chronicle* in Windsor reported that on Grosse Île "the living, the dying, and the dead are here mingled in promiscuous horror, and death reigns and revels amid this wreck of oppressed humanity." Alarmed, authorities in Vermont took steps to avoid contagion from spreading to the Green Mountains. Burlington appointed an inspecting physician to meet steamboats at the docks to turn away immigrants

Ships in quarantine at Grosse Île, Quebec. Sick or possibly sick passengers that inspectors found aboard were taken to "fever sheds" on the island. Thousands died there in 1847. (Courtesy of Library and Archives Canada.)

"unless they appear[ed] to be in good health." Handbills posted in St-Jean, Montreal, and Quebec City warned that diseased passengers would be sent back to Canada. But, while these warnings probably deterred some, still the Irish came.[5]

In the spring and summer of 1847, Champlain was an Irish lake. Sailing ships and steamers from St-Jean landed hundreds of famine survivors at the ports of St. Albans Bay, Plattsburg, Burlington, and Whitehall. Many had passed through the quarantine station at Grosse Île only to come down with typhus as they reached their journey's end. Burlington found itself engulfed in a humanitarian crisis unprecedented in its history. There are no statistics on how many died of typhus in the Queen City that summer, but there is much evidence of its widespread impact. In June 1847 Father O'Callaghan wrote his bishop of "the vast influx of immigrants who are prostrate with fever in every Irish house, shed and barn in the village [Burlington] craving for the sacraments," and went on to say that he had administered the last rites to seven dying patients. "What awful sickness and destruction is visible on all sides among the dying and the dead."[6]

Burlington's Poor Farm, a rudimentary facility used to shelter the indigent of the village, was hopelessly inadequate to meet the crisis. Usually home to no more than a dozen "inmates" at a time, in the summer of 1847 it was forced to hold over a hundred, and hastily enlisted workmen quickly erected hospital "sheds." At the annual town meeting in March 1848, the overseer of the poor reported that in the preceding year the Poor Farm had administered relief to 1,508 individuals, 121 of whom died, and of the dead, 107 were Irish. He cited "ship fever" as the cause of death in 108 cases. Other cases of "ship fever" were reported as far inland as Waterbury, Montpelier, Roxbury, and Royalton, towns that lay alongside the Central Vermont railroad line then being built by Irish labor. [7]

Only the onset of winter and the end of the sailing season temporarily halted the crisis; but each spring through the late 1840s, similar scenes repeated themselves. The year 1849 was particularly bad, although this time the culprit was not typhus, but cholera. On July 15 a young Irishman who had just arrived in Burlington from Ireland the day before fell ill and died. Other deaths followed. Panic spread through the village. The selectmen called for a conference of all local doctors to give a report on cholera in the area and make recommendations. When the doctors met, they confirmed eleven cases of cholera with eight deaths, but reminded townspeople that the disease was not contagious and was confined to those living in unsanitary conditions. Eventually, as the great wave of Irish emigration receded, so did Vermonters' fear of ship fever.[8]

Escaping the Famine

Many of the famine Irish entering Vermont followed the old Canadian route via Quebec City and Montreal that was such a regular feature of Irish immigration in the 1820s and 1830s. And many of them had Vermont connections—chain migration following its links. One transatlantic shipping firm—Harnden and Company—exploited the Vermont-Irish connection by opening an office in Burlington and advertising in April 1848 that "Passage Certificates" were available for "Old Countrymen who wish to bring out their friends from Ireland." What the advertisement failed to mention was that Harnden consistently overloaded their ships and skimped on provisions. Theirs were among the worst of the famine ships.[9]

The experiences of three families offer a glimpse into the journey from Ireland to Vermont. The most detailed account, written down in the early 1900s, described the 1846 voyage of John and Catherine Finnegan McElroy of Newtown Hamilton, County Armagh.[10] When the potato blight first struck in autumn 1845, John McElroy, twenty-three, had been married only a year but already had an infant son. To support his family McElroy helped on his father's farm and, when he could get a position, worked as a teacher. When the potato crop failed in 1845, and prospects for teachers looked dim, McElroy, his wife, and his brother-in-law, James

Finnegan, determined to emigrate in the spring. As Finnegan had a cousin in Fairfield, Vermont, they set their sights on the Green Mountains.

In early April they traveled overland to Warrenpoint, a small port town in County Down, and on April 14 sailed on the bark *Ayrshire*. On May 25, after forty-two days at sea, the *Ayrshire* dropped anchor at the Grosse Île quarantine station in the St. Lawrence. Apparently not finding disease present, the medical authorities waved the ship through. In Quebec City the McElroy party boarded another ship, this one a steamer, which brought them to Montreal, and sometime in mid-June the McElroys finally reached Fairfield.

After two months of continuous travel, John McElroy must have been exhausted, but his itinerancy was not yet over. Desperate for money, he scrounged for work, but there was little available in rural Fairfield. There was, however, employment available on the Lachine Canal back in Montreal. The canal, originally built in the 1820s to bypass the treacherous Lachine rapids on the St. Lawrence, was just then being expanded. With few options available to him, McElroy left his wife and child in Fairfield and walked the fifty miles back to Montreal. There, with pick and shovel, along with hundreds of other Irishmen, he toiled at the Lachine. The work was grueling. As the family account sadly lamented, "The handles of his implements were often stained with blood." He remained there until mid-September, when, the work complete, the bosses discharged him along with 1,600 other men.

Returning to Vermont, he sought work in Braintree, where a crew was laying tracks for the Vermont Central. Braintree lay sixty-five miles south of Fairfield, and McElroy probably walked the entire distance. When he arrived in Braintree and located the work site, he asked the foreman if he could hire on. The foreman told him he could start the next morning at a rate of a dollar a day, $1.75 taken out weekly for room and board. As it was then only three in the afternoon, the hungry and penniless young Irishman asked if it was possible for him to make twenty-five cents that day before quitting time. The foreman, probably out of pity, assented and let McElroy finish the day.

McElroy worked in railroad construction until Thanksgiving, when the first snowstorm of the season gave him a preview of a Vermont winter. Deciding on another line of work, he spent the winter in Williston threshing grain with a flail. Over the next few years he supported his family as a farm laborer, first in Williston, then among the Irish in Underhill, and finally in Westfield in Orleans County.

All this time his family was growing; five more children had been born since his arrival in America. Then disaster struck: in 1858 Catherine died, shortly after the birth of their youngest, a boy named Joseph. A widower with six children, one an infant, John McElroy was in a difficult position. For a man who

John Rowley awaited his wife's return from Vermont before he would undertake the dangerous crossing from Ireland to America. (Courtesy of Anne Rowley Howrigan.)

labored long hours to make ends meet, there was no time to care for his family. But, in a pattern that one saw time and again in immigrant Irish families, other family members offered help. John's mother, Bridget, who had followed her son and daughter-in-law to America, took over the care of John's "half-orphans," while little Joseph was given to Finnegan relatives in Hyde Park, Vermont, to be raised.[11]

In 1861 John McElroy's transient life came to an end when he purchased a small farm from another Irishman in the town of Lowell (the town formerly had been known as Kellyvale, after its original owner, the lawyer and land speculator John Kelly). McElroy must have found Lowell congenial, for although the town was sparsely populated, it had a significant Irish community of farmers strung out along Truland Brook on what became known as Irish Hill Road. There John McElroy resided the rest of his life, the farm passing to one of his sons when he died in 1913.

Another family that passed through Grosse Île on its way to Vermont was the Leddys. During the height of the Great Famine, the spring of 1847, Peter and Margaret Sheridan Leddy of Kilbride, County Meath, and their three children left Ireland for North America, despite the fact that Margaret was seven months pregnant. During their two-months-long voyage Margaret gave birth to a daughter, Ellen, who later in life frequently reported that she was born "on the banks of Newfoundland." Successfully passing through Grosse Île, the Leddys made their way to Vermont, stayed for a short time in Shelburne, and then moved to the Irish settlement in Underhill, where Margaret had relatives residing since the 1830s. By 1860 Peter owned his own farm and had a family of nine children. In the twentieth century, descendants of Peter and Margaret Leddy became important figures in Vermont politics.[12]

For sheer courage in those difficult times, few can compare with Elizabeth Flynn Rowley. In the midst of the famine, Elizabeth and her husband, John, and their six children decided to flee their native County Leitrim. Their destination was Fletcher, Vermont, just south of Fairfield, where Elizabeth's brother Thomas was already living. But lacking enough money to all go at once, they devised a plan. Elizabeth would go out alone, work in Fletcher as a domestic, and earn the money to send for the rest of the family. This she did; but when the money was sent home, her husband, apparently out of fear of the ocean voyage, refused to make the crossing without her. Elizabeth then sailed back to Ireland, using up some of her savings in the process, collected her husband and her four youngest children, and crossed the Atlantic again to return to Vermont. The two oldest children remained in the old country until enough money was saved for their passage. They finally made the trip in 1851. At a time when transatlantic travel took anywhere from five to eight weeks and was uncomfortable at best and deadly at worst, this resolute Irishwoman crossed the ocean three times to save her family.[13]

In each of the accounts mentioned, chain migration played an important role in bringing Irish immigrants to Vermont. This was also the case in the dramatic story of a group of evicted tenants from Ballykilcline, County Roscommon. Their story had roots in the seventeenth century. Since the late 1680s Ballykilcline, a township of about 600 acres, was owned directly by the British Crown. At the time of the famine it had between 500 and 600 residents, all poor tenant farmers. Since the mid-1830s many of them had engaged in a rent strike, the origins of which are obscure but seem to have been related to disagreement over leasehold terms. For a number of years farmers withheld rents and fought in the courts against eviction. Finally, in 1847, in the midst of the famine, the government put *finis* to the strike by turning out the tenants and at the same time agreeing to pay their passage to America. In the fall of 1847 through April 1848, approximately 368 Ballykilcline residents, in nine groups, left Ireland, first for Liverpool and thence to New York. According to recent research by historian Mary Lee Dunn, at least sixty-three of them made their way to Rutland, Vermont.[14]

The connection to Rutland was through John and Sabrina Hanley—the Hanley Mountain people—and a Maguire and a Colligan, all earlier immigrants from Roscommon. One can imagine that over the years letters had passed back and forth, the ones from Ireland detailing the hardships of everyday life, while those coming from Rutland extolled the abundance of America. When the Ballykilcline evictees discussed going to the New World, Rutland must have been constantly on their lips. And so they went. Among the sixty-three Ballykilcline immigrants who settled in Rutland, four were Hanleys, seven were Brennans—Sabrina Hanley was a Brennan—and one was a Colligan.

While family connections like those of the Leddys, McElroys, Rowleys, and Hanleys accounted for some of the famine migration to Vermont, an equally important factor was the availability of work. Though it was an agricultural state, just as hundreds of thousands of Irish landed in North America, Vermont was experiencing a mini–industrial revolution based on railroading, quarrying, and the manufacture of textiles. Employers needed laborers, and the Irish filled the need.

Working on the Railroads

Most important in bringing the Irish to Vermont were the railroads: most important because they not only employed a great number of Irishmen, but also made possible the expansion of other industries that required additional workers. Railroads came late to the Green Mountains. At a time when steel rails reached from the East Coast almost to Chicago, Vermont had not a mile of track. In the Green Mountains the railroad era began in 1846, when two competing lines, the Rutland & Burlington and the Vermont Central, starting laying track that by 1850 would connect Burlington to Boston, and eventually extend to Montreal. And when construction on those two lines ended, work continued for another twenty years as other smaller

Ireland and America.

Starving and destitute Irish peasants pictured America as a land of milk and honey.

lines crisscrossed the state. Through the period of railroad construction, contractors hired thousands of Irishmen to dynamite rock, move dirt, lay ties, build bridges and trestles, align steel rails, and hammer spikes. [15]

Now in addition to the Canadian route to Vermont, Irishmen poured into the Green Mountains from down-country: from New York, Connecticut, and Massachusetts. They differed somewhat from earlier Irish arrivals in that they tended to come from the southern counties—the counties most severely ravaged by the famine: Cork, Kerry, Clare, Tipperary, and Limerick. Unskilled and desperate for work, most of them were young, single males—or, if they were married, their wives and children were often left in the care of others. The railroad contractors offered steady pay and little else. Working conditions were primitive. The men lived near the work site in crews that ranged anywhere from a few dozen to a few hundred, putting down rails by day, and sleeping and eating in "breakdown" shanties at night. When a section of line was completed, the men dismantled the shanties, loaded them on wagons, and moved them to the next work site.[16]

While railroad construction provided immediate employment for the famine Irish, it also spurred the expansion of other industries that offered jobs. Quarry-

Railroad construction in Vermont boomed just as the famine Irish arrived in America. These men are railroad laborers in heavily Irish Northfield, Vermont, ca. 1880. (Courtesy of the Northfield Historical Society.)

ing was the most important. On the western edge of Vermont run extensive veins of both slate and marble. Both stones had been quarried since the late eighteenth century, but on a small scale. Distribution was the problem. Until the Champlain Canal opened in 1823, there was no inexpensive way to get Vermont products to a wider market. Even with the canal it was a laborious and time-consuming job to move the finished stone by wagon to Whitehall and then ship it by canal boat to points south and west.

The coming of the railroads changed everything. Now Green Mountain slate and marble could easily be shipped to customers in southern New England and New York and beyond. Orders piled up. Slate quarries in Fair Haven, Castleton, and Poultney scrambled for additional hands, as did marble works in the Rutland and Dorset areas. Irishmen who found the itinerant life of the railroad gangs not to their liking hired on as laborers in the quarries or as sawyers and stone polishers in the "shops."

The extractive industries attracted men who had worked in mining in Ireland. This was particularly true of the slate valley towns. Irishmen had long worked in the slate-producing regions of County Tipperary. No doubt some of them emigrated specifically to work in Vermont's slate towns; but far more probable is that Tipperary men originally came to Vermont to labor in railroad construction and then gravitated to the burgeoning slate works. Tipperary names became commonplace in the slate valley towns of Castleton, Fair Haven, Poultney, and Pawlet: Minogue, Durick, Keenan, McGrath, and Delahanty, to cite just a few. Local historian Peter Patten, himself a Minogue on his mother's side, estimated that two-thirds of the Irish in Fair Haven came from an area within a thirty-mile radius of Nenagh in the slate country of northwestern Tipperary.[17]

No such clear pattern of immigration can be found in Vermont's marble industry, although no doubt there was a connection to specific locales in Ireland: both counties Galway and Kilkenny are famous for their marble, Kilkenny City being known as Marble City. We do know that at least one Irish family, John Harrington and his two sons of Castletownbere in County Cork, an area once famous for its copper mines, specifically targeted Vermont for its mining opportunities, eventually settling in Dorset to work in the marble quarries. Other members of the Harrington family later joined them.[18]

Changing Settlement Patterns

The influx of famine immigrants impacted Irish settlement patterns. Unsurprisingly, given the importance of chain migration, the old centers of Irish population in Franklin County increased their Irish numbers dramatically. For years letters had been passing back and forth between Ireland and residents of Vermont's old Irish settlements. Perhaps the only place an Irishman in Leitrim or Cavan knew of in America was a little hamlet in the Green Mountains. When it came time to emigrate, that was where the Irishman headed. The farming community of Fairfield, which saw its total population increase by only 143 residents in the decade of the 1840s, saw its proportion of Irish residents double, going from 11.5 percent of the population at the beginning of the decade to 21.5 percent by 1850.[19] Similar increases occurred in the towns of Underhill and Moretown. If not for Irish immigrants, these rural communities would have experienced an actual population decline in the 1840s.

As the most important port on Lake Champlain, and a busy commercial and industrial center, Burlington saw its Irish numbers almost triple. As had been true before the famine, Burlington village continued to have the largest Irish community in the state. In the first census following the famine, that of 1850, Burlington had a population of 7,521. Of that number 1,660 were born in Ireland. The children of Irish parents, born either "at sea," in Canada, or in the United States, amounted to another 589. Together the two generations constituted a startling 31 percent of the population. One old man who came to the Burlington area as a young boy, as part of the great French Canadian migration of the 1860s, remembered years later that "it was all Irish and Yankee then." At midcentury, Burlington was as noticeably Irish as Boston or New York.[20]

Railroad construction added a new dimension to the pattern of Irish settlement in Vermont. Hundreds of Irishmen rushed to the state to build rail beds and lay down ties. They monopolized the work, and wherever the lines went, so too did the Irish. Towns that became railroad centers, with repair yards, depots, and offices, spawned extensive Irish neighborhoods. One such place was Brattleboro, in the southeast corner of the state on the Connecticut River. With hardly an Irishman in town in 1840, once the railroad came through in 1849 the Irish population shot up to constitute over 14 percent of the residents, many of them living in a congested district along the Connecticut River known as "the Patch."[21] Other railroad towns—St. Albans, Bennington, Bellows Falls, and Northfield—witnessed similar transformations.

The marble-rich town of Rutland, which was also an important railroad center, had only a handful of Irish prior to the 1840s. Then the steel rails came, and with them a great change. Irishmen poured in. In 1850, 852 of the town's 3,715 residents were immigrant or first-generation Irish Americans—almost 23 percent of the total population. They dominated jobs in the marble pits, in the marble-finishing shops, and in the railroad yards. Further west in Rutland County, the slate valley towns of Castleton, Poultney, and Fair Haven took on a similar Irish complexion. In 1850 the Irish constituted almost 25 percent of the inhabitants of

Castleton, the largest of the slate towns. Immigration of Poles, Swedes, Welsh, and Italians later in the century has tended to obscure the central role played by the Irish in the initial years of the slate and marble boom.[22]

The following table shows the Vermont towns with the greatest percentages of immigrant and first-generation Irish Americans in the 1850 U.S. census:

Town	Total population	Irish Americans	Percentage of Total
Burlington	7,251	2,249	31.0
Georgia	2,686	715	26.6
Castleton	3,016	743	24.6
Rutland	3,715	852	22.9
Fairfield	2,591	570	22.0
Moretown	1,335	281	21.0
Underhill	1,599	334	20.9
Fair Haven	902	157	17.4
St. Albans	3,567	619	17.4
Swanton	2,824	458	16.2
Middlebury	3,517	523	14.9
Brattleboro	3,816	542	14.2

With the exception of Georgia, Fairfield, Moretown, Underhill, and Swanton, the towns listed are industrial centers, and Georgia—an agricultural area—made the list only because at the time of the census a large number of Irish workers were building a rail line there connecting Essex Junction to St. Albans. Their presence was temporary. When the work was completed, most of the Irish in Georgia left. What the figures show is that most of the famine Irish who immigrated to Vermont did so because of opportunities in the industrial sector.

In the main, those Irish living in the old Irish communities of Fairfield, Underhill, and Moretown described themselves as "farmers" in the 1850 census, while the overwhelming majority of those residing in urban settings listed their occupation simply as "laborer"—a general term implying no more than possession of muscle, which was what the Irish provided in Vermont's mini–industrial revolution.

Within five years of the start of the Great Famine, over 15,000 people born in Ireland resided in the Green Mountains—almost 5 percent of the state's population.[23] And as they were concentrated in just a few counties—Chittenden, Franklin, and Rutland—the percentages in those places were significantly higher. Through the 1850s and 1860s, a period of significant economic growth in Vermont, the Irish constituted the largest ethnic group in the state.

Response to the Famine Irish

To the extent that they could, the Irish already resident in Vermont extended a helping hand to their incoming fellow countrymen. In Fairfield, a young couple, Bernard and Mary Finnegan, not long over from Ireland themselves but with their own farm, put up recent arrivals until they could get on their feet. In Burlington, grocer Patrick Cavanaugh lodged incoming Irish in tenements he owned on Water Street. In the early 1850s Rev. Edward McGowan, an Irish priest in St. Albans, "apprised newcomers from Ireland of available farms in his vast missionary territory."[24]

Many Vermonters mounted relief efforts for the suffering in Ireland. Rachel Robinson, a member of a prominent Quaker family in Ferrisburg, wrote her son George that "there is considerable sympathy manifested in this vicinity for the poor, famishing Irish" and urged her family to help. Burlingtonians collected food and clothing for Ireland. Timothy Follet, the village's leading citizen and most important ship and railroad owner, offered to transport provisions free of charge to New York City, from where they could be shipped to Ireland. A Barnet man reminded Vermonters that the people of Cork were generous in helping Ethan Allen in 1776 during his captivity by the British. "I do believe that the Green Mountain boys and girls will now acknowledge this debt of gratitude, and contribute generously to relieve the wants of the needy in Ireland." One zealous Vermont woman, Asenath Hatch Nicholson, went to Ireland and spent two years there distributing relief funds.[25]

But there was also hostility. It was one thing to have a few hundred, even a few thousand Irish living in settlements scattered around Vermont, but the seemingly unrelenting waves of destitute Irish now pouring in was a different matter. Cries of alarm rang out. One hears them in comments about Irish railroad crews. An East Braintree woman wrote a friend that she disliked seeing railroad construction going on in her neighborhood, for "I dislike to see so many Irishmen about." A paymaster with the Rutland & Burlington Railroad was even more telling in his remarks about visiting a shanty camp in Ferrisburg. He described the workers as "animals" and was fearful of being robbed because of the payroll he carried. A Braintree man told how he was returning from Randolph one evening when he passed an Irishman walking by the side of the road. When the man asked him for a ride, he remembered "having heard many gruesome tales about the fighting Irish" and whipped his horse on, and felt much relieved when he distanced himself from the Irishmen's camp. Even a priest, Rev. Joseph Coolidge Shaw, a convert to Catholicism and a Harvard graduate—the Irish called him "the Yankee priest"—who worked among the railroad Irish in Brattleboro in the summer of 1848, found them difficult. He wrote that "there were many things to discourage one in those hard railroad men." Natives reacted to these rough men in emotions that ranged from pity to fear. [26]

What Vermonters most objected to in the Irish, besides their Catholicism, was their intemperance. Whiskey and beer consumption was central to their culture. But what might have been a simple social habit in another context quickly turned to troublesome behavior among young single men who worked under horrendous conditions in railroad crews and in rock quarries, occupations in which maiming and even death were all too frequent. One Royalton woman noted that before the railroad gangs arrived, "The town could scarcely be called a prohibition town . . . but the drink habit was now deplorable."[27]

Violence often accompanied the drinking. Through the 1850s a steady stream of newspaper reports told about the drunken behavior of the Irish. In 1855 the *Free Press* lamented that "three miserable drunken Irishmen beat up a 16 year old in Rutland without any provocation," and went on to say that "whenever a Catholic meeting is held in [Rutland], drunken Irishmen are sure to abound in the streets." Another article noted a fight in an Irish boardinghouse and "groggery" in Springfield. Nor were Irishwomen exempt from this aggressive behavior. One *Free Press* report told how an inebriated Mrs. Gallagher on Burlington's Water Street tried to slit her husband's throat with a razor but only succeeded in cutting a gash from his cheekbone to his chin. Apparently an alcoholic, she was jailed a few months later for trying to hit her husband with an ax. Hardly a week passed without some incident involving the drunken behavior of the Irish, adding further evidence in the view of prejudiced Yankee Vermonters, if any was needed, of their natural depravity.[28]

This criticism of the "drunken" Irish increased in the 1840s and 1850s because at that time Yankee antipathy to alcohol was running at full tide. Since the 1820s there had been calls for temperance in Vermont, and over time the cry had become louder; and in the 1840s its supporters had shifted their goal from temperance to prohibition. They were motivated in part by the perceived threat of the "drunken" Irish. Even Rev. Theobald Mathew, the Irish "apostle of temperance," while on a visit to America in 1849 took time in Castleton to preach against alcohol.[29] In 1852 the prohibitionists succeeded in convincing the state legislature to pass the "Maine law" banning the sale of alcohol for any but medicinal purposes—a prohibition that lasted for fifty years.

During those long, dry years of Vermont's first experience with prohibition, the Irish were among the leading purveyors of illegal spirits. Unlike the descendants of New England Puritans, the Irish had few moral qualms about the "crature." In most railroad camps and Irish-owned grocery stores, one could find beer and whiskey sold under the table. One bootlegger, a woman, Catherine Driscoll Dillon, became something of a legend in her own lifetime. Described as a beautiful woman, Dillon arrived in Vermont from Ireland with her husband just as the railroad boom began. The railway camps became their ticket to prosperity. To make money they provided room and board for the workmen, and, much to the chagrin of the railroad bosses, always had liquor available. With the money they made they eventually settled in the railroad city of St. Albans, opened a boardinghouse, and continued to sell liquor even after passage of the Maine law.

It was while living in St. Albans that Dillon earned her notoriety. In one widely reported incident, she conspired to get rid of her husband by setting him up for the police by encouraging him to steal a valise from a train. When he did so, she turned him in to the authorities and then divorced him. On a number of occasions she was jailed for her bootlegging activities, and a few times managed to escape. On one occasion she let herself down from a second-story window by means of a cotton cloth forty feet long, which she had somehow managed to acquire, and when a deputy apprehended her not far from jail, she quietly informed him that she was "only going down to see the Governor about her fines, and would be back by Tuesday." When she died in St. Albans in 1872 at age forty-five, she left an estate estimated between $50,000 and $75,000. In its obituary, the *Burlington Free Press* said, "She was a remarkable woman, and no one had gained a greater local notoriety."[30]

The presence of characters like Catherine Driscoll Dillon, along with the perception of the Irish as a priest-ridden but wild, lawless people, led to an upswing in nativist sentiment in the years immediately following the famine. So strong was feeling against the Irish that in 1854 a slate of pro-Know-Nothing candidates swept the thirteen seats of the government's Council of Censors, a body in the executive branch that had the power to introduce amendments to the state constitution.[31]

Leading the campaign against the Irish in central Vermont was the weekly *Rutland Herald*. So hostile were its editorials that it raised the ire of the local postmaster, an Irishman named John Cain. Cain was no newcomer to America, having arrived in Vermont in the 1830s and since become a prosperous farmer. He was also outspoken and cantankerous. One contemporary described him as the type of person who held "his hand against everyman." To thwart what he believed was a Know-Nothing organ, he refused to deliver the *Herald* to its subscribers. How his protest played out is unrecorded.[32]

Only the fracturing of the national Know-Nothing Party over the issue of slavery, the emergence of the new Republican Party, and Vermonters' antipathy to the Know-Nothings' secretive deliberations ended its influence in the Green Mountains.[33] Though anti-Irish sentiment would exist into the next century, it was never again as virulent as in the 1850s.

The Catholic Irish

Continuing the trend that began in the 1820s, most of the famine Irish who settled in Vermont came from Catholic backgrounds, but not all. Because the Protestant Irish easily assimilated into Vermont society, it is impossible to assess their numbers; but a few stood out and attest to the presence of a larger community. John McCuen arrived in Vergennes with his parents in 1851 at six months of age and in the 1880s rose to become mayor of the city. In the 1860s Irish-born Rev. John Kiernan was the minister of the Methodist church in Pawlet village, where a good many members of his congregation were Welsh. Robert McLeod, who had left Ireland in 1857, began life in Vermont painting railroad cars, then went into farming, and by the end of the century represented Sheldon in the state legislature. Strictly speaking, Edward Bourne was not part of the famine Irish because he arrived in the United States in the 1830s, but he achieved prominence in the Green Mountain State in the years immediately following the famine: from 1851 to 1866 he was president of Norwich University. Just as in the days when the Scots-Irish settled Londonderry, there was an ongoing but difficult-to-quantify Protestant Irish presence in Vermont.[34]

The Catholic Irish are easier to count because they belonged to one church. Within a few short years of the famine, more than 15,000 Catholics lived in Vermont, the majority Irish.[35] To meet the spiritual needs of this growing population, the church hierarchy in Boston—Vermont was still a part of the Diocese of Boston—encouraged the building of new churches and the establishment of Vermont as its own diocese. Between 1847 and 1858 Catholics built ten new churches, the majority of them in the rapidly expanding industrial centers with their large Irish communities (see table, following page).

In 1853 Rome decided to create a new administrative jurisdiction, the Diocese of Burlington, to encompass the entire state of Vermont. But who was to be bishop? Father O'Callaghan, the pioneer who had guided Vermont's Catholics for over twenty years, was too old and had neither the tact nor the intellect to lead the new diocese. Instead, the church turned to a devout Frenchman from Brittany with proven administrative skills: the Right Reverend Louis de Goesbriand, most recently the vicar general of the Diocese of Cleveland. With de Goesbriand's appointment, O'Callaghan quietly moved to Holyoke, Massachusetts, where he founded a new parish, St. Jerome. He died there in 1861.

As Bishop de Goesbriand took office, he was faced with a growing problem in America's multicultural society: organizing a Catholic laity that encompassed different cultures—in this case, one Gaelic, the other Gallic. True, they were both Catholic; but they spoke different languages, revered different saints, remembered different histories, and sometimes viewed the others as not quite as Catholic as themselves. Even before de Goesbriand's arrival, church authorities in Boston had recognized this problem and permitted the French Canadian community in Burlington to build its own church, emphasizing French language and customs. St. Joseph, erected on a hill near the University of Vermont, opened in 1850, the first French national church in New England. Down the hill, closer to the bay, stood O'Callaghan's St. Mary Church. People referred to it as the Irish church, and St. Joseph's as the French. De Goesbriand wisely continued this duality as he later opened churches in Vermont's larger urban areas; this two-church pattern became commonplace throughout New England.

Immaculate Conception	St. Albans	1847
St. Patrick	Fairfield	1847
St. Louis	Highgate	1850
St. Joseph	Burlington	1850
St. Augustine	Montpelier	1850
Our Lady of Good Help	Brandon	1852
St. Bridget	W. Rutland	1855
St. Thomas	Underhill	1856
St. Vincent Ferrer	Waterbury	1857
St. Peter	Rutland	1857

De Goesbriand also knew that to best serve his ethnically divided flock he had to have both French and Irish priests. But in these early days of the Catholic Church in Vermont there was as yet no native clergy to draw upon. When de Goesbriand took office, there were only five priests in the state. In a letter he wrote at this time to a French bishop, he remarked that he "would need a dozen priests, for there are at least twelve Catholic centers which would require a resident priest in their midst." To fill this void he recruited abroad. On his periodic trips to Rome to report on conditions in his diocese, he usually included two additional stops: one in France and the other in Ireland. In both places he encouraged young seminarians

Louis de Goesbriand, first bishop of the Catholic Diocese of Burlington. (Courtesy of the Roman Catholic Diocese of Burlington.)

to think about joining him in the New World and advised prospective recruits in France to learn English and in Ireland to learn French.[36]

In Ireland he recruited at Dublin's All Hallows Seminary, an institution established in 1842 specifically to train priests for missionary work. In 1855, in his first trip to Europe after being named bishop, he returned with five priests, two of them, Charles O'Reilly and Thomas Lynch, from Ireland.[37] Lynch served the diocese for many years as a popular priest and administrator; two of his sisters later followed him to Vermont as members of the Sisters of Mercy. De Goesbriand returned to Europe many times during his bishopric, each time imploring young seminarians to join him in the Green Mountains. In the almost half century that de Goesbriand led Vermont's Catholics, his priests came almost equally from the French and Irish communities, a number of them directly from the Old World.

But even with his bridge-building efforts, the French-speaking bishop early on ran into a conflict with a group of his Irish co-religionists. The issue on which the sides clashed was centered in Highgate, in Franklin County. Adjacent to the border with Quebec, Highgate had, like Fairfield, an older Irish community and a large French Canadian population. Some of the Irish had been there since the 1820s and had established themselves as farmers, tailors, blacksmiths, carpenters, and shoemakers. In short, they were not the rough "shanty" Irish associated with the railroad gangs but a prosperous, settled community.[38]

In 1848 the Highgate Catholics, both Irish and French Canadian, felt sufficiently numerous to have their own church. Though the effort to acquire a church was a joint French Canadian and Irish endeavor, the driving force behind the project was a group of Irish people led by two carpenters, Thomas O'Heere and Adam Christie, and a farmer, Nicholas Hanna. Through local subscription they acquired a piece of land and bought a building that had once served as a Congregational church. To complete the renovation, Rev. Edward McGowan, the Irish priest in nearby St. Albans, advised them to raise funds by selling pews in the new church (a practice abhorred by Father O'Callaghan). In any case, the pews were sold, the money raised, and the new church completed in 1850. Perhaps as a compromise with the French Canadians, the church was named St. Louis.

All went well at St. Louis until 1855 when Jean Lionnet, a French priest, succeeded McGowan. In going over church finances, he came across records detailing the ownership of the pews. Father Lionnet had a problem. Canon law stipulated that laymen could not own church property. Clearly, pew ownership was in violation of church law; but given the embryonic nature of the Catholic Church in Vermont, plus the potential for ethnic factionalism, this was an issue best ignored. Lionnet, however, apparently was not a man of tact and may have already been at odds with his Irish followers. He informed his parishioners that they did not own the pews and in future would have to rent them.

To say that this did not sit well with the Irish is an understatement. In their eyes they had raised the money to acquire a church, had renovated it, and therefore it was *their* church. The bishop was called in to settle the dispute. This put de Goesbriand on the spot. Lionnet was clearly right, but the parishioners were adamant that Father McGowan had promised ownership in perpetuity. A decision either way was bound to have repercussions. The bishop, as he had to, came down on the side of canon law. At a parish meeting, he told the people their ownership could not continue. Most of the congregation immediately accepted the bishop's decision, but a small clique of Irishmen led by O'Heere resisted.

As often happens when people clash over principle, reason soon went out the window. De Goesbriand, who as a new bishop probably felt compelled to assert his authority, ordered the pews broken down and removed from the church. O'Heere and Hanna called the sheriff and had the bishop arrested and thrown in jail for stealing their property. Friends quickly bailed him out. Next, O'Heere filed suit against the bishop, charging that he had entered O'Heere's private property (the pew) and destroyed it. When the case came to trial, the court, not recognizing canon law, sided with the plaintiff and awarded O'Heere $20.83 in damages.

It was a Pyrrhic victory. For observant Catholics, de Goesbriand held the ultimate card: the interdict. He shut St. Louis down, instructing the priest there "to suspend all acts of public worship; [not] to celebrate Mass and marriages, [not] to preach the word of God, [not] to administer Baptism, [not] to perform the ceremonies of funerals." He did this, he wrote, because the Catholic community of St. Louis was in breach of the rules and canons of the Catholic Church. Highgate Catholics were free to worship at Catholic churches in neighboring towns, but as long as the interdict was in effect, the doors of St. Louis remained closed.

O'Heere and Hanna, probably bowing to pressure from their friends and neighbors, eventually saw the error of their ways and apologized to the bishop. Adam Christie had already left the scene, having moved to the Midwest in the early 1850s. (In a twist of history, one of his sons, Alexander, became the first archbishop of the Archdiocese of Portland, Oregon.) On his part, de Goesbriand, who had acted out of adherence to church law rather than any sense of vindictiveness, quickly forgave the protesters and reopened St. Louis. What the "Highgate Affair" all too visibly demonstrated was the power of latent ethnic tensions to disrupt and divide the Catholic Church in Vermont.

De Goesbriand's efforts to keep the peace with the "Canadians," as he called them, and the Irish were reflected in the building of Burlington's cathedral.[39] By the late 1850s St. Mary, Burlington's "Irish church" built in 1841 to replace the church destroyed by fire in 1838, was woefully inadequate to serve the village's English-speaking Catholics. Moreover, as the seat of the diocese, Burlington qualified for a cathedral to serve as Vermont's mother church. To satisfy both needs, construction of a cathedral began in 1862 but, as a result of labor shortages during the Civil War, was not completed until 1867. In recognition of the two communities that it served, the cathedral used the French fleur-de-lis as a

Burlington's Cathedral of the Immaculate Conception, under construction in the 1860s. It was thought of as the "Irish church," while nearby St. Joseph's was the "French church." (Courtesy of the Roman Catholic Diocese of Burlington.)

decorative motif, while its lone chapel was dedicated to St. Patrick. Significantly, when the church was consecrated as the Cathedral of the Immaculate Conception in December 1867, Archbishop John McCloskey of New York—perhaps in an effort to smooth ethnic tensions—preached a sermon entitled "Unity of the Catholic Church." Despite these efforts, well into the twentieth century the Irish thought of the cathedral as their church, while St. Joseph remained the "French church." In the years ahead, relations between the French Canadians and the Irish would at times become severely strained, sometimes resulting in violence.

The Bolton "War"

Karl Marx theorized that bringing workers together in factories and mills would socialize them: that is, they would come to understand their common needs and common plight, and the common utility of working together. Something along those lines happened to the famine Irish. Uprooted and thrown into an environment that was sometimes sympathetic, but often apathetic and at times openly hostile, the Irish usually grouped together, whether it was in living arrangements, in workplaces, in labor disputes, or in political contests. As early as the late 1840s and early 1850s, incidents occurred in Vermont that presaged the later involvement of the Irish in union activities and in politics.

An incident in Bolton in 1846 was the first example of an Irish work action in Vermont. In the spring of that year, two Irish crews of 300 men blasted a rail bed through a rocky stretch of the Winooski valley in Bolton, just east of Burlington. The men resided in two camps, one called Dublin and the other Cork, after their counties of origin. Amid constant dynamite explosions and the movement of steel rails and heavy wooden ties, accidents were common. When that section of the line eventually was completed in 1849, it had cost the lives of seventeen Irishmen.

In early July 1846, the contractor charged with building the section, a man named Barker, ran out of money. Word quickly spread that the workmen would not be paid. Disbelief soon turned to anger. Irishmen downed their tools and, in what one historian called "probably the first major work stoppage in Vermont history," walked off the job. Blocking the local road, they marched to nearby Jonesville, where Barker and his staff used a local hotel as their construction headquarters. Fearing he might be lynched, Barker sent one of his men to Burlington for help. The authorities there, probably from an inherent bias against shanty Irish railroad workers, mobilized the local militia, armed a volunteer fire company, and dispatched them to Jonesville. There the presence of Yankee bayonets and the counsel of a Catholic priest—most likely Rev. O'Callaghan—persuaded the strikers to disperse. The upshot of the Bolton "war" was that few of the workers were paid, their camps were broken up, the leaders arrested and jailed, and work on that section was curtailed for two years. What happened was so blatantly unfair that even the conservative *Free Press*, while critical of the work stoppage, argued that the workers had cause for complaint. The Bolton incident would not be the last time that unscrupulous employers took advantage of impoverished Irish laborers in Vermont, nor would it be the last time that workers struck back.[40]

O'Callaghan's Last Battle

Not many years after the Bolton "war," the Irish in Burlington demonstrated their political muscle. Just before de Goesbriand became Burlington's first bishop, Rev. O'Callaghan led his Irish followers in a fight over city incorporation. Whether to be chartered as a city as opposed to remaining as a town or village was a constant theme in Vermont's urban centers in the latter half of the nineteenth and in the early twentieth century. In Burlington, businessmen believed that establishment of a city would mean an increase in municipal services and lead to greater commercial activity. In 1852 the business interests persuaded the state legislature to introduce a bill that called for the urban section of Burlington to be incorporated as a city and the rural area chartered as a new township, South Burlington. Through partition, the business proponents of the plan hoped to assuage the reservations of farmers who were fearful of the taxes associated with city services. The legislature approved the bill but put it before the people of Burlington for ratification.

For reasons that are not totally clear, O'Callaghan opposed the plan. To him it may have smacked of big government and higher taxes. And, perhaps, being naturally conservative, he opposed change. He campaigned against cityhood, and he was a formidable campaigner, having fought for years to elect Democratic candidates on the state and national levels. In the fight he was assisted by an ambitious young Irishman, Cork-born James O'Halloran, who had graduated from the University of Vermont in 1843 and for a time was the editor of the Democratic-leaning *Burlington Sentinel*. (Later O'Halloran would become a lawyer, ending his career in Quebec as counsel to the Canadian-Pacific Railway.) With O'Callaghan in the pulpit and O'Halloran in the streets, they mobilized their "Irish Brigade," as O'Halloran called their followers, and the measure went down in defeat. The opposition of O'Callaghan and O'Halloran helped to delay Burlington's incorporation as a city by twelve years, by which time both men were no longer on the scene.[41]

What the contest demonstrated was the power wielded by the Irish in Vermont's largest urban center. It also previewed the influence the Irish would have in the state's other large cities and towns. In this vein it is significant to note that the year the cathedral opened its doors, 1867, a survey conducted by a local newspaper found that Catholics, Irish and French Canadian, constituted a majority of Burlington's residents.[42] Could political change be far behind?

The Vermont Irish on the Eve of the Civil War

At the end of the 1850s Vermont and its Irish community were much changed from what they had been in the early 1840s. Due to the influx resulting from the Great Famine, the Irish constituted the largest ethnic minority in the state, slightly ahead of French Canadians. In places like Burlington and Rutland they were an overwhelming presence. They could be found in most of the state's industrial centers, building railroads, quarrying stone, and manning looms; but they also worked the land on farms in Fairfield, Underhill, and Moretown. And while the pre-famine Irish came primarily from counties in the north of Ireland, evidence from gravestones and family histories suggests the famine Irish hailed from counties farther south. The famine Irish were also overwhelmingly Catholic, and with their French Canadian co-religionists they came to define the Catholic Church in Vermont.

By 1860 the Irish had become a stable community in the Green Mountains. In general, the patterns of Irish settlement that existed in 1860 continued down to the end of the century. There was, however, one major difference. With no continuing large-scale Irish immigration to Vermont in the latter half of the nineteenth century, the number of Ireland-born Irish in the Green Mountains continuously declined, while the number of second- and third-generation Irish Americans steadily rose.

The transition from fever-ship immigrant to settled Vermonter had been arduous. The Irish had taken the worst jobs and often lived in deplorable conditions, while Vermonters of old Yankee stock, shocked by the large numbers of newcomers, had often exhibited an anti-Irish bias exceeding anything seen before. Yet numerous examples of Yankee kindness and empathy toward the incoming Irish also suggested a degree of sympathy toward the newcomers' plight.

In 1859, on the eve of the Civil War, a minor election in Fairfield showed how far the Catholic Irish had come in a short time. At the annual town meeting in March, Michael McQueeney, forty-one, who had left Ireland in the early 1840s with his wife and young son, was elected a selectman—likely the first Irish Catholic in the state so honored.[43] The Vermont Irish were on their way to becoming Americans. In the next few years they would mark this transformation with their blood.

The 1860s:
The Turbulent Decade

Within a dozen years of Ireland's Great Famine, the Vermont Irish found themselves engulfed in that bloody calamity of nineteenth-century America, the Civil War. For many Irishmen it would be a defining experience, marking a transformation from emigrant green-horn to red-blooded American. A few Irish Vermonters returned from the conflict as genuine war heroes, capitalized on their reputations, and built successful business and political careers. A small minority, perhaps imbued by the martial spirit of the times, gravitated to the militantly nationalistic Fenian movement. Others simply returned to farms, quarries, and textile mills to resume their former lives. The war itself was a watershed, marking an end to the great wave of Irish immigration spawned by the famine, while also introducing the age in which the Irish began to successfully assimilate into American society.

How did Vermont's Irish perceive the Civil War? Not much differently from the rest of the North, it appears. There were probably as many opinions as there were Irishmen. For some adventurous young men, the conflict—particularly in its early days, before the horrors of the war were fully understood—may have been no more than a chance to see a bit of the country while drawing steady pay. Then, too, military life had a certain appeal to the Irish. For generations in Ireland impoverished men like William Gilliland in the 1750s had escaped bleak lives by taking the

British king's shilling as soldiers or seamen, or running off to join the Irish brigades in French and Spanish armies. In Vermont, putting on Union blue may simply have been a means to escape bone-wearying toil with pick and shovel.

Others may have joined the colors for ideological reasons. This was the case with Irish-born William White of Sheldon in Franklin County. While stationed in Maryland in 1863, he wrote a friend that he would stay in the army "until the victory is complete for the Union and these accursed rebels once more forced to return to their allegiance."[1] More than a few joined up simply because of bonuses offered by towns and the state. The question of slavery, while it was important in abolitionist Vermont, seems not to have been a major issue among the Irish. There were even one or two Irish voices that spoke in favor of the "peculiar institution." The Dublin-born Episcopal bishop, John Henry Hopkins, defended the institution of slavery on the grounds that it was found in the Bible—although his opinion may not have been widely shared among the Irish in Vermont.[2]

Did the Irish join the Union army in numbers commensurate with their share of the population? In the Union army as a whole, despite the fame of such Irish units as New York's "Fighting Sixty-ninth," the answer is no. This was also the case with the Vermont Irish. This is understandable. Most Irishmen were so new to the United States that the issues involved meant little. And, too, the all-consuming demands of making a living, and possibly supporting a family, precluded the military life as an option.[3]

At times there was real opposition to military service. This was particularly true in Irish reaction to the introduction of conscription in the spring of 1863. As passed, the Conscription Act made all men, age twenty to forty-five, liable for military service, but exempted those who paid $300 or who could provide a substitute willing to enlist for three years. As few workingmen could afford the exemption fee, the act was widely perceived as putting the burden of fighting the war squarely on the shoulders of the poor. Irish immigrants knew what this meant for them.

Reaction was sometimes violent. The most famous incident on the national scene occurred in New York City, where the draft riots of July 13–16, 1863, left 105 people dead, mainly Irishmen. But even before the New York riots, there had been trouble in Vermont. Less than a month prior to the violence in New York, an army officer entered the Adams and Allen Marble Works in West Rutland on June 16 to register men for the draft, but an angry crowd of quarrymen refused to give him any information. The next day a Captain Crane, the provost marshal charged with the task of enrolling area men for the draft, returned to the quarry, accompanied by a party that included the local sheriff and a few deputies. They intended to arrest the leaders of the resistance. What greeted them was a "well organized" throng of tough Irish quarrymen estimated between 200 to 500 strong. In a report filed later that day, Crane described what happened:

> Arriving at the place we quietly commenced a search for the offenders, when without provocation we were suddenly attacked by about 500 laborers, who appeared at a given signal armed with clubs and stones, which were mercilessly hurled upon us until we were driven entirely from the neighborhood. Both the deputy sheriff and myself were severely though not seriously injured. There are in and about the quarries about 1,000 laborers, all Irishmen. That they are organized and determined to resist the enrollment and draft I am entirely satisfied.

Crane omitted to report that in the melee he emptied his revolver into the crowd in an attempt to shoot the ringleader, although he must have been a poor shot, as no one was reported wounded.[4]

The situation was explosive. Following the confrontation, Crane rode to Montpelier and requested that 200 infantrymen be sent to West Rutland to quell the resistance. But there were no troops available: all active units were busy fighting in the South. It was even suggested that the Invalid Corps be sent, but the idea went nowhere. Finally, Montpelier advised Crane to avoid confrontation by getting the Irish enrolled "by reference to the pay-rolls of their employers." In the meantime, the authorities would put a force together before the draft took place.[5]

Through that summer, Irishmen around the state continued to agitate against the draft. In one incident in Burlington, crowds of onlookers pelted recruits who marched through the Irish neighborhood on the way to the train depot on Lake Street. In the end Vermont averted a crisis over conscription. Through bonuses offered by the state and towns, enough volunteers enlisted so that widespread use of the draft was unnecessary. Of the 34,238 Vermonters who served in the Civil War, only 437 were conscripts.[6]

John Lonergan and the Civil War

Despite widespread hostility toward the draft, hundreds of Vermonters from Irish backgrounds served in the war effort. Five Donnellys from Castleton enlisted, as did three McKeans, descendants of the Brian McKean who first settled in Castleton after working on the Champlain Canal in the 1820s. One of the McKean boys, John, never came home: after being wounded in the first battle of Bull Run, he died fighting in the Wilderness campaign three years later. Numerous McEnanys from Franklin County served, including forty-three-year-old Irish-born Barney McEnany from Bakersfield. Barney Leddy, who had come to America as a six-year-old in the worst year of the famine and who with his family settled in Underhill, enlisted in 1862 and was killed in the fighting around Petersburg, Virginia, in 1864. One Vermont Irishman, John Lonergan, became a hero of the war.[7]

Lonergan's beginnings were humble. He was famine Irish. Born in Tipperary in 1838, he received a rudimentary education at a Christian Brothers school and when he was ten years old fled with his parents to America, finally settling in Burlington. There his father worked as a cooper. From all accounts, young Lonergan was bright, quick-witted, humorous, a born storyteller, adventurous, and ambitious. By day he worked in menial jobs, and at night he continued his studies. Early in his life the military attracted him: in his free time he drilled with a militia unit in Brandon. In 1860 he opened a grocery store in the textile village of Winooski, catering to the hundreds of Irish who worked in the textile mills. There he continued his interest in military affairs by organizing a militia unit composed primarily of Irishmen from Burlington, Colchester, and Winooski.

The attack on Fort Sumter in 1861 changed Lonergan's life. From being a humble grocer he became a military man. When Governor Erastus Fairbanks called for the raising of a regiment of volunteers to meet President Lincoln's request for 75,000 ninety-day soldiers, Lonergan, on the recommendation of his militia commander, Colonel George Stannard, was appointed a recruiting officer. On May 7, 1861, he officially enlisted in federal service as a private. For the next few weeks he made the rounds among his Irish friends in Winooski and Burlington, encouraging them to join the ranks. What his motivation was is unknown. Perhaps it was love for his adopted land, for in later years he often expressed gratitude to the country that had given him so much. Or, more plausibly, it was simply a young man's attraction—he was only twenty-three at the time—to the adventurous life of a soldier. Whatever the source of his enthusiasm, he was a convincing recruiter. By June 1 he had enlisted a full complement of soldiers: Company K, First Regiment of Vermont Volunteers. The men elected him captain.[8]

His initial success as a leader, however, was short-lived. While his company was encamped at Fort Underwood in Burlington, where the Second Regiment was being organized, something happened, for on June 18 Governor Fairbanks disbanded Company K. A correspondent for the *Burlington Free Press* wrote that "Captain Lonergan's company has not answered the expectations of its friends, proving the reverse of orderly and attentive to duty, and that the unpleasant duty of disbanding the company has been forced upon the Governor." The writer gave no further details, but either Lonergan himself had been insubordinate, or he had been unable to keep his men in line. Probably the latter was the case. Since the mobilization of recruits in May 1861, Camp Underwood had been a mess.

Civil War hero John Lonergan was subsequently the leader of the Fenian movement in Vermont. (Courtesy of the Vermont Historical Society.)

The camp was makeshift, located in the fairgrounds in Burlington's north end. Nightly, raw recruits who were little more than civilians in uniform went AWOL by scaling the fence that surrounded the encampment and scurried off for quick visits to family, friends, and sweethearts. Most came back the next morning, but the constant comings and goings demonstrated a serious lack of discipline. There was also a problem with alcohol. Almost every evening bootleggers sold bottles of illegal liquor to the soldiers through the fence around the camp.[9]

Whether Lonergan and his Company K were more unruly than other units at Camp Underwood is unknown, but they were the only ones singled out for punishment.[10] Lonergan lost his command, and most of his men were reassigned to a unit from Vergennes.

Lonergan's movements over the next few months are vague, but he seems to have traveled down to Maryland with the Second Regiment and seen action in Virginia in the opening months of the war. However, when the ninety-day enlistment period ended, he returned to Vermont. In Burlington he joined another militia unit, this one also made up primarily of Irishmen, and calling itself the Emmet Guards, after Robert Emmet, the Irishman executed in 1803 for leading an abortive rebellion in Dublin. For the next eleven months Lonergan worked by day and drilled in the evening, closely following events in the South and no doubt chafing over the way

Second-in-command to John Lonergan in the Emmet Guards, Lieutenant John Sinnott died in the fighting at Gettysburg. (Courtesy of the Vermont Historical Society.)

he had been treated the previous summer. His military career, however, received a reprieve in August 1862 when President Lincoln called up 300,000 militiamen to serve for nine months. The call-up included Burlington's Emmet Guards.

By 1862 militia units across the North were grossly under strength, as many of their former members were already serving in the active military, and this included the Emmet Guards. To fill the ranks, Lonergan again recruited. The old Emmet Guards gave him a nucleus around which to build a new company, and Irishmen from Burlington and Winooski soon joined them. The Rutland Irish supplied another large contingent, although it took the promise of a $100 bonus to entice them. To round out the company, a group of Yankees from Westford added their names to the roster. How they felt about being thrown in with so many Irishmen can only be guessed at.

The Emmet Guards was a decidedly Irish unit. The company counted 83 members: 20 Yankee Vermonters, 5 French Canadians, and the remainder Irish. Initially 116 men enlisted, but only 83 showed up at the mustering point in Brattleboro. When the men elected their officers, as was customary in militia units, they chose Irishmen: Lonergan again became a captain, while another native of Ireland, John Sinnott, a schoolteacher from Rutland, was chosen first lieutenant. Another Rutland man, David McDevitt, became second lieutenant, and Burlington's James Scully became first sergeant. Onlookers at the drill grounds noted that when the company was ordered to assemble, the command given was a brogue-laden "fall in yees." One regimental officer later referred to the Emmet Guards as "my Irish Regulars."

As the men came in, the state put them up at Howard's Hotel on Court House Square (now City Hall Park) or at Murphy's Hotel on Water Street. Murphy's, situated in the heart of Burlington's Irish neighborhood, must have been a particular favorite for Lonergan's recruits. While they waited to be sworn in to federal service, the men filled their days drilling at the fairgrounds and at "the Battery" (now Battery Park).[11]

In late September the unit moved to Camp Lincoln in Brattleboro, where it officially became Company A, Thirteenth Regiment, Vermont Volunteers, and from there traveled to Washington, D.C., and finally to northern Virginia as part of Vermont's Second Brigade. From that time until Gettysburg in July 1863, Lonergan and his men saw little action, their life a constant routine of drilling, picket duty, tension, and boredom. There are, however, two incidents from this time worth relating, for they tell us something about the status of Irish Catholics in a Vermont unit, and also something about how Lonergan's superiors viewed him.

The first incident had to do with religious services. Since the outbreak of hostilities, Bishop de Goesbriand had asked Vermont military authorities to include a Catholic chaplain in their regiments. His requests were denied. To add insult to injury, soldiers in Vermont units were required to attend Protestant Sunday services. This did not sit well with the Emmet Guards. The issue came to a head at Christmas 1862. On that day the Thirteenth Regiment was ordered to attend divine services. Company A reluctantly complied, but there must have been rumbling and talk in the ranks, for on the following Sunday Captain Lonergan—never a man to run from a fight—as an act of protest refused to turn his men out for the weekly inspection. For his disobedience, the young Irishman was arrested and suffered the disgrace of having to relinquish his sword. The incident caused a furor in the regiment, and its leaders quickly realized their error. Lonergan was released, his sword returned, and attendance at Sunday services was made voluntary.

Lonergan's protest, his youth, his Irish Catholicism, and a general perception that he was hotheaded and quick to anger may have led to his being rejected for promotion in the spring of 1863. As the senior captain in the regiment, he thought himself first in line for a promotion. However, when a vacancy occurred, he was passed over. Some years after the war, his former regimental commander, Colonel Francis Randall, explained the rejection: "All colts have to be halter broke and

Encampment of Company A, Thirteenth Regiment, Vermont Volunteers, at Wolf Run Shoals, Virginia, prior to their deployment to Gettysburg. (Courtesy of the Vermont Historical Society.)

then we get good horses of them. I had some colts." In short, Randall thought Lonergan then unsuited for higher command. For Lonergan, the snub rankled.

The one good piece of news for Lonergan that spring was that George Stannard, his old mentor from Winooski militia days, had been raised to brigadier general and given command of the Second Brigade, the Thirteenth's parent organization. Stannard thought highly of the young Irishman: Lonergan could expect better treatment in the future. But time was running out for the regiment. As nine-month men, their enlistments were due to end in mid-July. If all went well they would be mustered out of the army and returned to Vermont, where they could regale friends and neighbors with their adventures in Virginia and Maryland—with nary a shot having been fired.[12]

But instead of a quiet exit from the war, Lonergan and Company A, just a few days shy of their mustering out date, found themselves engulfed in the greatest battle of the conflict—Gettysburg. When General Lee moved his army into Pennsylvania in June 1863, Vermont's Second Brigade was part of the Union army sent to blunt his invasion. Near the little hamlet of Gettysburg, 75,000 Confederates faced 90,000 bluecoats. There Lonergan and his "Irish Regulars" covered themselves in glory.

On July 2, the second day of the battle, General Winfield Scott Hancock ordered Colonel Randall to secure an artillery battery that was in danger of being overrun by rebels. With Lonergan and Company A, Randall "moved forward and secured the guns." Finding themselves being fired upon from a nearby building, Lonergan and his men "gave the Irish yell" and then charged and surrounded the structure, calling for its defenders to surrender. To their amazement, out came eighty members of an Alabama unit—more men than Lonergan had with him. For his actions that day Lonergan later received the Medal of Honor.

For all their heroics on July 2, Company A's finest hour still lay ahead. On July 3 the Thirteenth Regiment occupied ground just left of center of the Union line, with Company A on the far left of the regimental position. At about 3:30 in the afternoon, 15,000 rebels advanced on the Union lines in the attack forever famous as Pickett's Charge. As rows of rebel soldiers marched relentlessly toward the Union center, General Stannard noticed that the Thirteenth Regiment, by wheeling in a ninety-degree arc, would flank the advancing gray line. The order rang out, "Change front forward on first company." The entire regiment swung in an arc on First Sergeant Scully of Company A, who stood as a hinge while the line moved to its new flanking position. As soon as Company A came on line it opened a withering fire on the confused rebels. Later assessment calculated that the Emmet Guards each fired ten to twelve rounds at Pickett's men, double the number expended by the other flanking companies. Under fire from front and side, the rebels broke and ran.

In 1897, veterans of Vermont's Thirteenth Regiment attended ceremonies on the Gettysburg battlefield surrounding the dedication of a monument commemorating their service. Just visible between the two men sitting forward of the larger group is the head of Sergeant James Scully, the "pivotal" man at Gettysburg. (Courtesy of the Vermont Historical Society.)

In Vermont military lore, the Thirteenth Regiment is credited with breaking the last Confederate gasp at Gettysburg. And in this rendition of events, Company A is given pride of place. In the 1880s, George Benedict, who was present at Gettysburg as aide-de-camp to General Stannard, wrote a history of Vermont's participation in the Civil War. Of the Emmet Guards he said, "As the regiment turned on First Sergeant James B. Scully of Company A, he may be said to have been the pivot of the pivotal movement of the pivotal battle of the war." When Benedict made those remarks, Scully, now a war hero, was a successful businessman in Burlington.[13]

On July 21 the Thirteenth Regiment was mustered out and Lonergan and his men returned home as heroes—American heroes. In a sense, the Civil War experience forced native Americans to recognize their Irish comrades as fellow Americans. Too many Irishmen had fought and died in the Union cause for them to be considered outsiders. There were Irish people in Vermont, like Thomas and Elizabeth Henchey of Bakersfield, who had paid an awful price for their citizenship. Their three Vermont-born sons all served in the war, and one died in battle, while another failed to survive a Confederate prisoner-of-war camp. Dorothy Canfield Fisher, the Vermont writer, who was born not long after the Civil War and knew the generation that experienced that conflict, described the transforming experience of the war:

> The O'Haras and the McCarthys put on the blue uniform and marched beside the Hawleys and the Deweys into battle; they were sent back wounded, to lie in the same rough Vermont barrack hospitals. Some of them were killed in battle and their names were put on the bronze tablets on the town Roll of Honor. . . . The Irish soldiers, now G.A.R. men, were no longer immigrants: they were Vermont boys.

A similar sentiment was expressed while the war still raged. At a banquet held in Montpelier in June 1864 to honor General Stannard and the Second Brigade, a Protestant chaplain toasted the Irish: "At Savage's Station and Gettysburg, the shamrock of Ireland and the evergreen of Vermont were entwined around the staff of our victory flag."[14]

A visible metaphor for Vermont's acceptance of its Irish neighbors as full-blooded Americans following the Civil War is displayed in an oil painting that today hangs in the old library room of the State House in Montpelier. This monumental painting, ten by twenty feet, depicts scenes from the battle of Cedar Creek, fought on October 19, 1864, in Virginia's Shenandoah Valley. The Vermont legislature commissioned the painting shortly after the war to commemorate the battle in which more Vermont units took part than in any other engagement. Painted by Vermont artist Julian Scott, it is a montage of rearing horses, artillery smoke, flashing bayonets, unfurled flags, and advancing columns of soldiers. In the exact center of the painting—the point where the onlooker's eye is immediately drawn—are three soldiers in Union blue. One of them, a wounded redheaded officer with a goatee and mustache in the fashion of the day, is being carried off the battlefield by two comrades.

The redheaded officer is known to us. He was Captain Thomas Kennedy, commanding officer of Company K, Sixth Regiment, First Brigade—Vermont's famous "Old Brigade." He had enlisted as a private in 1861, saw action in most of the campaigns fought by the Army of the Potomac, and gradually worked his way up from enlisted man to commissioned officer. Unscathed through the first three years of war, he ran out of luck at Cedar Creek when a musket ball hit him in the hip. Lodged there permanently, the ball left him with a limp for the rest of his life. In preparations for the painting, Julian Scott wrote Kennedy, asking him for details of the fight, and specifically identified Kennedy as one of the eighteen officers depicted in the battle.

Kennedy was first-generation Irish American. His parents had come to America in the 1820s, may have spent some time in Pennsylvania, but by the 1830s were residing in Franklin County, Vermont. Thus it is interesting that in Scott's painting, meant to commemorate Vermont's contribution to the Civil War, the focus of the battle scene is a wounded Irish American being carried from the field. And this would have been well known to onlookers when the painting was first unveiled in 1874. By then Kennedy was a prominent Vermont figure. In the same year the painting was completed, the people of Fairfield elected him to represent them in the state legislature. To passersby, the Cedar Creek painting was a constant reminder that the Irish too had played their part in preserving the Union.[15]

Fenians or Finnigans

But they were still Irish. Among the generation that had experienced the Great Famine and the subsequent diaspora, there was intense bitterness against England—a degree of bitterness that had not been present before 1845.[16] This hatred led to the founding in 1858 in both Dublin and New York of a secret organization dedicated to the violent overthrow of British rule in Ireland. Officially, it was the Irish Republican Brotherhood; popularly, its members were known as Fenians, after an ancient warrior band, the fianna. Because its two founders, James Stephens and John O'Mahoney, had spent some time in France during the Revolution of 1848, they patterned their organization on the Blanquist model of cells, called centers, in which, as a precaution against informers, only one member of a center knew one member of another center. This was the theory, and while it was generally adhered to in Ireland, in America membership in the Fenian organization was quite open.

Initially slow to catch on, membership in the United States expanded rapidly during the Civil War. The war itself acted as a catalyst, bringing together thousands of Irishmen from diverse parts of the country and giving them military training. Fenian supporters found enthusiastic recruits in the Union encampments in Maryland and Virginia, and when those boys returned home they spread the word further. In 1864 Fenian speakers toured the country, bringing in converts. In December of that year a Fenian organizer spoke at a rally in Burlington. Significantly, the meeting was held in the city's Old Baptist Church: significant, because while the Fenian

movement was overwhelmingly Catholic in membership, as a secret organization it was proscribed by the Catholic hierarchy. This, apparently, did not deter the audience, for at the end of the session a large number of men joined up. Young Irishmen across the state flocked to Fenianism.

One of them was Captain Lonergan. After his discharge from the army following Gettysburg, Lonergan returned to Burlington and went back into the grocery business. With his gregarious personality and war hero reputation, he was soon the

A panoramic painting of the battle of Cedar Creek hangs in the old library room of the Vermont State House. In the center of the painting, the wounded Captain Thomas Kennedy is depicted, being carried from the battlefield. (Courtesy of the Office of Vermont State Curator.)

leader of the Irish community. His shop on the west side of Court House Square was a center for Irish activities. In 1864, as president of the local Hibernian Society, he organized Burlington's first St. Patrick's Day celebration. This was a festive affair, with a procession down the city's main street that included "bould soger boys" from Vermont's Seventeenth Regiment, Jericho's Cornet Band, and marching contingents from various Irish societies. In the evening there was a banquet at the American Hotel. That same year Lonergan organized a drama club to put on plays of Irish interest. For the young Irishman, these were heady days.

The leitmotif in all these activities was the Irish American's love both for his adopted and his native land. At the St. Patrick's Day ceremonies, Lonergan proclaimed "Here in America where we are permitted to unfurl it [the Irish flag], whilst we are ready to fight under the starry flag of our adoption, as we should do, no American will object to us fighting for it under the flag of our native land." Lonergan's constant referring to this dual allegiance reflected his growing involvement in the Fenian movement. When exactly he joined is unclear, but his public utterances beginning in 1864 leave little doubt as to where his sentiments lay. In April he was instrumental in bringing to Burlington Thomas Francis Meagher, the Civil War commander of the celebrated Irish Brigade and a rebel from the 1848 uprising in Ireland who had once been transported by the British to Australia. Before a packed house at Burlington's Town Hall, Meagher lectured on the life of Michael Corcoran, the late commander of the "Fighting Sixty-ninth," and noted "that as an Irishman his [Corcoran's] highest anticipation was to see his native country reestablished as a nation—in the effort for its restoration it was his highest hope to share." As the Civil War wound down, Irish American nationalists became increasingly bellicose in their rhetoric.[17]

Late in 1865 the American Fenians came under control of a faction impatient to strike a blow for Irish freedom. And, they believed, the easiest way to do this from the United States was to strike at Britain through Canada. Their strategy was to invade Canada and in essence hold it hostage in exchange for Irish independence. While today this seems a harebrained scheme, there were some solid reasons for believing it could work. First, with thousands of recently demobilized Irishmen, veterans of long years of war, the Fenian leaders believed they had the nucleus of a large, experienced army. Secondly, there was strong anti-British feeling in the United States over Britain's pro-Southern neutrality during the war, compounded by the Confederate raid out of Canada on St. Alban's, Vermont, in October 1864. This daring attack resulted in one Vermonter killed and the loss of $200,000 from the local banks. In this anti-British atmosphere, the postwar administration of Andrew Johnson seemed to be indifferent to a Fenian invasion of Canada. And finally, the Fenian leaders thought that once an invasion began, the thousands of Irishmen living in Canada, plus malcontent elements within the French Canadian population, would quickly join them. In the end, the plan was unduly optimistic, but it was not without its rationale.[18]

Vermont was central to the Fenian strategy. The national Fenian leadership envisioned a three-pronged attack, with one column entering Ontario from Detroit, another from Buffalo, and a third entering Quebec from upstate New York and Franklin County in northwestern Vermont. They set the attacks for June 1866.

Lonergan appears to have been key to the Fenian plan. As the de facto leader of the Vermont Irish, and a person attracted to the martial life, it was a foregone conclusion that he would become a Fenian. Moreover, he hated England. We do not know what horrors he witnessed as a young boy in the famine: perhaps family and friends slowly starving to death, the evictions of destitute families, or suffering the terror of crossing the Atlantic on a "coffin" ship where typhus and cholera took their toll. Whatever the memories that haunted him, in his public utterances he never ceased calling for rebellion against England.

Sometime in late 1865 or early 1866, the twenty-eight-year-old Lonergan became state "head center" of the movement in Vermont. Just as he had been for the Union cause, he was an energetic recruiter for the secret organization, traveling across the state to rally support. In his public utterances he often used coded language. His fellow countrymen understood what he meant when he said in January 1866 that "wherever ten Irishmen live who still remember Ireland, and have not forgotten England, prepare. Organize. There must and will be an exchange of prisoners." It was a clear hint that Canada would be used as a pawn in pursuit of Irish freedom. Moreover, using an image from the liturgy of the Catholic Mass, just as the rebels of the Easter Rebellion would do fifty years later, he warned that "the altar is prepared and the sacrifice to be offered."[19]

Lonergan's appeal was particularly strong in the state's industrial centers: among the railroad Irish in St. Albans, Northfield, Montpelier, Rutland, and Bennington; among the quarry workers in West Rutland and the mill workers in Burlington and Winooski. By early 1866 thirteen circles had been organized, with a combined membership of about 1,000. Burlington had the largest number with 140, while Montpelier was the smallest at 35. But not all Vermont Irishmen were as militant as those associated with Lonergan. One Irishman long resident in Vermont probably expressed the view of many when in a letter to the editor of the *Burlington Free Press* he said the Fenians had little chance of success because their plans were too well known to British authorities, that hostilities would lead to unnecessary bloodshed, and that the church was strongly opposed. Others thought it was ludicrous to attack the British in Canada rather than in Ireland. Despite these misgivings, the plan went forward. As a show of Fenian strength, Lonergan planned a great gathering for Burlington on March 17—St. Patrick's Day.[20]

Rumors spread on both sides of the Canadian-U.S. border that the invasion would take place on the feast day of the Irish saint. Canadian and British authorities positioned militiamen and regular troops at likely entry points along the border. But all was quiet there. In Vermont the action was in Burlington, at Lonergan's grand St. Patrick's Day celebration. At noon, in cold, blustery weather, a mounted "Captain" Lonergan led a parade. Following behind him were various Fenian units, including the Sarsfield circle from Burlington, Waterbury's Montgomery circle, the Corcoran circle from Rutland, and Montpelier's Ethan Allen circle. With them was a contingent from the St. Patrick's Benevolent Society of Winooski, which almost didn't march because its leader, a local harness maker named Charles Black, had opposed participation, probably because he did not agree with Fenian methods. Following the Fenian clubs were various local dignitaries and a number of horse-drawn carriages carrying thirty-two young, and probably quite chilled, ladies, each representing an Irish county.

After the parade through town, the festivities continued that evening with a dance and banquet at the Lake House Hotel situated on the waterfront, the heart of Burlington's Irish community. About 160 people attended. After dinner there were a number of speeches and toasts, the contents of which were both clear and confusing. One of the most avid Fenians present, John J. Monahan, a Civil War veteran from Rutland, toasted the brotherhood, saying, "May it increase in strength and numbers until Ireland is free, and Republican Government rise from the ruins of all monarchies." His belligerent remarks were followed by those of an even more defiant Lonergan, who said that before another St. Patrick's Day passed, "it would be decided whether Scotch sheep and English bullocks or Irish men would inhabit Ireland." But he went on to say, in a rather confusing twist, that there was no invasion of Canada intended.[21]

How to explain Lonergan's public remarks? Certainly he knew of the preparations for invasion then under way—his speeches over the previous few months attest to that. Perhaps he was dissembling, both to confuse Canadian authorities and to assuage the fears of Irish American Vermonters who were less than sympathetic to Fenian militancy. There were those even within the Fenian organization who thought the Canadian scheme foolhardy.[22] Whatever the reason, Lonergan publicly denied, but quietly planned.

In fact, the Canadian incursion—one hesitates to call it an invasion—took place in early June. It all began quietly enough. In late May bands of young Irishmen wearing civilian clothes, who walked about "with the drill of a soldier," said one observer, began disembarking in Burlington and St. Albans from trains from

New York, Connecticut, and Boston. A St. Albans resident years later recounted how the Fenians "[descended] on us like an army in Flanders, without notice or expectation. They were reticent and said they had come to St. Albans to look over the grounds and note the events made memorable by the rebel raid of 1864." The cover story fooled no one.[23]

In all, about 1,500 Fenians gathered in St. Albans, far below the 5,000 their organizers had anticipated. Their leader was "General" Samuel Spear, a Civil War veteran with thirty years of military service who had once commanded a Union division. Though their numbers were small, the majority were battle-hardened veterans of the recent war. After one night camped on the green in St. Albans, they dispersed to encampments in nearby Fairfax, Georgia, and in the long-settled Irish township of Fairfield. Were these newcomers supported by the Irish in Franklin County? There is evidence that at least some local Fenians had helped in preparing for the operation. In plans for the invasion, Fenian head-quarters in New York City received word that arms could be sent in advance to Peter Ward, the head center of the St. Albans circle. Ward was superintendent of a gasworks that had recently burned, and it was thought that as replacement equipment was coming in daily, additional heavy containers would arouse little suspicion.[24]

In a more general way, local Irish people welcomed the Fenians. A reporter from Burlington noted that in the towns along the Canadian border, "The latch string was out [to the Fenians] at almost every farmhouse, and their tables were spread with the very best which the dairy, pantry and cellar afforded." When one young Fenian, John Duffy, fell ill, he was put up at the Fairfield home of Francis Ryan, where he later died. He was buried in the Fairfield Catholic cemetery. Were actions like these evidence of sympathy toward Fenian militancy, or simply hospitality toward fellow old-countrymen who in many cases were also Civil War heroes? One suspects the latter.[25]

Moreover, there is some evidence that in the main, Vermont Fenians declined to actively participate in the incursion. Beginning on May 31, Lonergan's Burlington circle of Fenians met in discussion for three nights running, perhaps confused about what action to take. At one point Lonergan was described as "indifferent to the whole affair." On June 2 a Fenian from the St. Albans encampment met with the Burlington Fenians to try to enlist support, and all he got for his effort was a financial contribution, 60 weapons, and 500 "ball cartridges." There is no evidence that Vermont Fenians, with the exception of John Lonergan and a few others, joined in the campaign. On June 6 Lonergan "reported" to St. Albans and was assigned to "special service." Most Vermont Fenians, it seems, were reluctant to actively join in the hostilities, content to lend material, financial, and moral support. Lonergan, after all his drum-beating over the previous six months, no doubt felt compelled to participate or look the fool.[26]

Vermont Fenian reluctance may have stemmed from the doomed nature of the campaign from the start. It was poorly organized. Guns and ammunition transported by train were confiscated by U.S. authorities before reaching St. Albans. Moreover, the large numbers of Fenian soldiers planned for the operation failed to materialize. On June 4 "General" Thomas Sweeney, overall commander of the invasion and a Civil War veteran, arrived in St. Albans from Malone, New York, and hurriedly called a council on how to proceed in light of the situation. After much discussion, the decision was made to go ahead with the attack.[27]

On June 6 the "army" rendezvoused in the town of Franklin, about a mile from the border. After a miserable night encamped in the rain, the men marched into Canada. There was no opposition, as most local people had left in anticipation of hostilities, and Canadian forces had not yet arrived on the scene. The advance halted about a quarter of a mile into Quebec near the all-but-deserted villages of Frelighsburg and St-Armand. On the American side of the border, bemused Vermonters gathered in expectation of a great show, but at the Fenian encampment all was glum. There was much complaining: about the lack of arms and equipment, and increasingly about the lack of provisions. The men were hungry. On June 8 a detachment went into the town of Frelighsburg and plundered stores and shops. On the same day there was a short skirmish between Fenians and Canadian militiamen at nearby Pigeon's Hill. The Fenians' deteriorating situation was dealt another setback when, on June 6, President Johnson issued a proclamation against citizens breaking U.S. neutrality laws; this had the effect of further discouraging reinforcements from joining the Fenians. With an undermanned force, lack of weapons and ammunition, and inadequate supplies, "General" Spear faced reality and on June 9 beat a retreat back to St. Albans.[28]

Waiting for the bedraggled Irish were units of the U.S. Army under the command of General George Meade, the victor at Gettysburg. As Fenians straggled in in ones, twos, and in bunches, the waiting bluecoats surrounded them. Scenes on the green in St. Albans were almost comic. Just a little more than a year before, most of the Fenians had fought alongside the troops now arresting them. Both sides greeted each other as old comrades rather than as adversaries. One report noted that after their arrest, a band of Fenian prisoners serenaded General Meade at his quarters.[29] With the incursion over, and uncomfortable with what to do with so many Union veterans, the U.S. government simply let the Fenians go, even providing many of them transportation home.

The Fenian fiasco of 1866 was a major setback for the Irish community. On the one hand, it bolstered Yankee perceptions of Irish ineptitude. The *Rutland Herald*, in editorial after editorial, derisively referred to the Fenians as "Finnigans."[30] More important, the failure fractured the Irish community in Vermont. On one side were those who thought the Fenian plan was lunacy from the start, and on the other those who believed that with better planning and less opposition from the U.S. government, it could have succeeded.

This division was apparent in the festivities surrounding Burlington's St. Patrick's Day in 1867. Instead of one celebration there were two, one organized by local Fenians and one by those with a more moderate agenda. The "Fenian Guards" celebrated with a parade on Saturday, March 16, followed by a lecture in the evening given by "General" John O'Neill. O'Neill had served with distinction during the Civil War, and in the June 1866 invasion he had commanded a Fenian force that crossed the Niagara River into Canada. At the "battle of Ridgeway," O'Neill's men had sent a Canadian militia unit running. As the only Irishman to cover himself in even a modicum of success in the 1866 campaign, he was something of a celebrity. Wherever he spoke, crowds gathered. In 1867 he was president of the more militant wing of the Irish Republican Brotherhood. That he spoke in Burlington in 1867 underlines the strategic importance he attached to the movement in Vermont. The content of his talk that evening has not come down to us, but its title, "The Irish Revolutionist," and his subsequent career suggest it was a continued call to militancy.

The more moderate group, led by the Burlington Hibernians and Winooski's St. Patrick's Society, held its celebration on Monday, March 18, the saint's feast day falling on a Sunday that year. It was far less militant in tone and included a Mass at the cathedral—an option that was unavailable to the Fenians. In the afternoon there were the usual speeches, with the keynote oration given by Henry J. Clark, a leader of the Irish community in Montreal. His presence was significant. During the 1866 invasion, the Canadian Irish—who the Fenians thought would immediately rally to their side—had remained steadfastly loyal to their new country. Clearly, those Vermont Irish who opposed the Canadian adventure felt kinship with loyal Irish Canadians, and indeed, Clark's speech emphasized loyalty to one's new country, whether it was the United States or Canada. As in years past, the day's festivities ended with a banquet.[31]

Despite failure in 1866, the O'Neill wing of the Fenian movement continued to plot. There were rumors in 1868 and 1869 that the Irish would again try to cross into Canada, and each year the authorities in Montreal sent militia to the border; but nothing happened. In fact, there were plans to mount incursions, but either through internal bickering, money problems, inept leadership, poor logistics, or all four, the border remained quiet. In 1870, however, the Fenians mounted another attempt.

Like in 1866, Vermont and John Lonergan were central to the Fenian plans. The main thrust of this invasion was to be from Franklin County into Quebec. To avoid the logistical problems that plagued the 1866 venture, through the late winter and early spring of 1870 local Fenians stockpiled arms and munitions along the border. Lonergan continued to drum up support around the state. One of his most consistent themes—one meant to counter the criticism he had heard over and over again the previous few years—was that one could be loyal both to Ireland and America simultaneously. He used the analogy of a marriage: "When an Irishman takes a wife, as he is sometimes liable, does he therefore forget his mother? America is the Irishman's wife, but he does not forget his mother Ireland." In that spring of 1870, Lonergan was again to fight for his motherland.[32]

In late May Fenians from around New England and New York again began congregating in St. Albans. In all, about 700 showed up, led by "General" O'Neill. Included among his officers were Captains Lonergan and Monahan, who

One of the two Fenians killed in the 1870 attempt to invade Canada. (Courtesy of the Vermont Historical Society.)

were accompanied by a few other Vermonters. After rendezvousing in Fairfield, where they donned an eclectic assortment of green uniforms and received arms, on May 25 they attempted to cross into Canada. At Pike River, which straddles the border with Quebec at a point just north of Franklin, the Fenians met up with a unit of Canadian militia well protected behind a stone wall. In the intense skirmish that followed, two Fenians died, including one Burlington man, and nine were wounded, among them one fellow from Cambridge, Vermont, and another from Winooski. No Canadians were hurt. The unexpected resistance broke the invasion: the Fenians fell back, many of them to be arrested by U.S. authorities but, as in 1866, almost as quickly released.

The "battle" of Pike River ended Fenian attempts to invade Canada and marked the beginning of a long period of decline of militant Irish nationalism, in both Ireland and the United States. As the Fenian movement's popularity eroded, so too did the numerous St. Patrick's Day parades and festivities that were so popular in Vermont in the 1860s. In the future, festivities on March 17 tended to be church affairs, socials, and suppers, where the themes were less about Irish politics and more about community.

After a decade of conflict, by late 1870 Irish veterans of the Civil War, including those who had participated in the Fenian movement, were ready to put martial matters behind them and get on with their lives. James B. Scully, credited with being the "pivot" man in turning back Pickett's Charge, returned to Burlington, became the scion of a large family and a successful businessman, and one of the few Irish Republicans in town. Thomas Kennedy went home to Franklin County, married a Howrigan, and spent the rest of his life farming and dabbling in politics, twice serving as Fairfield's representative to the legislature, and in the 1880s as Franklin County sheriff. Civil War veteran and rabid Fenian John J. Monahan took up residence in heavily Irish Underhill, opened a law practice, served the town for many years as clerk, and three times represented it in the state legislature.

As for Lonergan, he managed his Burlington grocery business through the late 1860s, worked for a time for the U.S. Customs Service, and married and started a family. Shortly after the 1870 invasion he moved with his family to Lincoln, Vermont, a mountainous community southeast of Burlington, where he worked as a cooper—his father's old trade. Eventually he resumed work with the U.S. Customs and was assigned to Montreal, where he remained the rest of his life. He died there in 1903.

Dorothy Canfield Fisher was correct when she wrote that the Civil War had made Irish Vermonters simply Vermont boys. The war had made Scully, Kennedy, Lonergan, and hundreds like them Americans. How could it be otherwise for individuals who had risked their lives for the Union? Now, after suffering the disaster of the famine, enduring the difficulties of crossing the Atlantic and establishing new lives in an unfamiliar environment, and fighting in a war of unprecedented brutality, it was time to work and enjoy the bounty of their new homeland.

Demographics, Jobs, and Troubles: 1870–1900

I n 1879 a columnist for the *Poultney Journal* noted the large numbers of Irish in his town and had this to say:

> The Vermont Yankees . . . might take some lessons from the Irish who came here, with profit to themselves. The latter are rapidly becoming real estate owners in Vermont. I know of a town in the state in which nearly one-third of the farm lands are now owned by Irishmen. Twenty years ago, or thereabouts, there was not an Irish owner of a farm in the town. As the Yankee gets the western fever, he looks around for an Irishman to buy his farm, and sooner or later, finds one. The Irish in general with us are not model farmers, but are models of industry, hard work and rigid economy. . . . Paddy works and delves and buys only what he must have to sustain life. . . . Here is the secret of the Irish increase.[1]

The writer's comments are interesting not only because they are a backhanded compliment to the industriousness of the Irish (if not to their agricultural acumen), but also for the recognition that in the years following the Civil War, the Irish were present in Vermont in large numbers—"the Irish increase."

This was certainly true. The 1870 U.S. census reported that 14,080 people born in Ireland resided in the Green Mountain State, or about 4.2 percent of the total population of 330,551. After that date, the number of Irish-born living in Vermont gradually declined, as Irish emigration itself slowed. It should be pointed out, however, that the number of Irish-born living in the neighboring states of Massachusetts, New Hampshire, Rhode Island, and Connecticut peaked twenty years later, in 1890, suggesting that as time passed, newcomers may have found Vermont less attractive than other New England states. No doubt this was a reflection of Vermont's limited job opportunities.[2]

But the real story in the 1870 census was less about the number of Irish immigrants than about the first generation of Irish Americans. After the exodus spawned by the Great Famine, there had been a baby boom among the immigrant Irish. Many immigrants had come to the United States either as young couples or as single people, many of whom married as soon as circumstances permitted and began families—large families. Families with six, seven, and eight children were common among the Irish. Patrick and Catherine Howrigan, who had settled in Fairfield in 1849, were typical. They had seven children—three born in Canada and four in Vermont. One Yankee resident of Fairfield, perhaps surprised at the number of freckle-faced redheads in the neighborhood, referred to the Irish section of town as Young Ireland, a play on the name of the nationalist movement of the 1840s. One historian who studied large families in Rutland town in the late nineteenth century found that of the eleven families with ten children or more, nine were Irish.[3]

Thus in addition to the 14,080 immigrant Irish living in Vermont in 1870, the state had a conservatively estimated 21,120 first-generation Irish Americans.[4] Collectively the two groups made up almost 11 percent of the total population; but given the consistent underreporting of the Irish in the U.S. censuses in these early years, plus the numerous second- and even third-generation Irish Americans in Vermont, the total number of Irish Americans in the state probably was somewhere between 15 and 20 percent. For a state that has been traditionally portrayed as quintessentially Yankee in the nineteenth century, this is a dramatic revision.

Though the Irish lived in every corner of the Green Mountains by 1870, they tended to concentrate in five of the state's thirteen counties: Rutland, Chittenden, Franklin, Washington, and Bennington. These five counties were home to 74 percent of the state's Irish-born (10,445), while only 47 percent of all Vermonters lived in them.[5] What these counties had in common, in an overwhelmingly agricultural state, was the presence of industrial jobs: Rutland had slate and marble works, manufacturing plants, and railroad yards. Chittenden had shipping, manufacturing, and textile mills. Franklin contained massive rail yards (in addition to farming). Washington was home to granite quarries and shops, textile mills, and manufacturing. And Bennington had manufacturing and textile mills, along with extensive marble quarries.

Rutland County was the center of Irish Vermont. In a population of 40,651, some 23 percent were immigrant or first-generation Irish Americans. A number of county villages and towns had much greater concentrations. Rutland town, the urban center of the county, with its extensive marble quarries, the massive Howe Scale works (after 1877), and the depot and maintenance facilities of the Rutland & Burlington Railroad, was the greenest community in Vermont, with anywhere from 35 to 40 percent of its residents Irish. The slate-producing towns in the western part of the county also had a significant Irish presence. For example, of Poultney's 2,836 residents in 1870, over 22 percent were Irish.[6]

The marble vein that passed through Rutland and gave it such an Irish complexion continued south into northern Bennington County and attracted numerous Irish workers. They worked primarily at Mount Aeolus—"Marble Mountain"—in Dorset. In 1870, when demand for marble for Civil War monuments and public buildings ran high, Dorset's population peaked at 2,195, some 33 percent of them Irish. In nineteenth-century Vermont, the Irish and the marble industry went hand in hand.[7]

In Chittenden County the sons and daughters of the Emerald Isle concentrated in two industrial centers—Burlington and Colchester. Burlington had been attracting Irish immigrants since the 1820s to its docks, manufacturing operations, and commercial establishments. Irish residents in the city composed 20 percent of the population in 1870. In nearby Colchester, the Burlington Woolen Mill Company and various other industrial establishments employed hundreds of workers, many of them Irish. West Allen Street in Colchester's Winooski village was so heavily Irish that residents referred to it as Cork Alley.[8]

Bennington, in the extreme southwest corner of the state, was another industrial center that attracted large numbers of Irish. From its beginnings in the eighteenth century, Bennington had a number of Scots-Irish immigrants associated with the family of William Henry. The crossroads around which these early settlers clustered became known as Irish Corners. Around 1800, Thomas Trenor, or Traynor, a leader of the radical United Irishmen in Dublin, escaped imprisonment by the British for his political activities, fled to America, and settled in Bennington. By the beginning of the nineteenth century there was a small but significant Irish presence in Bennington.[9]

In the 1830s and 1840s, Bennington began to grow as investors built a large complex of mills on the Walloomsac and North Branch rivers producing cotton and linen cloth. When the railroad came to town in the early 1850s, the number of manufactories again grew, and so too did the number of Irish. So many famine Irish moved to the mill town that in 1854 Louis de Goesbriand, the bishop of the newly created diocese of Burlington, established in Bennington the first Catholic church in southern Vermont—St. Francis de Sales. By 1870 almost a quarter of Bennington's residents were Irish.[10]

Though the counties of Bennington, Franklin, and Washington all had significant percentages of Irish, overall those counties were far less populous than either Rutland or Chittenden counties, so their absolute numbers of Irish were lower. In sheer numbers Rutland and Chittenden counties were the epicenters of Vermont's Irish community.

Irish Farmers

What do we know about the occupations of the Vermont Irish in the post-famine period? Information compiled from the 1880 federal census showed that for Vermonters born in Ireland, the single most common occupation was farmer or agricultural "worker"—"worker" being an individual employed in agriculture, oftentimes a son who worked on his parents' farm, while a "farmer" was one who owned his own farm. After farmer came laborer, then railroad worker, and finally marble or stone worker.[11] Unfortunately, no such statewide breakdown exists for first-generation Irish Americans.

That most Irish in nineteenth-century America resided in cities has obscured the fact that across the United States were pockets of Irish who made their living in farming. Vermont agriculture attracted the Irish for a number of reasons. For one, land was inexpensive. As the *Poultney Journal* commentator noted at the beginning of this chapter, Yankee Vermonters gave up their hardscrabble farms in droves to move to the more fertile fields of the Midwest and West; this pattern went back to the 1820s. When Yankees left, the Irish stood ready to replace them. In addition, Vermont agriculture in the latter half of the nineteenth century came to rely principally on dairy farming, perhaps the one type of farming the Irish knew best. Working with milk cows in Vermont was little different from working with milk cows in Ireland. Then, too, there was that intense Irish need—obsession, really—to own land, the reaction to years of denial in Ireland.[12] Finally, among the Irish in Vermont who owned farms in the latter part of the century, many of them had come to Vermont prior to the famine, or had family connections in the state predating the famine. No doubt brothers, sisters, aunts, uncles, cousins, and friends who had arrived earlier helped the newcomers to purchase farms.

Up and down the Green Mountains were many examples of Irishmen making good in farming: men like Kilkenny-born Francis Ryan. Ryan bought his first farm in 1833, a parcel of 134 acres in North Fairfield, then bought up to a better piece of land in Fairfield in 1858, eventually passing it on to his Vermont-born sons. They added to the family holdings, and when they passed on at the turn of the century, the Ryans owned over 1,200 acres in the adjacent towns of Fairfield and Georgia. In like manner the family of Patrick Howrigan, who bought his first farm in 1849 in Fairfield, increased their holdings in 1882 and became one of the most prosperous farming families in the region.[13]

But it was not solely the pre-famine Irish who did well in farming. John Hart arrived penniless in the United States just as the Civil War broke out, and by the mid-1880s he operated a 600-acre farm in Ira, in Rutland County. James Sheridan, born near Drogheda, County Meath, in 1800, came to the United States just as the famine began, worked in Shelburne as a farmhand for eleven years, then at age fifty-six bought a one-acre plot and over time increased that to forty-six acres. Trucking his apples, potatoes, and other produce into Burlington, he built a prosperous business, which he later passed on to his son.[14]

The story of the farming Gilfeather family has an interesting twist. The Gilfeathers arrived in Vermont in 1863 and established a farm in Wardsboro, a hilly region northwest of Brattleboro. One son, John, who farmed there until his death in 1944, developed a white turnip that gained a local reputation for its sweet, mild taste. To this day it is farmed in southern Vermont, and root crop connoisseurs consider it a rare treat.[15]

Though many Irishmen aspired to the independence of the farmer's life, and some achieved it, for most it was an unattainable dream. Lack of capital and the necessity of immediately earning an income meant taking whatever work was available: and these were virtually always the lowest-paying, most physically arduous, and most dangerous jobs. A *Burlington Free Press* editorial that appeared in 1869 aptly described the Irishmen's position:

> It is the Irish, and the Irish alone, who clean the streets, dig gutters, build the road, make the sewers; the farms teem with Irish laborers; they are the best fellers of wood and diggers of potatoes. They are, in America, emphatically toilers by the sweat of their brow.[16]

In short, along with a growing number of French Canadian immigrants, whose numbers shot up in Vermont during the Civil War decade, the Irish provided the muscle that built and maintained industrial Vermont. This was particularly true in the slate and marble industries.

Irish "Slaters"

The Vermont slate and marble industries, which had only begun to expand at mid-century with the introduction of railroads, exploded in activity in the century's closing decades. Early on, slate was used primarily as school writing tablets, but when railroads made transportation inexpensive, slate became a popular roofing material and an inexpensive substitute for marble fireplace mantels. Demand for the colorful stone rose dramatically. Towns in slate-rich western Rutland County—Castleton, Fair Haven, and Poultney—became the center of this burgeoning industry.

Quarry and sheds of a slate company in Poultney, ca. 1890. (Courtesy of the Vermont Historical Society.)

By the 1880s Vermont was the nation's second-largest slate-producing state, after Pennsylvania.[17]

Historians have tended to describe the workforce in Vermont's slate industry as composed mainly of Welshmen.[18] This is an oversimplification and overlooks the important role played by the Irish. As the slate industry began to expand in the late 1840s and early 1850s, its workforce was primarily Irish, composed of men originally drawn to Vermont by railroad construction but who later switched to quarry work. As noted earlier, many of them came from Tipperary, which had a long history of slate quarrying.

Demographic figures for the town of Fair Haven point out the evolution of the slate region's ethnic workforce. In 1850, 308 Irishmen resided in Fair Haven, and 7 of them described themselves as either quarrymen, stonecutters, or "slaters." Another 34 simply said they were laborers; and no doubt a number of them worked in the slate industry but had no particular skill. At the same time only 14 Welsh people lived in Fair Haven—all members of two families—and only 3 of them worked in slate. Ten years later there were 324 Irish in town, with only 10 specifically working in slate, although another 44 were laborers or day laborers, and many of them probably worked at tasks associated with the quarries. But for the Welsh the situation had changed dramatically. Now 249 Welsh resided there, and almost all the males worked in the slate industry: 73 as "slate makers," 7 as "ledgemen," and 1 who described himself as a slate "manufacturer"—probably a quarry owner or manager. That only 2 Welshmen described themselves as day laborers or laborers, while a large number of Irish did so, suggests that the Welsh held the more-skilled positions in the industry, while the Irish filled the unskilled. In short, in the decade of the 1850s, the Welsh came to dominate in the Fair Haven slate business.[19]

But this was not true of nearby Poultney. Of 157 slate workers there in 1870, more than half, 81, came from Irish backgrounds, and the remainder were Welsh. That the Irish held their own in the Poultney quarries reflected their overwhelming presence in the town. They constituted over 22 percent of the town's inhabitants, versus fewer than 5 percent for the Welsh. Moreover, while the Welsh toiled almost exclusively in the slate works, the Irish held a variety of occupations: tailor, tinsmith, blacksmith, machinist, porter, gardener, railroad worker, to cite just a few. This exclusivity on the part of the Welsh suggests that they came to Poultney specifically to work in slate, while the Irish were opportunistic in their approach to jobs: they took what opportunity presented.

The greatest concentration of immigrant and first-generation Irish residing in the slate belt lived just east of Fair Haven in Castleton, which had had a significant Irish population going back to the 1830s. In 1870 more than a third of Castleton's residents were immigrant or first-generation Irish American, while fewer than 5 percent of the town's residents were Welsh, most of them living in the village of Hydeville.[20]

The Irish could be found everywhere in Castleton, but the remote village of West Castleton, then called Screwdriver, was uniquely Irish. West Castleton lies in the northwest corner of Castleton along the western shore of Lake Bomoseen. For most of its history it was difficult to get to: it lay four and a half miles up a dirt track off the main Rutland–Fair Haven road. Snow and ice in winter and mud in spring made traveling the Castleton road difficult much of the year. In 1851 an investment group took advantage of the extensive slate formations there plus the water power from a stream that ran between Screwdriver Pond (now Glen Lake) and Lake Bomoseen and opened an extensive quarrying and slate-milling operation. From a dock on Lake Bomoseen boats carried the finished slate down-lake to be off-loaded onto railcars. By 1854 the West Castleton Slate Company employed 250 men, almost all Irish.[21]

West Castleton was a "company" town. To house the workers, the Slate Company built two rows of simple wood-frame houses on "stacked" slate foundations. Managers lived in dwellings constructed entirely of stacked slate, as was the company store. The extensive use of slate as a building material gave the little company village of West Castleton a look entirely different from the wood-frame or brick houses so typical of Vermont. A few of these structures can still be seen today. In this place apart, the "Screwdriver" Irish—as outsiders referred to them—toiled in the slate works and raised families.

Life for slate workers was harsh. Hours were long, and pay was poor. A typical workday in the Fair Haven quarries in 1880 was ten and a half to eleven and a half hours, at $1.59 a day for skilled workers and $1.23 for unskilled—the latter amount

Slate workers' housing in West Castleton, ca. 1880. (Courtesy of the Vermont Historical Society.)

insufficient to sustain a family. To survive, a family had to supplement the father's income. Children frequently had to take up the slack. Out of forty-two employees of the Castleton Slate Company in 1870, seven were age fifteen or younger. In the McKinney family, fourteen-year-old Thomas and his eleven-year-old brother, John, both labored in a slate mill to support themselves, another brother, and their widowed mother. Single daughters worked as domestic servants, and wives lessened the pressure on the family's meager income by maintaining kitchen gardens and keeping a few chickens. If everyone worked, a family could make ends meet.

But in the slate works, employment was irregular. In the winter months, when ice and snow made outside work nearly impossible, quarrymen either worked at reduced pay or were laid off entirely. Survival often meant running up large bills at company-owned stores, where goods cost 30 to 40 percent more than in conventional establishments.

The work itself was dangerous. A report issued by the U.S. Bureau of Mines in 1920, when conditions were much safer than in the nineteenth century, found that one in every ten men in the slate industry suffered an injury. Accidents were common. How could it be otherwise? The work entailed explosives, tons of rock, heavy machinery, and rock-cutting saws. The ordeal of Jack McCann was horrendous but hardly unusual. In March 1880 McCann, an employee of Vail's Slate Mill in Fair Haven, while oiling overhead shafting caught his coat sleeve in the gearing and was carried three times around, striking his head on surrounding timbers, cutting him seriously. Some accidents ended more tragically. In one winter incident, a pile of icy slate slag broke loose and knocked a man into a quarry, killing him. In the extractive industries, workers lived on the edge in more ways than one.[22]

Marble Workers

The situation in Vermont's marble industry paralleled that of slate. The coming of the railroads to Vermont in the 1840s opened new markets for what had been small-scale operations. With the widespread demand for marble gravestones and monuments following the Civil War, and the stone's use in classically styled public buildings, the marble-producing region of Rutland County entered a period of unprecedented prosperity. By the 1880s Vermont was the largest producer of marble in the United States.[23] Rutland village briefly eclipsed Burlington as the most populous town in the state. In time Rutland became known as Marble City.

In 1881 Rutland's ten marble companies, with the two firms of Sheldon & Slason and the Vermont Marble Company being the largest, employed 1,500 men, with six out of every ten workers being Irish.[24] While the Irish could be found in Sutherland Falls (later renamed Proctor) and Rutland Center, they concentrated in two areas: the village of West Rutland and on the southwest side of Rutland village (the village became Rutland city in 1892).

West Rutland was the heart of the marble-quarrying district. Until 1886, when it was chartered as a town, West Rutland was a village in the town of Rutland. Most West Rutlanders lived in a village in a lowland area surrounded by mountains. One part of the village on the east side was known as "the Swamp," because of frequent flooding in springtime. Here deep quarry holes pitted the landscape from the bottomlands up into the hillside. Two company-owned tenement complexes—one called Baxter's Yard and the other Parker's Patch—standing near the "holes," housed over 400 workers and their families in the early 1870s. Outsiders in the late nineteenth century called the tenements Red City—probably as much due to the occupants' perceived political orientation as to the buildings' red-painted color. Because of unsanitary conditions, cholera and typhus frequently afflicted the residents. It was a tough place to raise a family. People of means lived on the west side of the valley, away from Red City and the quarries.[25]

Locals referred to West Rutlanders as "Stonepeggers." The origin of this appellation is obscure, but apparently it is either related to the antidraft incident of 1863 when quarrymen chased off recruiters by pegging (throwing) stones at them, or to a fracas at a baseball game when West Rutland fans pelted a visiting baseball club with marble chips. Whatever the source, the moniker stuck, and whether intentional or not it suggested a rough and tough people.

Like parts of the slate valley, West Rutland was an Irish enclave. In the first census that counted residents of West Rutland separately from those of Rutland, that of 1900, over 30 percent of West Rutland's 2,914 inhabitants were immigrant or first-generation Irish Americans. And this census came at a time when the Irish population was dropping off, as newer immigrants, particularly Swedes and Poles and a smattering of Italians, began moving in. Earlier the percentage of Irish would have been even higher. Records of the Roman Catholic Church show that in 1857, three-fifths of all Catholics living in Rutland town—the majority of whom would have been Irish—lived in West Rutland.[26]

Two of West Rutland's leading institutions—its Catholic church and its public school—reflected the village's Irish orientation. In 1855 the Sheldon & Slason Marble Company deeded a piece of hillside land to the Catholics for a church. There the Catholic community built a small wood-frame structure and dedicated it to St. Bridget, a popular Irish saint. It was quickly outgrown. By the late 1850s plans were under way for a larger, more-impressive edifice. To keep construction costs down, the new church was built of local marble and with volunteer labor. Each Sunday at Mass, Rev. Thomas Lynch—one of the first priests from Ireland recruited by Bishop de Goesbriand—read out a list of names, assigning each individual to an evening's worth of work on the new church. On the designated evening, after a long day in the "holes," a quarryman or mill-shop worker had a quick dinner at home and then spent his evening hours at the church site. Because the labor was volunteered, and the principal material used was local marble, the structure was inexpensive to build. When construction ended in 1861, St. Bridget's stood as a shining ornament to the religious commitment of the West Rutland Irish.[27]

*Workers in the "hole" of a marble quarry
in East Dorset, ca. 1880. (Courtesy of
the Vermont Historical Society.)*

High above West Rutland, St. Bridget Church dominated the landscape. (Courtesy of Mary Kenny.)

The public school in the village also had a curious Irish-Catholic orientation. In the 1850s, Rutland had a dozen small schools scattered throughout the township. School No. 7 served West Rutland. By the mid 1850s almost all its pupils were Irish. When the Irish, desirous of having a parochial school, realized they could not afford it, they struck a deal with the town school board that was unique in Vermont and perhaps in America. The Catholics asked that at School No. 7 they be allowed to appoint a Catholic principal and hire Catholic teachers and to select Catholic textbooks. The school board agreed, with the proviso that it could inspect the school at any time and that all teachers and administrators be suitably qualified. Throughout its existence, Public School No. 7 was known as "the Catholic school." This unique blending of public and religious education lasted to the late 1920s.[28]

In nearby Rutland, the southwest corner of the village—Ward Seven—was the Irish neighborhood. Its grid of streets straddled the railroad lines that ran through town and was adjacent to the manufacturing sheds of the Howe Scale Company. Like West Rutland, Ward Seven also had its Irish Catholic church, St. Peter's, established in 1857, as well as a convent school for its children. Rutland residents called the area "Nebraska," after a sermon by the local priest in the late 1800s; despairing of so many parishioners leaving to seek their fortune in the Midwest, the priest chided his congregation that their "Nebraska" was right there in Rutland.[29] The name stuck. And like West Rutland, it was a tight-knit community. Besides its church and school, it had an Irish literary society, an all-Irish volunteer fire company, and in the mid-1880s a chapter of the Irish Land League.

Each day the quarrymen of West Rutland and Rutland rose early and made their way to the quarry holes and marble shops. The day was long. Work began at six in the morning and ended at six in the evening. Some men toiled in the holes using heavy steam-channeling machines to cut out the marble, while others operated derricks to hoist marble blocks to the surface. Once the blocks were aboveground, workmen placed them on flat "boats," which oxen and later steam engines hauled to the shops, where the stone would be "dressed" for shipment. For their efforts, marble workers in the early 1880s received one dollar a day.[30]

Rutland's quarry owners exploited their workers through the company-store system and the seasonal nature of quarry work. Up through the 1880s they laid off most quarrymen on December 1 and then rehired them at the end of winter, usually April 1. Those who worked in the sheds and mills were kept on, but at reduced wages. Often when laid-off quarrymen resumed work in the spring, their first pay envelopes were empty, their wages having gone to pay debts run up in winter at the company store.[31]

The company store, Proctor, ca. 1890. (Courtesy of the Vermont Historical Society.)

Work in the marble quarries was dangerous in the extreme. In the spring of 1868, for example, there were two serious accidents in the West Rutland quarries alone. On March 9 a charge to blast open a wall between two quarries went off in an opposite direction, severely lacerating and breaking bones in five Irishmen. Two months later, a massive block of marble crushed and killed James Carrigan. A particularly bad accident occurred in 1893 when a mass of stone dislodged from the ceiling of one of the Vermont Marble Company's quarries and killed five men and injured ten others.[32]

Over time, myths surrounding the danger of quarry work grew and became part of the folklore of Rutland's Irish community. One story held that back in the 1850s, to encourage the faithful to attend Mass on holy days of obligation, Rev. John Daly promised the quarrymen that if they did so, no harm would befall them while at work. As the story went, the men complied, and although numerous incidents occurred of marble crashing into the quarries, miraculously no one was hurt. There must have been a statute of limitations on Daly's promise, however, for in reality the work continued to be as dangerous as ever.[33]

Strikes and Stoppages

Given the difficult conditions under which the slate and marble workers labored, it is not surprising that the Irish of Rutland County lashed back at their employers from time to time through work actions. At times protest took the form of solitary actions. When steam-powered jackhammers replaced the work formerly done by twelve hand-drillers in the Dorset marble quarries, a disgruntled Patrick O'Keefe frequently stole onto the work site at night and sabotaged the jackhammers. Other angry quarrymen did the same.[34] More-organized protests took the form of strikes.

Strikes were fairly common, particularly in the marble industry. Beginning with a strike in 1859, there followed strikes in 1864, 1868, and 1880. Always the fight was over wages and hours. For example, in the 1880 strike against the Rutland Marble Company (forerunner to the Vermont Marble Company) and Sheldon & Sons, workers demanded $1.25 for a ten-hour day but eventually had to settle for $1 for ten hours. This was at a time when common laborers who performed maintenance on the Erie Canal earned $1.75 a day and carpenters $2.50.[35]

Against striking workers the quarry owners employed two tactics: the "turnout" and the use of "scab" labor. The turnout was an intimidating weapon in the hands of the employers. Most workers lived in company-owned housing: all the dwellings in West Rutland's "Red City" were company owned, as well as those of the slate workers in "Screwdriver." In Proctor, home of the Vermont Marble Company, there were only thirty-five independently owned homes; the rest belonged to Vermont Marble.[36] When strikes loomed, the owners threatened to turn the workers out of their homes. It was not an idle threat.

In a bitter strike in West Rutland in spring 1868, quarry owners evicted all the families of striking workers. The "Great Turnout," as it came to be called, left lasting scars in Rutland, with many Irish workers forced to leave the area. Years later old-timers remembered watching evicted families walking with their one cow in tow as they trudged south to seek work in the Dorset quarries. So many left that, in the space of a year, the rolls of the Irish in St. Bridget Parish dropped by almost half: from 350 families in 1867 to 200 families in late 1868.[37] For people who had suffered evictions during the Great Famine twenty years before, this latest setback must have been a particularly cruel punishment.

The other tactic used by employers was the introduction of strikebreakers, or "scabs." Once workers struck, company agents went to Quebec and recruited French Canadians. During the Great Turnout, dozens of strikebreakers came down from Quebec. At one point, strikers vowed to give them a hostile reception. To avoid a confrontation, quarry owners had strikebreakers unloaded from a train before reaching West Rutland and then marched them surreptitiously to the recently vacated tenements of Red City. Though numerous altercations took place over the following weeks, there was far less violence than anticipated. The *Rutland Daily Herald*, never sympathetic to the Irish, had an explanation for the quiet after the strike: "There is not a sufficient number of the strikers now resident there to raise much of a disturbance, and those remaining seem thus far quite peaceably disposed." Evictions had broken the strikers' will to resist.[38]

The friction often found in Vermont between the Irish and French Canadians had its origin in incidents like the Great Turnout. Quebec, with its surplus labor and limited job opportunities, could always be tapped for manpower. For Irish workers struggling to make a living, French Canadians were a tool of management.

Interestingly, labor-management relations in the slate regions of Poultney, Fair Haven, and Castleton were less volatile than in the marble industry. From 1870 down to 1907 there were no major strikes in the slate valley, although on one occasion in 1870, workers at the Scotch Hill Slate Company near Screwdriver, having gone unpaid for six months, refused to work any longer.[39] Why there were so few strikes is unclear. Perhaps the fact that slate companies were smaller than the marble enterprises, with many of them locally owned—some even owned by Irishmen—made employers more sensitive to the needs of workers. Whatever the reason, the slate workers struck only under dire circumstances.

The Vershire or Ely "War"

A case that echoed the Bolton "war" of 1846 and the Scotch Hill work stoppage was the Vershire or Ely "war" of 1883. The town of Vershire lies in east-central Vermont, not far from the Connecticut River. Copper ore had been mined there since the early 1800s, but in 1854 a group of investors led by entrepreneur Smith Ely established the Vermont Copper Company and began operations on a large scale. By 1881 the company produced 60 percent of the copper output of the United States and employed 851 men.[40] At the apex of the Vermont Copper Company's success, the Vermont legislature temporarily changed the town's name from Vershire to Ely, after the company's principal owner.

Two characteristics of Vershire stood out. One was the ecological blight caused by the huge smelting furnaces that separated copper from ore. Visitors to Vershire frequently commented on the bleakness of the landscape. A young doctor, John Goodrich Henry, practicing in the Vershire village of West Fairlee in 1881, described Vershire as "the most awful looking country I ever saw. The smoke and fumes from the furnaces kill all the vegetation for a mile around and even have some effect on the vegetation here." A newspaper reporter visiting the area two years later echoed the doctor's impression: "And prevailing everything is a most beastly odor from the roasting beds, caused by the noxious gases from the ore by heat—the gases which are responsible for the killing of vegetation in the vicinity. Altogether, the spot is the most utterly God-forsaken in the whole world." What the gases were doing to human lungs can only be imagined.[41]

The other noticeable aspect of the copper community was the foreign-born composition of its workforce. Smith Ely liked to hire men from Cornwall, England. Just as Welshmen had a reputation as slate workers, so too did the Cornish enjoy fame as copper miners. The first manager of the company was Thomas Pollard from Cornwall, as were most of his successors. By 1880 English immigrants, mainly from Cornwall, constituted 18 percent of Vershire's population and just under 14 percent of the company's workers. Even with the strong Cornish connection, however, the Vershire copper district was predominately Irish. The Irish accounted for 24 percent of the town's residents and 22.5 percent of the copper workers. Though some of Ireland's counties (Cork, Wicklow, and Waterford) had, like Cornwall, a tradition of copper mining, most of the Irish workers in Vershire seem to have held unskilled positions.[42]

Trouble in Vershire began in 1880 as continuous mining operations depleted the more easily accessible veins of copper ore and extraction became more expensive. With financial troubles mounting, in early May 1883 the company failed to make payroll. Anxious about their future, but afraid of losing their jobs, the men continued to go to work. For two months they went without pay. With cupboards bare, mothers and children went without. Then, on June 29, concern turned to panic, as the Vermont Copper Company announced it was closing permanently without any back pay forthcoming.[43]

The announcement came on a Friday. Through the weekend the stunned miners mulled over their situation, their anger mounting. On Monday, July 2, frustration erupted into violence. With a clique of Irishmen in the lead, a mob brandishing revolvers and knives ransacked the company store, ran a former mine manager out of town, took control of Vershire and West Fairlee, and threatened to destroy the two villages and all Vermont Copper Company property unless they were paid. At one point a crowd went to the West Fairlee mansion of Smith Ely and extracted a promise from him that they would be paid on Friday, July 6—a promise he gave only to save his own hide. When the crowd left, he quickly exited the scene, further inciting the miners.[44]

With the miners in control of Vershire and West Fairlee, sensational reports appeared in the Vermont press. Under bold headlines that proclaimed "Ely War" and "Civil War," the *Burlington Free Press* warned that the miners had 150 kegs of blasting powder in their possession and would make good on their threat to destroy the villages if not paid. Other reports described drunken men parading about, fueled by "a moonshining distillery . . . supplying the mob with raw cider brandy," while the miners' wives stockpiled stones in anticipation of a confrontation.

Alarmed at events in Vershire and at the role his Catholic Irish were playing, Bishop de Goesbriand dispatched Rev. Daniel O'Sullivan, a Winooski-born priest who had once served in the Vershire area, to calm the miners. Governor John Barlow took more drastic action, calling out militia units from St. Albans, Northfield, Montpelier, and Rutland. The latter unit was commanded by Redfield Proctor, a Civil War hero, former governor, and president of the Vermont Marble Company in Rutland.

The militiamen rendezvoused in Montpelier, and a train took them to Vershire, where they arrived on Saturday morning, July 7. To their surprise the scene was eerily calm. Perhaps the visit by Father O'Sullivan had had its effect. Instead of angry mobs, the militiamen found starving men, women, and children who greeted them as saviors rather than oppressors. As one reporter noted, "The troops, instead of finding rioters to deal with, had their sympathies strongly appealed to by women, at the point of starvation, coming to them with children in their arms and begging for assistance." When the soldiers later that day broke for lunch, many of them gave their surplus rations to famished villagers. Order was restored, a few token arrests made, and the "war" was over.

Once the facts of the Vershire riot became widely known, sympathy in Vermont turned in favor of the miners—but they still were the losers. The copper works remained closed, and back-wages were never paid. Quietly the miners and their families drifted away, some traveling to Butte, Montana, to work in the Anaconda Copper Mine owned by Irishman Marcus Daly. From 1,875 residents on the eve of the "war," seven years later Vershire's population had dwindled to 754. The town never recovered; in 2000 it had only 629 residents.[45]

What to make of Irish labor unrest in Vermont in the nineteenth century? The Irish were in the vanguard of labor agitation. But only when conditions went beyond stressful, to intolerable, did they engage in strikes. It is worth noting that three of the most important incidents in Vermont involving Irish labor—the Bolton "war," the Scotch Hill work stoppage, and the Vershire "war"—were not fought for increased wages or better working conditions but for pay honestly earned but unpaid. What is remarkable in the Vermont context is not the aggressiveness of Irish labor but its patience. Perhaps this was related to the paucity of alternatives for industrial workers in Vermont. Outside of the extractive, textile, and railroad industries, little work was available in the Green Mountains. A worker contemplating strike action had to think long and hard before subjecting his family to unemployment and possible homelessness. As described in the next chapter, even when the Knights of Labor began organizing in Vermont, they emphasized a program of influencing government policy rather than promoting strike action.

Irishwomen in the Workforce

Irishwomen made up a significant number of the female workers in nineteenth-century Vermont. One reason for this was simply that there were so many Irishwomen in the state. Records show that in the long history of immigration to America, only among the Irish did women exceed the number of men.[46] With few options at home, single, young Irishwomen left the old country in droves and flooded the American job market. In addition, because a laboring man rarely earned enough to maintain a family, single daughters by necessity often had to go to work. Once a woman married, however, she was expected to leave her job to "keep house." Thus it was mainly young, single girls, along with spinsters and widows, who made up the female Irish workforce.

For work, they had limited options. The vast majority of working Irishwomen in Vermont took positions as domestic servants. In figures for Rutland town in 1870, of 145 Irish-born women working outside the home, 114 worked as domestic servants. They dominated the market. In 1886 the wife of Percival Clement, one of Rutland's leading businessmen, wrote in frustration to a family member that she was looking for new help in the house but "would like to try something else besides Irish." Chances are she searched in vain.[47]

For Irish girls, working "in service" had a certain appeal. It required skills that could easily be learned, while it brought in a small but steady income. And, as historian Hasia Diner has pointed out, because employers provided room and board and at times even work clothing, domestics were financially better off than their contemporaries in other occupations. They could put money aside either to help relatives in Ireland, to support their church, or to buy a fashionable outfit. Moreover, domestic service provided the security of a home—no small benefit to young women who might have survived the voyage to America alone and had no family to fall back on.[48]

Besides domestic labor, Irishwomen could be found most noticeably in other service-related jobs. In large towns like Rutland, Brattleboro, and Burlington that had hotels, Irishwomen labored as cooks, "table girls," chambermaids, and washerwomen. The same was true in boarding schools, colleges, hospitals, and asylums. In the 1860s and 1870s, almost all the help at the Troy Conference Academy of the Methodist Church in Poultney, the forerunner to Green Mountain College, was Irish, as was the help at the state insane asylum in Brattleboro. A few skilled women worked in the "needle" trades as seamstresses, dressmakers, and "tailoresses."[49]

Unlike in Massachusetts, where the textile mills of Lowell, Springfield, and Chicopee hired thousands of Irishwomen, mill work in the Green Mountains was relatively unimportant as an employer of Erin's daughters, primarily because there were so few mills. By the later decades of the nineteenth century, many of Vermont's once-numerous small textile works had closed in response to competition from Massachusetts. In the few places where textile mills survived, however, Irishwomen constituted a significant but not overwhelming portion of the female workforce. A woolen mill in Ludlow in 1870 employed 60 women, and 18 of them were Irish. In Winooski's extensive woolen and cotton mills, about 200 women toiled at looms and jennies. The vast majority of them were French Canadians, and only about 40 were Irish immigrants or their daughters. And as historian Jan Albers has pointed out, Vermont's textile workers, men and women, even at the industry's peak in 1850, never amounted to more than three-quarters of 1 percent of the total population. Unlike Massachusetts, where the popular image of the female Irish worker was either Bridget the domestic servant or Tessie at the loom, in Vermont Bridget was joined by Maggie at her farm chores.[50]

The one genteel occupation where Irishwomen in Vermont had a noticeable presence—particularly among first-generation Irish Americans—was teaching. One historian has written that "the Irish-American teacher joined the Irish-

American policeman, fireman and motorman as the stereotypical civil servants in large American cities." And this was as true across Vermont as it was in American cities. By the late 1800s, dozens of public schools in villages and towns throughout Vermont had teaching staffs that were primarily Irish. As early as 1869, West Rutland's Public School No. 7—the "Catholic" school—had five female teachers, all Irish: Bridget Gaffney, Bridget O'Neill, Mary Maloney, Kate Carmody, and Margaret Boyle Leonard, the latter the wife of the only male member of the faculty, Principal Joseph Eugene Leonard, also Irish. Given its designation as the "Catholic" school, it is not surprising that the faculty was all Irish. But even elsewhere in Vermont, wherever there was an Irish community of significant size, the public schools had large numbers of Irish teachers. In the old Underhill Irish settlement at the turn of the century, at least six of the fourteen schoolteachers were Irishwomen, while at the same time the equally old Irish town of Fairfield had eleven Irish teachers out of fourteen—four of them from the same family, the Rooneys. In the marble-quarrying town of Dorset in 1900, nine of seventeen teachers were Irish; and in the opening decades of the twentieth century, Irishwomen predominated in schools in the textile village of Winooski.[51]

What was the attraction to teaching? A number of factors seem to have been at play. One was availability. Because the job paid poorly—wages were often less than those of dairy maids, shopgirls, and house servants—there was constant turnover, a situation accentuated by the widespread requirement that a woman leave teaching upon marriage. Another factor was the entrance requirement. Owing to Vermont's decentralized educational system, where each school district established its own standards for teachers, oftentimes little more than the ability to read and write and do simple math was necessary to teach. Some Irish teachers were hardly more than children themselves: Jeannie Foren and Mary Hassett in Moretown were only fourteen when they stood before their young charges in the 1880s.[52]

Irish fathers, worried for their daughters' future economic well-being, oftentimes encouraged them to get an education and become teachers. This was the case with Patrick Duffy, an Irish immigrant who had come to America at the time of the famine, settled in Georgia, Vermont, near many of his County Louth neighbors in Fairfield, and practiced his trade as a blacksmith. In time Patrick married and raised six children—a son and five daughters. As the son, John, apprenticed to his father, his future seemed assured. But Patrick worried about the girls. They needed a skill to make a living. Patrick determined that they would get an education. Thus at a time when the education of girls was generally considered of less importance than that of boys, the five Duffy girls received more formal schooling than their brother. Eventually all five girls became teachers. This served them in good stead, as three of them never married, and supported themselves as teachers throughout their lives. In an ironic twist, John Duffy had to give up blacksmithing with the advent of the automobile and went into farming.[53]

Finally, and perhaps decisively for Vermont Irish girls, a young female teacher could board at home. There were multiple benefits in this. Living inexpensively with family, the teaching daughter could help her parents financially, often a necessity among struggling immigrants. Religious concerns also may have played a role. Because Catholic churches existed only in Vermont's few cities and in rural communities with concentrations of French and Irish, families may have been reluctant to let their daughters seek employment in areas where the only religious institutions were Protestant.

Another factor tending to keep Irish girls close to home was the reluctance of predominately Protestant communities to hire Catholic teachers. Parents of students at Northfield Academy were assured in 1857 that the new teacher on the faculty was a Protestant. The hiring of a Catholic to be principal of Rutland High School in the late 1870s resulted in heated letters to the editor of the local paper, and it was widely rumored that in a town near Rutland a teacher was forced to resign when it was learned she was a Catholic. The end result of these restraints was that female Irish teachers tended to work primarily in heavily Catholic communities and to live with their parents until married.[54]

The Second Generation

Looking back at the Irish in Vermont from the vantage point of the early twenty-first century, it is easy to forget that from the time of the famine to the end of the 1800s there had been fifty years of change. The Irish of the 1890s were different from the Irish of the 1840s. The *Burlington Free Press* commented on the transformation that took place when it declared in 1869 that "the second generation of the immigrant Irish are educated at the public schools, rise to a higher sphere of labor than their parents, in many cases become Prodestants [*sic*], and then freely mingle with the rest of the community as thoroughly American citizens."

W. Scott Nay, a country doctor who practiced in Underhill around the turn of the century, echoed similar sentiments in a memoir he set down after retirement in the 1930s. Looking back on his Irish neighbors, he recalled that "nearly all had large families, and the members of the second generation were among the most intelligent and influential personages in the town."[55]

But progress was uneven. Some families and individuals got on better than others, and too many stagnated, little improving their lot over that of their parents. How could it be otherwise? Too many children of Irish immigrants had to leave school early, at age twelve or thirteen, to supplement family income by working in marble shops, in homes as domestics, or as pickers or dyers in textile mills. School enrollments bear this out. Up until the seventh or eighth grade, Irish children in the Green Mountains attended school at about the same rate as did Yankee children, but after that their numbers dropped precipitously. While many of their elementary school chums carried lunch pails to high school, too many Irish youngsters carried them to mills and quarries.[56]

The Mooney family of Bennington was probably typical of many struggling Irish in the 1870s. John and Sallie Mooney, both from Ireland, had four children born in the United States. At age fifty, John Mooney worked as a farm laborer, a poor-paying job that left the family with little to live on. Sallie remained at home to "keep house," but her four children—two boys and two girls between the ages of eight and sixteen—all worked in a local cotton mill. While the jobs held by the children helped the family to make ends meet, they also restricted the children's options for the future.[57]

But the sons and daughters of immigrants did advance economically. The examples already mentioned of first-generation Irish American women becoming teachers in the late nineteenth century are evidence of that. And in the only study that tracked the occupations of male Irish workers in Vermont in the late 1800s, Brian Walsh reported evidence of steady progress. Walsh's work on Burlington, covering the half-century from 1850 to 1900, found that the percentage of Irish working in unskilled or semiskilled jobs was over 78 percent at the beginning of the period and down to less than 37 percent by the turn of the century. At the same time, the percentage of Irishmen working in skilled, craft, or commercial work went from about 15 percent to over 35 percent. Life for the Irish was getting better.[58]

Urban political power accounted for some of the economic progress of the Irish. As their numbers grew in Vermont cities and towns, so did their political influence, and that influence often translated into public-sector jobs. As elsewhere in America, Vermont Irishmen played important roles in police and fire departments. In 1890 some 37 percent of Burlington's firemen were Irish and 20 percent of its policemen. In the 1860s and 1870s Vermont-born Noble Flanagan served the city successively as sheriff, fire chief, and then its police chief. He was followed in 1903 by Patrick Russell. In nearby Winooski village, the Lafayette Hose Company—despite its French name—was exclusively Irish. Besides being a part-time firefighting organization, it also functioned as informal men's club, supporting sports teams and sponsoring social events. Its chief, Plattsburg, New York–born Patrick McGreevey, was a popular local merchant and dealer in real estate. He was also a notorious bootlegger (perhaps that was why the Lafayette Hose Company was popular as a social organization). By the end of the first decade of the twentieth century, there had also been an Irish fire chief in Bennington and Irish police chiefs in St. Albans and Northfield. A few years later Brattleboro had an Irish police chief, Patrick O'Keefe. Local residents long remembered him as the person who officially announced the beginning of spring each year when he appeared on city streets in his straw hat.[59]

First-generation Irish Americans also rose in prominence in the business world. One could draw up a long list of Irish doing well in various business endeavors in the late nineteenth century, but citing just a few should suffice. In Rutland, Hugh Duffy operated a successful coal and wood business; in Burlington, John McKenzie first owned a grocery store and then established the region's premier meat-packing company; in Montpelier, Frank McMahon Corry, whose immigrant father had once operated a truck farm, successfully ran a grocery store, then went on to own two granite companies, and eventually became president of a local bank.

Irish American businessmen in Vermont were particularly successful in the slate industry, perhaps owing to the long tradition of working with slate in Ireland. In 1879 Martin and William Bolger established the Bolger Brothers Company, with a quarry in Poultney and a mill in nearby Hydeville. For the Bolgers, slate working was in their bones. Their father had worked the colorful stone in Tipperary before immigrating to the United States in the early 1850s. The same was true of the Delehanty family, which operated the Bomoseen Slate Company in Hydeville. The father of its founder had also worked the Tipperary slate ledges before sailing for America. This Tipperary heritage served them well: men like the Bolgers and the Delehantys knew how to work the ledges, how to shape the raw slate, and how to get it to market. With the wealth generated through the Bomoseen Slate Company, the Delehanty progeny built careers of their own. Of eleven children of the founder, one became a nun, two took up the law, one went into medicine, and two became teachers. Clearly the Irish were on the rise.[60]

These successes, however, were mere shadows compared to the accomplishments of John J. Flynn. In the realm of business, no first-generation Irish American in Vermont achieved as much as Flynn. Long before his death in Burlington in 1940 at age eighty-six, he was not only the Queen City's most important businessman, but also one of the most influential in the state. His business interests were so diverse that the *Burlington Free Press* in his obituary proclaimed that "no man in Burlington was able to list them [all]." They included extensive real estate holdings and ownership in utility companies, light rail lines, movie theaters, and banks. From the 1890s through the 1930s there was hardly an area of industry and commerce in Burlington in which Flynn was not involved.

Flynn came from a typical Irish Catholic immigrant family. His parents and his older sister, Mary, had arrived in Vermont in the early 1850s. His father initially worked in the marble quarries in Dorset and then later for the Bennington & Rut-

From the 1890s through the 1930s, John J. Flynn dominated business in Burlington.

land Railroad. John, born in 1854, was the first of four American-born Flynn children. Like so many other Irish children, as soon as he completed primary school he went to work; but rather than staying near home, he moved to Burlington, a city that had expanded greatly during the recently ended Civil War. There he first worked on a dairy farm and was so successful that he soon became its manager and then its owner. From dairying he went into the grocery business and finally into real estate. By 1900 he was one of Burlington's wealthiest capitalists.[61]

The son of poor immigrants, Flynn never forgot his working-class roots. Despite his wealth and prominence, in a business community that was staunchly Republican Flynn actively supported the Democratic Party. In the early 1900s he helped Democrats organize voters in Burlington's heavily ethnic north end, and this in turn helped the Democrats to challenge Republicans for control of city hall. During the Depression Flynn took a particular delight in treating the city's numerous newspaper boys to a sumptuous banquet at the elegant Hotel Vermont each New Year's Day. After the meal he gave the boys tickets to attend a movie at one of his theaters. Though Flynn never had children of his own, concern for the well-being of young people was one of the principal interests of his life.[62]

But there was one way in which Flynn was an atypical son of Irish Catholic immigrants: he abandoned the church of his forefathers and became Protestant. Over the years there has been some speculation about this, usually related to his marriage to Nellie Waite. Nellie was the descendant of an old Yankee family whose roots in Vermont went back to the eighteenth century. And Nellie was proud of her lineage: she actively supported the Daughters of the American Revolution. She and John probably knew each other as children, for she grew up in Peru, a town adjacent to Dorset. They may even have gone to school together. And John would have noticed her: she was a bright, studious girl, and photographs of her in middle age show a still-attractive woman. In her youth she must have been a beauty. Those who knew Nellie and John Flynn said he "idolized" her, but it was not a match that would have pleased either family.[63]

Did he change religions in order to win Nellie's hand? Possibly, but there is no evidence. He may have been just as motivated by a sincere desire to subscribe to a less dogmatic church: throughout their lives together, John and Nellie worshipped as Unitarians, one of the most liberal Christian churches in America. Equally plausible is that he abandoned Catholicism for business reasons, to get ahead in a sphere dominated by Protestants. Or it may have been a combination of all three factors.

Despite his apostasy, Flynn never abandoned his respect for Catholic institutions. In his will, after first providing for nieces, nephews, and longtime employees—his wife had died before him—and leaving real estate to the city for a park and a home for aged men, Flynn bequeathed a substantial portion of his estate to Burlington's St. Joseph Orphanage, the Bishop de Goesbriand Hospital, and the Catholic Fanny Allen Hospital in Colchester. His largesse to these Catholic institutions suggests that early-life influences never entirely left him.[64]

In our own time, Flynn's name, though not the man, is well known in Burlington. Flynn Avenue in the city's south end runs through property he once owned; while on the opposite end of town, the John J. Flynn Elementary School sits near real estate formerly part of his extensive holdings. The most conspicuous display of the Flynn name, however, is on the marquee of the art deco–style theater he built on Main Street in 1930. Today, the elegantly restored Flynn Theater in downtown Burlington is the center of the Queen City's cultural life and a testament to the achievements of this once-poor son of Irish immigrants.

Irish Americans in the Professions

Almost as much a cliché as the Irish policeman and the Irish teacher are the Irish attorney and the Irish physician. First-generation Irish Americans and those that followed swarmed to these two professions. Their motivations are understandable. For generations the great mass of the Irish people were landless peasants, while lawyers and doctors were gentlemen, men of refinement and education. Among the impoverished Irish, the doctor stood only a notch below the parish priest in the village hierarchy. To become a lawyer or doctor was to cross the divide that separated the nameless masses from middle-class respectability. In the case of doctors, there was also the need to serve one's fellow man, a strong trait in the Irish character. Partly motivated from an intense sense of Christian charity, many Irish gravitated to the helping professions: clergymen, nuns, teachers, nurses, and physicians. Moreover, there was a ready market for Irish attorneys and physicians. Like all ethnic groups, the Irish preferred a person from their own background to treat them; thus every industrial center in Vermont, from Brattleboro and Bennington in the south to Burlington and St. Albans in the north, could support three or four Irish professionals.

Beginning in the 1860s, a steady stream of Irish Americans received degrees from the Medical College of the University of Vermont. At the turn of the century there were 32 Irish-surnamed physicians practicing in Vermont, out of a total of 180. Within one generation of their exodus from Ireland, the Irish constituted a significant part of Vermont's medical community. By the 1930s, 16 of Burlington's 60 physicians were Irish, over 26 percent of the total.[65]

Some of them stood out, as much for their accomplishments in their private lives as for their successful medical careers. Three whose lives bear recalling were Burlington's Patrick McSweeney, Rutland's John Hanrahan, and Brattleboro's James Conland.

McSweeney is remembered as *the* Irish doctor in Burlington from the late 1880s through the 1930s. There were other Irish physicians in the city at this time, but Irish and Yankees alike held McSweeney in high esteem. In addition, so many other members of his family later became physicians that the McSweeney name became synonymous with the medical profession in Vermont. Many Vermont families cherished stories about Patrick McSweeney.

The Rowley family of Milton recounted one episode. In 1889 the family of Elizabeth Flynn Rowley—the brave woman who three times crossed the Atlantic to keep her family together—came down with diphtheria. Dr. McSweeney attended them. Elizabeth and one son died, but three sons survived. In later years, one of the Rowley boys who came through that ordeal ascribed his narrow escape from death to McSweeney's prescribing that he swallow a full glass of whiskey a day.[66]

The Irish doctor was also called to the scene of one of Burlington's most heinous crimes. On May 13, 1904, police officer James McGrath cornered Benjamin Williams, a deserter from the army post in Colchester, in the lumberyards on the city's waterfront. Williams, still in possession of his service revolver, shot McGrath three times and fled. Witnesses rushed to get a priest from the nearby cathedral and to summon Dr. McSweeney, who lived just a few streets away. There then occurred an unusual act of solidarity with the wounded McGrath. While the priest and the doctor administered to the dying officer, a crowd from the heavily Irish waterfront neighborhood quickly gathered and publicly prayed the rosary. Sadly, neither prayers nor the doctor could save McGrath.[67]

McSweeney's stature as a physician extended beyond his Irish neighborhood. At one time he served as chairman of the University of Vermont's Depart-

A Civil War hero, immigrant Irishman John Hanrahan was a leader of the Irish community in Rutland in the 1870s and 1880s.

ment of Obstetrics and Gynecology and as president of the state medical society. Less well known was the role he played in putting other family members through medical school. After he received his medical degree, he helped two younger brothers and two cousins through medical school. The strong connection of the McSweeney name with the Burlington medical community continued down to the end of the twentieth century: Patrick's daughter Katherine and his grandson E. Douglas McSweeney both became physicians.[68]

In Rutland, John Hanrahan played the role filled by McSweeney in Burlington. But there were differences between the two. Where McSweeney was first-generation Irish American, Hanrahan was born in Ireland and came to America in 1856 at age seventeen. In addition, while McSweeney maintained a citizen's interest in politics, Hanrahan lived for politics. One contemporary described him as a "perennial office seeker." During the 1870s and 1880s, he was president of almost every Irish organization in town, was a prominent member of the Grand Army of the Republic, and a committed and active Democrat. Politically moderate, he garnered support from a broad spectrum of Rutland's citizens. This served him in good stead: For eight years he was a trustee of Rutland village and twice served as its president. A key figure in state Democratic politics, he often represented Vermont at the Democratic Party's national conventions. At the height of his career, he formed and supported an Irish volunteer fire department in the village, the Hanrahan Hose Company Number 7.[69]

Part of Hanrahan's popularity in Rutland stemmed from his Civil War service. When the war erupted, Hanrahan was studying with a physician in New York. Though he possessed no medical degree, he was commissioned a surgeon in the U.S. Navy by examination and served on Union ships through the course of the war. The nadir of his military career came when rebels captured his ship at the mouth of the Rappahannock River and for six weeks he was held at a prisoner-of-war camp near Richmond. During his incarceration the prison authorities asked him to treat sick and wounded Union prisoners, which he happily agreed to do. In later years he never failed to mention how well treated he was while a guest of the Confederacy.[70]

When the war ended Hanrahan returned to New York and resumed his medical studies, this time at New York Medical College. After four years of caring for sick and wounded sailors and soldiers, he probably had more practical medical knowledge than his instructors. His degree complete, in 1869 he moved to Rutland and opened a practice. There, as physician, Irishman, and Civil War veteran he played a key role in the civic life of the Marble City.

A third physician of note, not because of his medical prominence or political activism, but because of a connection to the literary world, was James Conland. Born in Brooklyn, New York, in 1851 of Irish parents, Conland as a young man worked as a seaman, but by 1875 he had removed to Brattleboro and began the study of medicine with a local physician. Later he matriculated at the University of Vermont's College of Medicine. Once he received his medical degree, he returned to Brattleboro.

In Brattleboro Conland became the personal physician of Rudyard Kipling, the English writer who after marrying an American lived in Brattleboro for four years, 1893–97. The two enjoyed each other's company. Kipling called Conland "the best friend I made in New England."[71] In the evenings at Kipling's exotic home, Naulakha, Conland often regaled the Englishman with adventurous stories of his early seafaring days. The tales recounted by Conland later appeared in Kipling's *Captains Courageous*.[72]

Irish *and* American: 1870–1900

O n Saturday morning, August 9, 1902, Captain John Lonergan, Civil War hero and unrepentant Fenian, was laid to rest in Burlington's St. Joseph Cemetery. Present at the funeral were many of his longtime Irish friends, including James Scully—the "pivotal" man at Gettysburg—and John J. Monahan, his old Fenian comrade. There was also a large contingent of gray-haired GAR men who had no Irish connections but were there to honor a fellow Civil War veteran. Among them were prominent Burlington attorney and leader of the state Democratic Party, Bradley B. Smalley, and former Republican governor Urban Woodbury.[1]

The diversity of the mourners underscored the two great themes of Lonergan's life: his devotion to Ireland and his love for his adopted land. That dual attachment was eventually proclaimed in the inscription on his gravestone. It noted that he was born in Ireland, fought at Gettysburg, and that he died "believing in everlasting life and in the destiny of this dear land." In these few words, etched in granite, John Lonergan proclaimed himself both Irish and American.

This was the great duality of the immigrant and first generation of Irish Americans. They carried with them the beliefs and biases, the customs and habits, and the world view of their ancestors, while at the same time hungrily taking on the behavior and outlook of Americans. In late-nineteenth-century Vermont, this duality exhibited itself in a number of ways.

Identity and Religion

In the century following the Great Famine, perhaps nothing characterized Irish Americans more than their Roman Catholicism. In an America that had been almost exclusively Protestant, the Irish were intensely, even militantly Roman Catholic, the result of long centuries of nurturing their faith as a cornerstone of national identity. This connection between identity and religion carried over to the New World. In general, to be Irish in Vermont—as in the rest of the United States—also meant being Catholic.

In an ironic twist, American Protestants from an Irish background actually helped to solidify the equation of Irish with Catholic. In the main, Irish Protestants had arrived in America under different circumstances and in an earlier time. By the time the famine Irish, who were overwhelmingly Catholic, began entering the United States, many Americans of Protestant Irish descent had been in the country for generations, and they sought to distance themselves from the ragtag and often disease-ridden refugees of the 1840s and 1850s. It was only at this time that the term "Scots-Irish" came into popular use, as a means to differentiate the two groups. Previously, Americans labeled anyone from Ireland, Catholic or Protestant, as Irish.

"Scots-Irish" was code for sober, hardworking Protestants, unlike the "hard-drinking, shiftless followers of the popish church." Another phrase Vermonters at this time used to denote a Protestant Irishman was to say he was from the "North of Ireland." One finds this in numerous Vermont town histories published in the 1870s and 1880s, which usually included a section of short biographies on an area's leading businessmen and farmers. Hamilton Child's *Gazetteer and Business Directory of Chittenden County*, published in 1882, described William McBride, a prosperous Protestant farmer in Colchester, as from the "North of Ireland." Lewis Aldrich's *History of Franklin and Grand Isle counties*, which appeared in 1891, described a John Butler in the same way.[2]

In differentiating themselves in this way, Protestant Irish Americans made clear their separateness from mainstream Irish America; and in some ways they *were* different. In Vermont, in general, they supported the Republican Party, unlike the strongly pro-Democratic Catholic Irish. Moreover, as Protestants, they intermarried more readily with their Yankee neighbors than did Catholics, and were more readily integrated into mainstream American society. Thus while the Catholic Irish retained a strong sense of group separateness through religion, for the Protestant Irish, religion was a vehicle of assimilation. And for them assimilation occurred so quickly that they virtually vanished from the ethnic scene, leaving the Catholics in sole possession of the appellation "Irish."

One way Irish Americans remained connected to Catholicism was through a reluctance to marry outside their faith. There are no statistics to document apostasy among post-famine Irish Catholics in Vermont, but anecdotal evidence suggests it was minimal—although some, like John J. Flynn, did drift away. No doubt matters of the heart often played a role in this, but romantic attachments also worked the other way. In the early 1900s John Sheehey of St. Albans, the grandson of Irish immigrants, married a Protestant who converted, and their son Robert became a priest.[3]

Lack of access to religious instruction may also have accounted for some Catholics abandoning their church. Take the family of James and Kitty Brennan. As a young couple at about the time of the Civil War, they left their hometown of Fairfield and bought a farm in Eden, in north-central Vermont, far from any Catholic church. There they raised five sons, and while the parents clung to their Catholic religion despite the hardships of distance, two of the boys strayed from the church of their birth.[4]

Far more noticeable than apostasy in the late nineteenth century was the intense adherence of the Irish to the Catholic Church. By the early 1870s, a growing number of young Vermonters entered the religious life as priests, brothers, and nuns, thus lessening—thought not eliminating—the need to recruit from abroad. For the devout Irish Catholic, entering the religious life was a special calling. Listen to the excited words of John Rowley, who, while living in Maryland in 1867, wrote his immigrant parents on the family farm in Milton that he had decided to enter the Society of Jesus (Jesuits):

> My dear parents it has pleased our good god two bestow greater favors
> on me than you or myself could ever have imagined . . . it has pleased
> his divine madgesty two call me out of the world and placed me in the
> walls of his own house in religion thanks bee [to?] his goodness and his
> blessed mother mary.[5]

The joy Rowley expressed in his announcement could not have been greater had he struck gold in California. Though his parents' response to this news is unrecorded, they probably beamed with pride over his decision. Rowley lived his life as a Jesuit brother, doing maintenance work first at Georgetown College in Washington, D.C., and later at the College of the Holy Cross in Massachusetts, where he died in 1910.

Bishop de Goesbriand found young men among his Irish flock eager to enter the priesthood. The first native Vermonter ordained a priest for the Diocese of Burlington was John Stephen Michaud in 1873. Despite his French name, Michaud was partly Irish American. His French Canadian father died when Michaud was

*John Rowley,
son of the courageous
Elizabeth Rowley,
who crossed the
Atlantic three times
to keep her family
together, became
a Jesuit brother.
(Courtesy of Anne
Rowley Howrigan.)*

four, leaving his Irish mother—Limerick-born Catherine Rogan—to raise him. The impecunious Mrs. Michaud resorted at times to the Irish widow's occupation of selling bootleg liquor to her Irish neighbors along Burlington's waterfront. Michaud himself identified strongly with his Irish ancestry: in 1865 he was vice president of Burlington's Hibernian Society.[6]

Around the state other Irish boys followed in John Michaud's footsteps. From Winooski came two brothers, Daniel and William O'Sullivan, sons of a woolen-mill worker from Cork. Another O'Sullivan brother, Thomas, chose a different path, went into the law, and lived his life as part of the Tammany machine in New York. James Shannon, destined to be one of the leaders of the diocese in the early twentieth century, was the son of an Irish immigrant who had become a successful farmer in Enosburg. By 1900 about half the Catholic clergy in the Green Mountains came from Irish backgrounds; the other half had roots in Quebec and France. In Vermont the Catholic Church was a Franco-Irish enterprise.[7]

Irish Catholic Education

While the free education offered by Vermont's public schools was a boon to poor immigrant families—and a key instrument in the assimilation process—many Irish and French Canadian Catholics gravitated to convent or parish schools as a means to instill their own beliefs, histories, and values in their children. In this sense Catholic schools were antiassimilationist, sheltering young Catholics from the perceived evils of Protestant America.

As soon as he was appointed bishop of Burlington, de Goesbriand turned to the question of education. In 1854, just one year after his appointment, he established in Burlington the St. Joseph's Orphanage and Hospital to educate and care for orphans and young girls. Four years later he hired a remarkable young Irishman, Michael Mulqueen, to operate a school for boys. Mulqueen was well suited for the task. In his native Limerick he had attended a Jesuit school where he studied to be a teacher, but in the mid-1850s he immigrated to America, probably due to a lack of prospects at home, and found his way to Winooski, where he initially took work as a clerk in the textile mills. There de Goesbriand discovered him. Accepting the bishop's invitation, Mulqueen opened a school in his Burlington home on Cherry Street, close by the cathedral.

A strict disciplinarian in the Jesuit tradition of education, Mulqueen was an excellent teacher. In later years his former students remembered him with fondness, and it became a mark of pride among Burlington's Catholic professionals to note that one had been educated by Michael Mulqueen. Moreover, as a result of Mulqueen's commitment to Catholic values, many of Vermont's first native sons ordained to the priesthood passed through his classrooms. Quite possibly he was instrumental in the decision of the two O'Sullivan boys to become priests, perhaps less because of his role as a teacher than the fact that he was their uncle.[8]

Mulqueen's prominence as an educator made him a leader in Burlington's large Irish community. He was an active member of the city's Hibernian Society and sat with John Lonergan at the dais at many St. Patrick's Day banquets—although his views on the captain's Fenian activities are unknown. Until his retirement in 1876, he was one of Burlington's most important Irish American citizens.

Mulqueen's pioneering work in Catholic education was carried on by an Irish order of nuns, the Sisters of Mercy. Founded in Dublin in 1831, the Mercyites began sending sisters to the United States in the 1840s, and by the 1860s had established convents across the country. In casting about to find teachers for his diocese, de Goesbriand contacted Sister Frances Warde, the Irish-born leader of the American Sisters of Mercy and an old acquaintance of the bishop's. Warde, residing in New Hampshire, responded positively and in 1874 sent four sisters, including energetic

Sisters of Mercy were photographed with their students in front of the former St.
Mary Church in Burlington. The church was built in 1841, but by the time of this

photograph it had been converted to a school. (Courtesy of the Roman Catholic Diocese of Burlington.)

twenty-six-year-old Galway-born Sister Stanislaus O'Malley, to Burlington. Under Sister Stanislaus's leadership, Mulqueen's old school, renamed by the sisters St. Patrick's Academy, thrived. Teachers like Mulqueen and the Sisters of Mercy transferred Irish Catholic values to succeeding generations of Vermont Catholics.[9]

Despite the best efforts of Bishop de Goesbriand, however, Catholic schools were few and far between in nineteenth-century Vermont. Most Irish American children walked daily with their neighbors to the little public schoolhouses that dotted the countryside. In most cases the experience was a good one. There were times, however, when the public school was the center of a cultural clash, pitting the newcomers with their foreign traditions against the dominant Protestant culture. One such incident occurred in the Connecticut River town of Brattleboro in 1874.

Brattleboro was one of Vermont's boom towns in the closing decades of the nineteenth century. The arrival of a rail line at midcentury linked it to Boston and Montreal and made it an important commercial and manufacturing center. Brattleboro was also home to the largest maker of reed organs in the world, the Estey Organ Company, which employed hundreds of workers. Other residents found employment in cigar-making shops, paper mills, the various spa-hotels for which the area was famous, and at the Vermont State Insane Asylum.

In 1870 the town had almost 5,000 inhabitants, with close to 15 percent of them from Irish backgrounds. While the Irish held a diversity of occupations, from carpenters to plumbers to blacksmiths and carriage makers, the vast majority of the men were common laborers. Irishwomen who worked outside the home did so either as cooks, laundresses and kitchen girls at the insane asylum, or in private domestic service.[10]

Bustling Brattleboro supported a number of public schools, from the primary grades through high school. With large Irish families, it is not surprising that Catholics made up about a quarter of the town's student population of 600, although this figure included some French Canadian children as well. Directing policy over the school system was a prudential committee composed of influential citizens drawn from the town's dominant Protestant community.[11]

Apparently there had been tension in town for some time between the large numbers of Irish that had settled there since the late 1840s and the older Yankee community, for when the Catholics desired to buy land in the 1860s to build a church, they felt compelled to resort to a ruse. Rather than having the local priest or Bishop de Goesbriand approach potential sellers, an Irish coachman named O'Hara acted as front man and made the purchase. Only later, and with some surprise, as workmen began building St. Michael Church near the center of town, did townspeople learn the true nature of the transaction. Some suppliers of building materials refused to sell to the church builders.[12]

The tension that existed between the two communities came to a head on June 4, 1874, the feast of Corpus Christi. This day in honor of the Eucharist had long been celebrated by European Catholics as a "holy day of obligation," meaning attendance at morning Mass was obligatory, followed by a holiday from work and school. Because American society did not recognize "holy days," their observance was a problem for devout Catholics: to miss a day of work or school might put one's job or education in jeopardy. As mentioned earlier, Rev. John Daly back in the 1850s had to bribe West Rutland quarrymen to attend Mass on holy days with the promise that if they did so, God would protect them from harm while they worked in the quarries. Catholics found themselves caught between their religious duties and the demands of life in America.

The series of events that precipitated the crisis in Brattleboro began with the coming of a new priest to St. Michael, the Reverend Henry Lane. Lane was a greenhorn. In 1874 he was twenty-eight years old and had been in America only five years—one of de Goesbriand's Irish recruits. Lane spent his first few years in Burlington under the bishop's guiding hand and had only taken up the Brattleboro post on May 26, 1874, just nine days before the incident in question. Brattleboro was the young priest's first independent assignment.

Lane was the type of man who tackled his responsibilities head-on. His fellow priests described him as "zealous" and "energetic." The bishop thought highly of him. Lane also had a reputation for physical strength. He was a big man, and it was said that he had been a champion hammer thrower in Ireland; in later years onlookers saw him heave the hammer over the fence at the Rutland County fairgrounds. Both mentally and physically, he was not the type to back away from a confrontation. In his first Sunday sermon, just a few days after arriving in Brattleboro, he reminded his parishioners that they were to observe the feast of Corpus Christi by attending Mass. That year the feast day fell on a Thursday, June 4. Whether intentional or not, the gauntlet was down.

On Wednesday, June 3, some of the Catholic students informed their teachers that they would be absent the next day, only to be told that they were not excused. Up to this point no one had notified the school authorities of the feast day, a serious oversight. On the morning of the fourth, just moments before the beginning of school, Father Lane shot off a quick note to the head of the prudential committee: "Sir—You will confer a favor on us Catholics, by exempting the Catholic children from attending school on all holy days. I should have called and explained our reasons, but have not had opportunity yet."

Perhaps piqued that he had not been contacted earlier, the head of the committee fired back his response: "To comply with your request involves closing two of our schools, and greatly interrupting several others. This we have never done, and cannot do." The children were not excused, but sixty of them chose to attend church services and absented themselves from school.

This challenge to the school authorities was met with a harsh response. When some of the absented children attempted to enter school after attending Mass that day, they were refused admission, as were all the truant children when they tried to gain admission on Friday. School administrators told irate parents that according to school policy, truant students were not to be readmitted for the remainder of the school term, which in any case was just a few days away. When the parents of the offending students objected, the prudential committee responded that the children would be readmitted only if the parents promised not to absent them on holy days.[13]

With his ire raised, Lane went on the offensive. In a letter to the local paper, the *Vermont Phoenix*, he argued that the school authorities were interfering with the right of the children to practice their religion, which was guaranteed by the U.S. Constitution. Further, he charged that Catholic children had been discriminated against in the public schools, for they had been forced to recite Protestant prayers, required to purchase Protestant Bibles, and in one instance had been told "that it was the Catholics that had banished the Puritans out of England."[14]

While Lane fought the battle in the press, he and his parishioners moved on two other fronts. On the one hand they began discussing the possibility of starting their own parochial school, while on the other they filed suit against the prudential committee on the grounds that their children were being denied a public school education, and that they, as parents, had the right to send them to religious services, as they were the ones responsible for their children's spiritual and moral upbringing. Lawyers for the prudential committee argued that to make special provisions for adherents of one religious group would open the school authorities to special requests from others, and given the numerous denominations in town besides the Catholics—Presbyterians, Methodists, Unitarians, Congregationalists, and Baptists—the schools would quickly become chaotic.

One school attorney introduced a note of condescension into his argument when he argued that Irish children should be the last ones to miss school, "as the regular attendance of said Catholic children is especially important, for the reason that they receive less aid and encouragement in learning at their homes than do the children of Protestant parents." In the end a local court decided in favor of the prudential committee's position, and when that decision was appealed before the Vermont Supreme Court, the lower court's ruling was upheld.[15]

That summer, as lawyers argued the case before the courts, Brattleboro residents wondered what would happen when the fall term commenced in September. In any event, the opening of school went off smoothly, with all the Catholic children again in attendance. But what would happen when another holy day of obligation fell on a weekday? That occurred on December 11, the Feast of the Immaculate Conception. Again Catholic children attended Mass and missed school, and again the school authorities refused them readmission.

Having lost their case in the lower court (the State Supreme Court had not then decided), Father Lane and his followers took the only action they saw available to them—they opened their own school. For the remainder of the school year, two young Irishwomen, Annie and Mary Burke, taught Catholic children in a makeshift school building, with boys in one room and girls in another. The following year, 1875, the parish replaced the interim school by building a wing onto the rectory with four classrooms. It opened as St. Michael's School, the first parochial school in the Green Mountains.[16]

The Brattleboro incident underlined the separate world views of the town's two communities. Irish Catholics assumed that church attendance trumped school attendance, while the Yankee community demanded conformity to the established order. Interestingly, some liberal-minded Protestants sided with the Catholics on the school issue, but for different reasons. The *Vermont Phoenix*, for example, criticized the prudential committee for its hard-line position because it forced the Catholics to establish their own school and thereby lost the chance to use the public schools as a vehicle for assimilation.[17]

Accepting the special religious needs of Vermont's Catholics took a long time. In her old age, Veronica Maloney Ryan of Fairfield remembered with bitterness that as a young schoolgirl in nearby Hyde Park in the 1920s, she was punished with detention when she arrived late to class after attending Mass on a holy day. Moreover, because her school graduation exercises took place in a Protestant church, her family's Catholic sensibilities forbade her participation. In time Vermont became more accepting of the diverse cultural and religious needs of its citizens, but through the early years of the twentieth century differences still rankled.[18]

Cultural Carryovers

The devout Catholicism of the American Irish was only the most visible of the cultural characteristics carried by them from the Old World. There were others, sometimes so subtle that few people would have guessed their Irish roots. Take the circumstances surrounding the wedding of Luke Barrett to Aurelia Peria in Shelburne in 1888. Barrett, born in Vermont in 1859, descended from Waterford immigrants who settled in Underhill in the 1830s. As a young man he became a master carpenter. When the Shelburne Shipyard on Lake Champlain learned of his skills, they hired him to build boats and dock facilities. While there he met and fell in love with a French Canadian girl, Aurelia Peria. Soon a "mixt" marriage was in the works. As the wedding day approached, Luke's Irish friends and family planned a "horning," the gathering of revelers with tin horns and pots and pans to joyfully harass the newlyweds on the first nights of their honeymoon. Learning of their intentions, Luke and the Peria family let it be known that the young couple would spend their first few nights at the home of the bride's family—while in fact they had booked a room at Burlington's fashionable Van Ness Hotel. Thus it was only after two nights of raucous drinking and noisemaking that the horners learned their efforts had done little more than disturb Aurelia's parents.[19]

Horning was an old Irish tradition, particularly strong in the Barretts' ancestral county of Waterford. In that region marriages were often accompanied by young men serenading the newlyweds by blowing horns, particularly if the match was an unpopular one, as would be the case when a significantly older man took a young bride. But, as in the Barrett example, it had also become an accepted prank at any wedding. Aurelia's parents probably went along with this ruse, since French Canadians had a similar custom, called charivari.[20]

There were cultural carryovers in language, too. Long after the great influx of Irish arrived in Vermont in the famine years, the Irish language could be heard in the hills and valleys of Vermont. Down to the time she died in the 1880s, old Bridget Wall, who had arrived with her husband in Underhill in the early 1840s, walked the back roads smoking her corncob pipe and visiting with her Irish-speaking neighbors. In 1900 there were still members of the aging immigrant generation who spoke Irish—although their numbers were decreasing with each passing year—and while their American-born offspring were raised speaking English, it was an English peppered with words and phrases echoing the language of the "Old Sod." This was not peculiar to Vermont but was happening all over America. From Irish, words like "shenanigans," "smithereens," and "galore" entered the English language.[21]

There are a number of examples of Irish words surviving in the Green Mountains. Frank Patten, whose parents had arrived in Fair Haven before the Civil War, always referred to a stupid fellow with the Irish word *amadán* well in to the twentieth century. Tim O'Connor, Speaker of the Vermont House of Representatives in the 1970s, remembered that when he was a boy in the years around World War II, his father used the Irish *cé hé sin* (pronounced *kee-a-shin*)—"Who is that?"— when desiring to know who someone was. O'Connor's father learned that from his Irish-born parents. A song popular in the Rutland area in the 1870s and 1880s, "Castleton Rippers," mentioned a *pocha*, which Irish listeners knew was a mischievous hobgoblin. Quarry workers often described the color of Rutland marble as *bawn*—Irish for "white." Into the twentieth century some Vermonters of Irish lineage prayed in the old language: Bessie Connor Ryan of Fairfield always recited the Lord's Prayer in Irish, the language in which she first learned it.[22]

A vivid example of Irish words slipping into the vernacular of Yankee Vermonters comes from the Civil War diary of Charles Mead. Mead, from an old West Rutland family, served with Company F, First U.S. Sharpshooters, from 1863 until his death outside Petersburg, Virginia, in 1864. In his entry for Sunday, February 21, 1864, he recorded that he and a few of his friends "had a 'shindee' in the street." Growing up in heavily Irish West Rutland, he must have heard this word many times. It comes from the Irish *seinnte*, meaning a musical gathering with singing and celebrating and probably the origin of the word "shindig."[23]

Besides Irish words creeping into Vermonters' everyday speech, Irish syntax and expressions found a fertile home in the Green Mountains. Tom Howrigan, great-grandson of the Patrick Howrigan who settled in Fairfield in 1849, remembered family members noting "it fell upon my ears" when relating that they had just heard some bit of gossip or news, or that they "took advice" when seeking counsel in some grave matter. Tom and his brothers also related that their parents had taught them to say a short prayer whenever leaving their house or one of the farm buildings: "In thy name O God please care for it always but especially until I return." Expressions coming from Gaelic Irish were a commonplace, two of the best known being "Keep the wind always at your back" and "May ye be in heaven three days before the devil knows y'er dead."[24]

Not only did words and sayings live on, but in some places the very cadences of Irish-English—the brogue—passed from generation to generation. This was particularly true of the more remote areas of Vermont. In the out-of-the-way village of West Castleton—the old Screwdriver slate-working community—the brogue had a long life. As late as the 1970s there were still old-timers who spoke with a distinct Irish lilt. People referred to it as the Bomoseen or West Castleton accent. Similar cadences could be found in the hilltop Irish communities of West Rutland.[25]

Echoes of Ireland could also be heard in the music and songs of the Green Mountain Irish. Music was and is central to Irish culture. No other country has a musical instrument (the harp) as its symbol. In the old country, isolated farm people met in the evenings at crossroads or at someone's house to dance to the tunes of fiddlers, pipers, and accordion players. If a musician could not be present, someone would mouth out a tune by lilting. With its landscape of remote valleys dotted with widely scattered farms, something similar occurred in Vermont. Gerald Heffernan, a young boy in the 1930s, remembered many such evenings in his family's farmhouse on Little Ireland Road in Starksboro. Most of the neighboring families were descended from Irish immigrants who had settled there following the famine. On a Saturday night with the chores done, Conways, Butlers, Caseys, Hannons, and others would gather at the Heffernan house for a "kitchen tunk" or "tonk." Strapping farmers pushed the furniture aside, spread cornmeal on the floor, and an evening of music and dancing followed. Kevin Heffernan, Gerald's father, provided the melody on his button accordion.[26]

Songs were part of this revelry. John Brennan, who left Ireland in the 1840s, regaled his Fairfield neighbors with verses he wrote and put to well-known old Irish tunes. Often their themes described callous Yankee attitudes toward the Irish. In the 1930s Mrs. Harry Thomas of Springfield remembered her Irish-born mother singing the tragic love story of "Johnny Doyle." The most popular Irish songs, however, were those known as "come all ye's," where the singer in the opening line invited a specific audience to listen—as in "Come all ye young maidens," or "Come all ye brave men," and so on. Unlike ballads, the "come all ye's" usually had a basis in fact, built around some known incident, individual, or circumstance.[27]

The work of one nineteenth-century Vermont Irish "come all ye" composer has come down to us. His name was James "Jimmy" Carney. Carney was born in Tipperary in 1823 and came to America in 1856, and like so many other Tipperary men he first worked in the West Rutland marble quarries. After a number of years in the holes, however, he found a position as a gardener on the estate of a wealthy Castleton family. In his spare time he composed and sang songs. Popular, energetic, and witty, Carney was in demand at social events and concerts throughout Rutland County.

Carney created songs out of the stuff of everyday life, inserting names and incidents that were well known to his audiences. One example, "The West Rutland Marble Bawn"—its title a play on the well-known Irish song "Molly Bawn"—exhibits all the characteristics of a "come all ye":

> Come all ye good people attend for awhile to a story I
> will unfold;
> The truth I'll tell you'll know right well as I was
> plainly told.
> A dollar a day it will be your pay, and go work at the
> earliest dawn:
> It is a weary life to be pleasing a wife and cutting
> the Marble Bawn.
>
> The Irish boys that fear no noise, they will stand on
> the rock so brave;
> The noise of their drill will be never still but
> echoing in your ear;
> They'll stand in a line like the wild geese flying, and
> they never will be scolding or jawing;

They are the very best boys that ever wore frieze for
  chipping out the Marble Bawn.

When I came into this State it was very late, about
  nine in the afternoon;
The night was dark and I being strange, I knew not
  where to roam;
But I started on the train and to West Rutland I came,
  where the steam mill is always sawing
The beautiful stone that the like was never known;
  they call it the Marble Bawn.

There is one man still, they call John Gill, I must
  not forget to praise;
He's working hard from morning till night, and he
  never stands at ease;
The noise of his sledge on an iron wedge like a shot
  when the trigger is drawn;
He's the best in the State, of his size or weight,
  for raising the Marble Bawn.

Now Sheldon has a ledge, it lies to the south, it is
  the deepest in the diggings all around;
And Parker has a ledge, it lies in the north, it is
  the latest that has been found.
But Sherman has a ledge in the midst of them both,
  that the like of it never was known;
There's nothing can compare, but the snow from the
  air, to that beautiful marble stone.

So now when you are dead and a stone at your head to
  mark where your body do lie;
Your parents will lament, they'll be discontent, and
  bitterly weep and cry;
And then it will be your doom to lie beneath a tomb,
  that the Cross will be so neatly on it drawn;
Your name will be enrolled, and prayers for your soul,
  will be engraved on the Marble Bawn.

So now my song I'll end, and success to every friend
  that ever left the Shamrock Shore;
May they live in peace with the Yankee race, and each
  other dearly adore.
So now as we are free in the land of liberty, where
  no tyranny over us will be drawn;
We will sit down at ease and sing the praise of West
  Rutland Marble Bawn.[28]

This "come all ye" was full of meaning for Carney's listeners. Rutland folks certainly knew the details of marble quarrying, and the quarries of Sheldon, Parker, and Sherman were familiar workplaces. Mayo-born John Gill was a West Rutland marble worker, apparently with a "John Henry"–like reputation. Carney's "come all ye" reflected the experience of the Irish in Vermont's marble industry.

Collar-and-Elbow Wrestling

Another cultural carryover from Ireland to Vermont, but one little commented on, was collar-and-elbow wrestling, sometimes called Old Sod wrestling, or Irish country wrestling. Wrestling has a long tradition in Ireland. The sport is mentioned in ancient sources. Ireland's most famous epic, *The Táin Bó Cuailnge*, which dates from about 600 AD, describes the great hero-warrior Cúchulainn wrestling victoriously over 150 foes. As late as the seventeenth century, Irish villages supported their champions against stalwarts from other villages in brutal matches that frequently ended in death.[29]

In the nineteenth century Irish immigrants brought collar-and-elbow wrestling to America. The name collar-and-elbow came from the initial stance of the wrestlers. It resembled two men dancing at arm's length. Facing each other, the combatants stretched out their left arms, putting their left hand on the other's shoulder. The right hand grasped the opponent's left elbow. In Ireland, and at times in the United States, each man wore a tight-fitting shirt or vest, with his opponent's left hand grasping the collar of the shirt—thus collar-and-elbow. From this position the objective was to get the opponent on the ground—to "bring him to grass," as the saying went. This was done through lightning-fast pushing maneuvers and tricky legwork calculated to trip one's adversary. Once on the ground the contestants struggled to force a three-point pin on their opponent. Because the feet were used, the wrestlers fought either barefoot or in light slippers. Agility and quickness counted as much as strength, and it was not unusual that a smaller, lighter wrestler defeated a stronger, brawnier one.

In the years following the Civil War, Irish collar-and-elbow enjoyed wide popularity across America. Like with boxing, promoters arranged matches wherever a large crowd could be gathered: in fairgrounds, music halls, theaters, or saloons. Wrestlers made their money in "side bets"—betting on themselves—or from a guaranteed purse, or a percentage of the gate, or from a combination of all three.

Unsurprisingly, Irish Americans excelled at this form of wrestling. They were raised as boys with the sport, mastering numerous intricate holds and tripping tricks, and worked at physically demanding jobs that kept them in top physical shape. Moreover, the Irish in the New World as in the Old embraced physical competition, the athlete and the strongman a figure of prominence. In late-nineteenth-century Vermont, stories of Irish feats of strength circulated from neighborhood to neighborhood. One told of two Irishmen working at the Fairbanks Scale Company in St. Johnsbury who hand-loaded for weigh-in fifty-six tons of pig iron in a single day. Underhill Irishmen marveled at Francis Cahill's strength. Cahill frequently hired out to carry spindly-legged tourists to the top of nearby Mount Mansfield, Vermont's tallest mountain. And, as already mentioned, Irish Vermonters admired Rev. Henry Lane's prowess with the hammer. The farm boy or quarry worker who proved himself in the ring enjoyed an exalted standing among his peers.[30]

The Vermont Irish played a leading role in the brief heyday of collar-and-elbow-wrestling. Vermont, particularly the old Irish enclave of Franklin County, was arguably the center of collar-and-elbow wrestling in the United States in the 1870s and 1880s. Three of the seven grapplers who held the U.S. championship in these years were farm boys from Franklin County: James Owens of Fairfield and John McMahon of Bakersfield (both born of Irish parents), and Richford's Henry Dufur, whose family name was originally Dunn. Charles Morrow Wilson, the authority on the sport, estimated that in the latter half of the nineteenth century, twenty-one Vermonters earned accredited championships in the sport; fourteen of them came from Franklin County and nine of them from Fairfield. Moreover, of the twenty-one champions, seventeen had Irish backgrounds. Around the country they were known as the "Fairfield trippers."[31]

What accounted for Vermont's preeminence in the sport? Three explanations have been offered. One is that Rev. James McQuade, an exponent of the sport, popularized it when he spent a year in Vermont in the early 1820s. Another source points out that three of the first five priests recruited by de Goesbriand in Ireland were collar-and-elbow enthusiasts, while a third suggests that a number of Irish immigrants in Vermont came from County Kildare, where the sport was particularly strong. Whatever the genesis, by the time of the Civil War, young men across Vermont, and particularly in Franklin County, were well acquainted with collar-and-elbow wrestling. In time, no parish picnic or fair day was complete without a series of matches.[32]

The greatest of all the Franklin County wrestlers was John McMahon, the "Green Mountain Boy." McMahon was a Vermont farm boy, having grown up in the 1840s and 1850s in the rural township of Bakersfield, adjacent to Fairfield. When John had time off from his farm chores, he passed the time wrestling, besting his neighbors and acquiring a reputation as a real comer. Perhaps his best competition came from his cousin on his mother's side, James Owens of nearby Fairfield. No doubt many a Sunday afternoon found the two cousins putting each other through their paces.

After years of playful wrestling, in 1861 McMahon made his professional debut, when at age twenty he made $100 in side money in a match against a highly regarded opponent held in Port Henry, New York, just across Lake Champlain. From there, aided in part by the Civil War, his sporting career took off. When the Thirteenth Regiment of Vermont Volunteers formed in 1862—the same unit that included Lonergan's Emmet Guards—McMahon along with his Bakersfield neighbors joined its Company G. As with all soldiers in all wars, much of their time was spent in drilling and waiting. When not marching on the parade ground or assigned to some detail, the men often engaged in sporting contests. Baseball, for example, was first popularized by men in garrison during the Civil War. McMahon spent his free time wrestling. Late in life he wrote a friend that once while encamped, "we had a wrestling match one evening, when I threw 17 men. We wrestled the old fashioned collar and elbow hold. I have won several hard contests since then, but then and even now when I think of it, that evening seems to be the best work I ever did in this line."[33]

Once home from the war, McMahon bounced around, sometimes farming with his brother Tom in Bakersfield, at other times working at laboring jobs in Rutland, but always making extra money from wrestling. In 1873 he arrived on the national scene when in Troy, New York, he defeated the far more experienced Homer Lane for the American "championship." Perhaps even better than the title, the jubilant McMahon, a heavy underdog in the match, pocketed a purse of $3,000—big money for a Vermont farm boy.

With his national reputation established, McMahon traveled the rails, taking on challengers. Through 1877 and early 1878 he was on the West Coast, putting down burly loggers and hardened miners. In a famous match in Chicago's McCormick Hall in November 1878, McMahon defeated another claimant to the national title—Colonel James McLoughlin, a Civil War veteran from upstate New York. When the athletic McMahon abruptly tripped the larger McLoughlin for the decisive fall, the large crowd that had gathered to witness the match erupted in cheers. An exhausted but beaming McMahon accepted the championship belt, saying, "Gentlemen, I have been after this for five years, and now I have got it at last."[34]

Ironically, some of McMahon's greatest challenges came from Franklin County neighbors. On numerous occasions he fought Richford's Henry Dufur, sometimes winning, sometimes losing. In a grueling match in Boston that lasted six hours, the contest was declared a draw when at midnight the promoter's lease on the hall expired with neither man being able to force a fall. But perhaps the match that underlined the dominance of Vermont's Irishmen in collar-and-elbow was the one contested in Boston in the summer of 1880. Fighting for the U.S. championship were cousins John McMahon and James Owens. The two boys had grown up together, gone to school together, and wrestled together. McMahon was the reigning champion, but Owens had briefly held the title in the mid-1870s. As cousins and old friends, they took the train together down to Boston for the contest. Once in the ring, however, they put kinship aside, and the contest was hard fought, lasting a muscle-numbing three hours. McMahon eventually prevailed and kept the championship belt.

Through most of the 1880s McMahon was the wrestler to beat, and he cashed in on his fame. When opponents in the United States grew scarce, he traveled abroad. Working his way on freighters and cattle boats, he went to England and downed the British champ, John Tedford, the "Terrible Welshman," then sailed to Argentina and Australia and garnered more titles. When there were no opponents, he joined the P. T. Barnum Circus, giving exhibition matches. His opponent in those contests was fellow Vermonter Ed Decker, himself a former world champion. By agreement they alternated "victories" as the circus moved about the country.[35]

McMahon fought his last professional fight in 1891 and then retired. The time was right. The "Green Mountain Boy" was a boy no longer—he was fifty-one. And the sport itself was changing. The popularity of collar-and-elbow was in decline. The Greco-Roman style, which prohibited the tripping legwork used in collar-and-elbow, was in the ascendant, particularly in the growing number of high school and college wrestling teams. Then, too, the team sports of baseball and football had come to dominate the American sports scene. The day of collar-and-elbow wrestling had passed.

Among the Irish farmers of Franklin County, however, it lived on for another fifty years. In the summer months, sales drummers making their appointed rounds put up at Soule's Hotel in the center of Fairfield village and in the evening often challenged locals to wrestle. Farmer Michael "Mick" Brennan frequently took up those challenges and quickly dispatched the unwary visitors. Sometimes after Sunday Mass men would gather on the green in front of St. Patrick Church in Fairfield and challenge each other to a bit of scuffling while onlookers bet on the outcomes. Probably to the surprise of no one, one of the best grapplers in these impromptu contests in the 1920s was the parish priest, Irish-born Rev. Thomas McMahon (no relation to John McMahon).[36]

By the time of the Second World War, however, even in Franklin County collar-and-elbow wrestling was but a memory—but it was a memory of a time when an Irish sport, transplanted to the New World, had put northern Vermont atop the sporting world.

Baseball

Though many Irish Americans retained an interest in sports brought from the old country, the vast majority became enthusiastic supporters of the new American game of baseball. In the closing decades of the nineteenth century, the Irish so completely dominated the game that the era has been dubbed baseball's "Emerald Age." One writer for the *Sporting News* opined in 1872 that fully one-third of all major league players came from an Irish background, and one historian has concluded that there were times in the late nineteenth century when as many as half of all professional players were Irish. Early heroes of the game included such icons as Mike "King" Kelly, Charlie Comiskey, Connie Mack (Cornelius McGillicuddy), and John McGraw. And, in the most famous baseball poem ever penned, first published in 1888, it was an Irishman, "mighty Casey," who struck out. In its earliest days, the all-American game was almost an all-Irish game.

Irish interest in baseball probably came from a number of sources. One was the Irishman's keen delight in competition when it involved athletic prowess and physical strength. Baseball was also democratic, nonelitist, open to anyone with talent and the drive to succeed. Poor Irish American boys who worked in mines, textile mills, and on farms used baseball as a means to gain respect, even acclaim, and for some, a job—a pattern later followed by other immigrant groups. One historian has suggested that Irish experience in a bat-and-ball game—hurling—made for a natural transition to baseball.[37]

Baseball has always had a strong appeal to Vermonters. A summer sport, baseball offers young men and rabid fans a welcome release from long months of snow and ice. This was even more important in the nineteenth century, when fewer entertainment options existed. Back then in the hot, humid days of July and August, teams representing businesses, churches, schools, clubs, and fire departments competed against one another. Town teams were particularly popular. By the last quarter of the nineteenth century, every Vermont town had at least one amateur baseball nine, and towns with a heavy concentration of Irish frequently had an all-Irish team. In the 1870s, Rutland had an Irish team called the Excelsiors, and the textile village of Winooski and the quarry town of West Rutland both had Irish teams named the Emmets, after Robert Emmet, the United Irishman executed in Dublin in 1803.[38]

Underhill-born Patrick Dealey was a catcher with the Boston Beaneaters in the 1880s. (Courtesy of the Library of Congress.)

Some of the Green Mountain Irish ballplayers were talented enough to play for professional teams. Underhill's Patrick Dealey played for the colorfully named Boston Beaneaters in the 1880s, while Bennington-born Tom Lynch suited up with the Wilmington Quicksteps and later with the Philadelphia Quakers. James "Sun" Daly escaped Rutland's marble quarries by playing with the Baltimore Orioles.

In terms of longevity in the game, the most successful Vermont Irish baseballer was Dave Keefe. Keefe came from a pre-famine Irish family that had settled in

James "Sun" Daly played outfield for Minneapolis in the late 1880s but in 1892 went to the Baltimore Orioles. (Courtesy of the Library of Congress.)

DALY, L. F., Minneapolis
COPYRIGHT BY GOODWIN & CO., 1889.
OLD JUDGE
CIGARETTE FACTORY.
GOODWIN & CO., New York.

Vermont in the 1830s. His grandparents had farmed in Richmond, just east of Burlington, and he grew up on a farm in nearby Williston. It was while living in Williston that Keefe suffered a traumatic accident that changed his life. While playing around a corn-cutting machine, he lost his middle finger on his right hand. But, as can happen in life, tragedy turned into opportunity. When he took up baseball as a pitcher a few years later, he found that by grasping the ball between his index and ring fingers he could hurl it with a spin that dropped the ball sharply as it entered the strike zone. This forkball, or split-fingered fastball pitch, eventually became a staple change-up pitch among baseball moundsmen. Some baseball historians credit Keefe with inventing it.

While Keefe was playing for his high school team at the time of World War I, a member of Connie Mack's Philadelphia Athletics Club saw him pitch, whereupon Keefe was invited to play for the A's. Between 1917 and 1922—with a short break for military service—Keefe played for the A's and the Cleveland Indians. But except for a game in which he struck out Babe Ruth three times, his career as a major league pitcher never took off. He spent the next ten years moving from team to team in the minor leagues. Then, in 1932, a whole new career opened to him. His old boss, Connie Mack, asked him to be the batting-practice pitcher for Philadelphia, which later evolved into a coaching job. Eventually he became the team's traveling secretary, managing all the details of their road trips, a job he thought the best in the world. It kept him around the game he loved. After fifty years in professional baseball, Keefe retired in 1967. He died in 1978 and was buried in Richmond, Vermont, near his birthplace.[39]

If Keefe's story is one of a sportsman's life well lived, that of Ed Doheny was one of tragedy. Doheny was born in 1873 in the textile and railroad town of Northfield, one of eight children of immigrant parents. Life must have been difficult for the Dohenys, for in various census reports the father's occupation was listed either as "day laborer" or "railroad laborer"—work that produced only meager wages. Despite this rough beginning, at least five of the Doheny children led successful lives. One son, Patrick, became a priest, and four girls followed the path then so common to Irishwomen and took up teaching. Ed Doheny took another route.

From an early age Edwin showed promise as a baseball player. By the late 1880s he was a star pitcher on various Northfield teams, and his prowess eventually landed him a position on a club in St. Albans. It was while playing for St. Albans in 1895 that he came to the attention of the New York Giants, who signed him the same year. For six years he wore a Giants uniform and then went to the Pittsburg Pirates in 1901. There he had his greatest baseball success, winning sixteen games in both 1902 and 1903. On the field he was a winner, but off it his life was in turmoil.

There was something wrong with Doheny. Even in his early years with the Giants, his behavior was often erratic, leading to arguments with teammates and disciplinary measures from management. While he was with the Pirates, his conduct grew more violent. Drinking heavily, he frequently came to blows with fellow players and suffered delusions. At one point he believed that detectives were following him. The Pirates had to let him go. For a year or two he drifted. In 1905 his clergyman brother committed him to an asylum in Danvers, Massachusetts. He died at the Medfield State Asylum in 1916 at the age of forty-three. Whatever the cause that brought Doheny down, it ended a promising baseball career.[40]

The First Hurrah

From the days of Matthew Lyon and Michael "Squire" Flynn, Protestant Irishmen had been active in Vermont politics. In every decade since the founding of the Green Mountain State, Protestant Irishmen could be found serving as aldermen in town governments or traveling to Montpelier to sit in the legislature as representatives and senators. They were either Scots-Irish or what could be called Yankee Irish— descendants of Irish immigrants of unknown religious background and for so long resident in the New World that culturally they were indistinguishable from their Yankee neighbors. Only their surnames hinted at an Irish connection. If they had Catholic ancestors—and no doubt many of them did—they had nonetheless become thoroughly Americanized Protestants. This may have been the case with Peter McLaughlin, who represented the remote mountain town of Groton almost continuously from 1813 to 1830, and Martin French, who sat in the House for Bloomfield in the 1830s. Besides McLaughlin and French, in the years preceding the Civil War there was a Casey, a Crowley, two Kellys, a McAuley, and a Dunn in the Vermont legislature. To be sure, one or two of them may have been Catholics, but given the general antipathy toward Catholics at the time, this seems unlikely.[41]

At about the time of the Civil War, however, Irish Catholics began to enter the political scene in Vermont. Not surprisingly, their political presence was first felt in communities where the Irish concentrated. Possibly the first Irish Catholic selectman in Vermont was Michael McQueeney of Fairfield, elected in 1859.[42] In following years Irish Catholics were elected in other towns with large Irish concentrations: places like Underhill, Moretown, Burlington, Fair Haven, and West Rutland. In 1879 four of the seven trustees in the textile mill village of Winooski, adjacent to Burlington, were either born in Ireland or the sons of Irish immigrants. At the same time, in Rutland, in the most heavily populated part of Rutland town, residents elected Dr. John Hanrahan village president.

Success in winning town offices was followed by entrée to the state legislature. The election of 1867 returned the first known Irish Catholics to the Vermont House—thirty-one-year-old John H. Ryan of Fairfield and thirty-eight-year-old Patrick Barrett of Underhill. The backgrounds of both men were similar and tell us something about the social advance of Irish Americans in Vermont. Both men, while the sons of immigrant parents, were born in the state, members of the pre-famine generation of Vermont Irish. Both resided in communities with a large concentration of Irish: the Irish vote alone would have counted for much at the polls. That they were also successful, hardworking farmers probably commended them to their Yankee neighbors. As native Vermonters with agricultural backgrounds, they had broad appeal.

Barrett's success underscored another characteristic of Vermont politics at this time—the importance of Civil War service. Having worn Union blue in the recent conflict qualified one as a genuine patriot, a true American. In this sense the Irish of the Civil War generation were both fortunate and unfortunate: they had the misfortune of experiencing the horrors of that bloody conflagration, but as participants in one of the great defining events in American history, they had a unique claim to being Americans. For many Irish veterans, war service opened the door to politics.

This had been true for Barrett. He joined the army as soon as war broke out and served almost two years with the Third Regiment of Vermont Volunteers, part of Vermont's famous First Brigade. Three years after the war ended, as Vermonter, farmer, and veteran, he was elected by the citizens of Underhill to serve in the Vermont House.

Others followed Barrett's route into politics. Felix McGettrick from Fairfield joined the army in 1864, when he was only seventeen, fought through the end of the war, and once discharged became a lawyer in St. Albans. Active in Democratic Party politics, he held numerous local and state offices and in 1892 was the Democratic nominee to serve in the U.S. House of Representatives. He lost that election, but in 1902 he ran for governor. Given the strength of the Republican Party in the Green Mountain State, however, it was a foregone conclusion that McGettrick would again lose.

Thomas Kennedy, the central figure in the Cedar Creek painting hanging in the State House, was another Irish veteran turned politician. Once returned to civilian life, he settled in Fairfield, married a Howrigan, and eked out a living as a farmer and merchant. Always interested in politics, he served his town as selectman, tax collector, constable, and head of the schools. In 1874 and 1878 the people of Fairfield elected him to the Vermont Legislature. He ended his public life serving for many years as sheriff of Franklin County. As with Barrett and McGettrick, service in the Civil War had opened for Kennedy a long career in state politics.[43]

By the mid-1880s anywhere from two to four Irish Catholics—almost always from small rural communities with large concentrations of Irish—regularly sat in the Vermont House, although they had little impact on Green Mountain politics. Vermont was staunchly Republican, and Irish Catholics were Democrats. Since before the Civil War, no Democrat was elected governor, and Republicans routinely held all 30 Senate seats and over 200 of the 240 seats in the House of Representatives. House makeup in the biennial session of 1888–89 exemplified Republican dominance in this era. Of 240 members, 219 were Republicans, 19 Democrats, 1 an Independent, and another described himself as an Independent Democrat. Of the 19 Democrats, 3 were Irish Catholics, as was the sole Independent Democrat. Moreover, three of the four Catholics served in the Civil War. So closely associated were Irish Catholics with the tiny Democratic Party that it was derisively referred to as the Irish Catholic Party.[44]

Significantly, two of the Republican members of the House had been born in Ireland: Nicholas McCuen, a former mayor of Vergennes, and John Thompson of Fayston. Both men were Protestants. Through the middle of the twentieth century, Democrats could only watch from the sidelines as Republicans set the political agenda. But there were signs that Irish American political power was on the rise.

Marble City Politics

In Vermont's two most heavily Irish urban centers, the city of Burlington and Rutland town, political progress was uneven. Burlington by the turn of the century was an ethnic town that included Italians, Jews, Germans, French Canadians, and Irish, the latter of whom made up over 19 percent of the city's population. The third ward, which encompassed much of Burlington's waterfront and contained 25 percent of the city's Irish population, was an Irish stronghold, returning Irish aldermen to the city council beginning in the 1870s.[45] While Irish representation on the police force and fire department grew dramatically, and even Irish representation on the board of aldermen increased over the years, down to the turn of the century city government remained firmly in the hands of the Republican establishment. This would change early in the twentieth century.

Rutland, the "Marble City," was a different story. There Irish political power asserted itself in the 1880s. But the story of how this came about is a complex one. It involved large numbers of Irish and other "foreigners," union organizing, "unity" candidates, and a tragic death.

Until the late 1840s, Rutland was a sleepy town on Otter Creek in the center of the state. Most people farmed, although there were a few small-scale manufacturing works and some small marble quarries. That all changed with the advent of the railroads. By the late 1850s, six railroad lines passed through Rutland, making it the most important railroad center in the state. Moreover, the presence of so many rail lines dramatically decreased the cost of transportation, leading to an explosion in the growth of the local marble industry. The relocation of the Howe Scale Company from Brandon to Rutland in 1877 only increased the town's prosperity.

The industrial engines of marble quarrying, railroading, and manufacturing led to a rapid increase in population. From 3,715 residents in 1850, Rutland town's population mushroomed to 12,715 in 1880, temporarily eclipsing Burlington as the most populous community in the state. Most Rutlanders lived in urban settings. More than half the town's 16,000 inhabitants resided in Rutland village, a few thousand in West Rutland, and about 1,500 in Sutherland Falls. And, as pointed out in the previous chapter, the Irish made up a good chunk of the population— anywhere from 35 to 40 percent.[46]

Despite their numbers, prior to 1886 the Irish were only marginally successful in Rutland politics. Town politics was controlled by a business elite associated with the marble industry, particularly Redfield Proctor of Sutherland Falls and his rivals, the Clement family and their allies, the Ripleys and Dorrs. The attitude of this elite toward the Irish newcomers was expressed in an editorial in the *Rutland Herald* when the Howe Scale Company sought to eliminate Irish houses in "Nebraska" to make way for its manufactory: "The bog-trotters will have to dig up their taties and go elsewhere."[47] A callous statement, considering that people's homes were at stake.

Typically, the town's select board consisted of five members, with only one coming from an Irish background, and that one was from West Rutland village, which was overwhelmingly Irish. The other four members were bankers, merchants, and quarry owners, including Redfield Proctor's son Fletcher. At town meetings Redfield Proctor himself played a vocal role, and as he was the area's leading employer, his opinion carried weight. Already he had represented Rutland in the Vermont House, the Senate, and the state as governor.

Even in Rutland village, where most residents of Rutland town lived, the Irish by the mid-1880s had made little political progress. This was due to a ward system of voting that marginalized the large Irish electorate. While the Irish could be found almost everywhere in the village, they were most concentrated in "Nebraska"— Ward Seven—and to a lesser extent in Ward Three. Thus they would always win in Ward Seven and sometimes in Ward Three, but the other ward representatives could always outvote them. Ironically, voters elected the president of the trustees on an at-large basis, and this was why the Civil War veteran Dr. John Hanrahan frequently held the office of village president, beginning in the late 1870s.

Notwithstanding Hanrahan's success, the solid phalanx of Republican businessmen on the board of trustees ensured that Rutland village stayed firmly in the hands of the Yankee Republican establishment. In the mid-1880s that changed. The catalyst was labor agitation. In 1885 the Knights of Labor decided to organize Vermont workers. They launched their Vermont campaign in Rutland, the Green Mountain State's most heavily industrialized area. Quietly, behind the scenes, an organizer from Boston met secretly with local workingmen. First to join were the cigar makers, followed by railroad workers and then the quarrymen. By early 1886 recruitment was well under way. A newsman from the *Rutland Weekly Herald* met with the Knights' leadership and, pledging to keep their identities secret, reported that "a remarkable number of workingmen representing almost every department of work in town had been enlisted."[48]

Among the quarrymen, recruitment may have been enhanced by a tragic incident that rocked the Irish Catholic community just as the Knights' efforts began to take hold. This was the horrific death of Eddie Copps. In 1886 Copps was thirty-two years old, recently married, and a member of a large family that had left Ireland in the early 1850s. By the mid-1880s the Coppses were an influential West Rutland Irish family, particularly noted for their musical skills—as the Irish say, a musical family. When in 1867 the principal of Public School No. 7 organized the General Sarsfield Cornet Band, six of its sixteen members were Coppses: Eddie Copps, Big Ned Copps, Red Ned Copps, Jim Copps, Mike Copps, and Patsy Copps. Eddie was particularly talented, described as "one of the most promising musicians in the state." Through the 1870s and 1880s, the Sarsfield band performed at county fairs, St. Patrick's Day parades, and entertained in hotels and concert halls.

By the mid-1880s Eddie Copps was one of the leaders of West Rutland's Irish community. He was the director and business manager of the Sarsfield band, a leader in the St. Patrick's Benevolent Society, and a foreman in Proctor's Vermont Marble Company. His marriage in the early 1880s to Bridget Moloney connected him to another well-known Rutland Irish family. Bridget's brother Edward was a priest at St. Stephen's in Winooski, and another brother, Thomas, was a successful Rutland attorney. When another family member married into the Durick family of Fair Haven, Eddie's Irish connections extended across Rutland County.[49]

On February 10, 1886, Eddie Copps led a crew laying tracks on a ledge of the Vermont Marble Company's Foster Quarry, to bring in a diamond boring machine. When a marble overhang broke loose, the men scrambled for safety, but Copps was not fast enough. A marble slab knocked the young foreman off the ledge and into the hole of the quarry, a drop of 150 feet. As workers peered over the edge when the dust settled, all that could be seen was Copps's ghostly face encased in ice, amid tons of marble. News of the accident quickly spread. One by one workmen lay down their tools and huddled near the quarry. The pit was so deep and access so treacherous that the body could not be immediately retrieved. For over a week rescue teams worked desperately to chip away ice, pump out water, and remove debris. Finally, on February 19, Copps's body was brought to the surface.[50]

Irish funerals are legendary. In the old country they were often accompanied by grief-masking merrymaking or sometimes used—as in the funerals of nationalists like Terence Bellew MacManus and O'Donovan Rossa—as rallying points for political causes. Copps's funeral may have played a similar galvanizing role, for it came in the midst of the Knights' organizing campaign.

Whether there was a causal relationship between Copps's death and the success of the Knights is unknowable, but his funeral on February 20 touched a deep chord in the Irish community. Across Rutland town all the quarries and mills shut down, and although the day was "very stormy," a huge throng—described as "perhaps the largest congregation ever assembled in St. Bridget's"—descended on the West Rutland church. There Father Moloney celebrated a requiem High Mass, and the dead quarryman was laid to rest in a nearby graveyard.[51]

Eddie Copps's death long remained in the memory of Rutland's Irish community, and a story about it eventually took hold. In the late nineteenth and early twentieth century, some people in West Rutland believed that there had been a sort of curse on Eddie Copps. In the folk memory, the curse had come about as the result of a confrontation Copps had had with Rev. Charles O'Reilly, the Irish-born pastor of St. Bridget's, a few weeks before the quarryman's death. Apparently Copps aspired to be president of the parish temperance society, but his candidacy was opposed by O'Reilly. Why the priest disapproved of the quarryman's candidacy is unknown, but whatever the reason, according to oral tradition the confrontation ended in a heated exchange in which the priest banished Copps from St. Bridget's, with the admonition that while the quarryman lived, he would not be allowed inside the church. And, of course, the next time Copps entered the church was at his own funeral.[52]

Coming at a time of intense unionizing activity, Copps's death must have forced many workers to reevaluate the conditions under which they labored. Knights membership steadily grew. Across Rutland County, workingmen formed Knights assemblies. By the end of the year, most quarrymen belonged to the Knights. New leaders came to the fore, and while they included Germans, Englishmen, and French Canadians, two Irishmen played central roles: Thomas A. Brown, a young West Rutland marble polisher whose oratorical gifts roused vast audiences of working people, and quarryman James C. Gillespie.[53]

As the Rutland Knights grew in numbers, employers looked on in trepidation. Since 1877, when workers had struck against the eastern railroads, a series of strikes had swept across the country. And it had been only a few years before, in 1883, when unpaid copper miners took over Vershire and West Fairlee. Already in January 1886 there had been a strike among slate workers in Fair Haven, and in May the infamous Haymarket Square Riot in Chicago had resulted in the deaths of six policemen and others in the crowd. The *Rutland Weekly Herald* expressed the business owner's antipathy toward the local Knights and underlined the close association the latter had with the Irish when it said that to strike is "a wrong and a crime. . . . It was born of revolution in Ireland, and is out of place in time of peace in a land of universal freedom." The reference to Ireland was to the recently concluded Land War, which introduced the word "boycott" to the English language.[54]

But in keeping with the policy of the national organization, the Rutland Knights were little interested in striking. Eschewing strikes as counterproductive and a tactic of last resort, they emphasized entering labor candidates in local and state elections in order to influence policies that affected working men and women. Through the summer of 1886 the Knights invited anyone who sympathized with the plight of the working class, whether they were Democrats, Republicans, Greenbackers, or Independents, to join in supporting United Labor candidates in the September elections to the Vermont House of Representatives and for Rutland town's fifteen justices of the peace.

To nominate candidates and agree on a program, the Knights called a public meeting for August 26 in the town hall. Before the meeting took place, however, the leadership of the Knights caucused secretly to come up with a strong candidate to run for Rutland town's seat in the Vermont House of Representatives. Shrewdly, they chose an individual calculated to appeal to a broad spectrum of voters—James F. Hogan. An Irish Catholic, Hogan, thirty-six, owned a clothing store on Rutland's Merchant Row, had worked as a young man in the quarries, as had his immigrant father before him, and through the savings of his brothers and sisters had been able to attend the College of the Holy Cross in Massachusetts. Educated, a pillar of the business community but with working-class roots, Hogan was a strong candidate.

Rumors that the workingmen planned to run Hogan sent chills through the leadership of the local Democratic Party: they knew that the ex-quarryman-turned-merchant posed a serious threat to their former hegemony over the workingmen. Party stalwarts like Dr. Hanrahan and one of the party's rising young men, attorney John Spellman, opposed the workingmen's plans and went as far as to try to persuade Hogan to run as a Democrat; but loyal to his working-class background, he turned them down.[55]

With feelings running hot on both sides, the stage was set for a confrontation at the workingmen's caucus announced for the twenty-sixth. It was open to the public, and anyone from any party and any class background could attend. Organizers ensured a large turnout of quarrymen by laying on a special train to bring in workingmen from West Rutland, six miles away. Leading Democrats planned to attend to try to convince the caucus that putting up a third-party candidate would be disastrous for labor.

When the workingmen's caucus convened, it was a raucous affair. An audience of tough quarrymen, shop machinists, cigar makers, and common laborers crowded the Rutland Town Hall. The assembled crowd quickly elected quarryman James Gillespie to chair the meeting. From the podium, Gillespie set the tone for the evening, telling his listeners that he was pleased to see so many workingmen present, for "it demonstrates that the time has come when they propose to have a share in the legislation by which they are governed." The workers, excited by the strength of their numbers, were in no mood for the old-style politics. When a Democrat in the crowd asked that John Spellman be given a chance to speak, the crowd hissed him down. Chairman Gillespie, refusing to give Spellman the floor, said "this [is] purely a workingman's meeting, and . . . there was no need for lawyers in it."

In "response to hearty calls," the excited throng called on Thomas Brown to say a few words. Unknown before his unionizing activity with the Knights, the young marble polisher had become a crowd-pleaser owing to his oratorical gifts. Before the enthusiastic workingmen Brown was at his best. Knowing how to play the crowd, he poured himself some water and drew laughter when he said that he "would begin by taking a drink." Then he launched into his talk, reminding his listeners that

> they had not come here in obedience to the crack of any ringmaster's
> whip, but to take independent action on matters of personal interest
> to every man who works for wages and to nominate a man who will be
> elected and who will truly represent our principles.

He went on to say that they were about to nominate a man who

> is better than an experienced politician, an honest, God-fearing man,
> who will work for justice and right and not in the interest of monopoly;
> who grew up here from a barefooted boy to a quarryman, then to a
> student in college then to a merchant; who has not been a politician
> because he was too honest to have anything to do with their dirty,
> contemptible tricks.

With the preliminary remarks over, the gathered workingmen under the banner of United Labor nominated Hogan for the Rutland seat in the Vermont House and selected a slate of fifteen candidates for justices of the peace in Rutland town.

In addition, as United Labor they drew up a platform of political objectives. The platform's six planks reflected conditions peculiar to Vermont, alongside goals long cherished by the national Knights organization. It asked for the repeal of a law known as the "trustee process" whereby the owners of a bankrupt company were not liable for the debts of the company. This was a response to situations like that in Vershire, where a company declared bankruptcy while leaving its workers unpaid. The second plank stipulated that workers be paid weekly in

Thomas Moloney was one of Rutland's leading political figures at the turn of the twentieth century; in 1890 he represented Rutland in the state legislature and later was an unsuccessful Democratic candidate for governor and U.S. senator. Moloney was a brother-in-law of Eddie Copps, who died tragically in a quarry accident.

cash, not in company chits redeemable only at a company store. Another asked that the people, rather than the board of civil authority, elect the overseer of the poor. Perhaps with the recent death of Eddie Copps in mind, a fourth plank demanded that employers be held liable for injuries to their workers due to carelessness on the part of the employer. They also stipulated that free evening schools be established in every town over 7,000 population. Finally, the caucus laid out that the workday be limited to ten hours. It was a progressive agenda, one bound to cause alarm among employers.[56]

In the days leading up to the election, United Labor exhorted its followers to get out the vote. At a massive rally held at the Rutland Skating Rink on the eve of the election, labor leaders exhorted the crowd to vote for Hogan and requested that workers stay away from saloons as long as the polling places were open. Workers followed the advice. Election day, September 7, was a sober day; most saloons did not bother to open. All day long a steady stream of voters entered the polls. Abstinence paid off. When the results were announced that evening, they were a decisive victory for labor. Hogan became the first Irish Catholic from Rutland elected to the Vermont House, defeating his Republican rival 1,645 to 744. The candidate from the fractured Democratic Party finished a distant third with 247 votes. To make the victory complete, the entire United Labor slate of fifteen candidates for justices of the peace was elected. As the Republican-leaning *Rutland Weekly Herald* conceded, "the Workingmen carried the day."[57]

Labor's victory resulted in an unanticipated turn of events. To some people in Rutland and around the state, the town seemed to be in the hands of a lawless minority. No one felt this more than the marble baron Redfield Proctor. Moreover, he believed that someday Rutland town would be incorporated as a city—there had been discussions about this since 1880—and he would lose his iron grip on the village that bore his name. To forestall such an eventuality, Proctor lobbied his political cronies in Montpelier and succeeded in having his village set off from Rutland and chartered as the town of Proctor.[58]

Ironically, the residents of West Rutland village, whose Irish quarrymen had been so conspicuously in the vanguard in United Labor's Rutland campaign, also petitioned the legislature to separate their village from the town, although their motives were different from Proctor's. While Proctor was interested primarily in retaining control over his town, West Rutlanders sought to eliminate the financial burden of supporting a two-tiered system of town and village government. They also believed that they had not been well represented at the town level, for being situated six miles away from the center of Rutland town, it was a hardship for residents to attend the annual town meeting and other special meetings called by the town. As noted by one West Rutland Irishman—mindful of events then taking place in the British parliament—the demand for separation from Rutland town was a call for "home rule." In the end, West Rutland, like Proctor, broke away from Rutland and became its own town.[59]

In the ensuing years Irish Catholics came to dominate politics in Rutland and West Rutland. After Hogan's election to the Vermont House, Rutland sent a long line of Irishmen to Montpelier, including Thomas Moloney, the brother-in-law of the late Eddie Copps. And after Rutland, as Redfield Proctor had always feared, became a city in 1892, the board of selectmen came under control of a rejuvenated Democratic Party, which itself was led by Irish Americans.[60] In 1896 the voters of Rutland elected the former marble polisher turned labor organizer, Thomas Brown, as the city's third mayor, and he was followed a few years later by his onetime Democratic opponent, John Spellman. The days when an oligarchy of wealthy Republican capitalists controlled Rutland were over.

By the end of the nineteenth century, Irish Americans were not only an established part of Vermont life, but in some cases had come to play leading roles in the state. They formed the vanguard of labor agitation in the state, constituted the nucleus of a growing Democratic Party, rose to leadership in the Catholic Diocese of Burlington, and stood ready to wrest control of Vermont's cities from the old Yankee establishment. They had come a long way from the days when they had arrived as a ragged, dispossessed people in the 1840s. Even greater success lay ahead.

Yet they still stood apart from mainstream Vermont. This stemmed from their religion, their separate schools, their tendency to live among kith and kin, and their shared heritage of language, customs, and mores. They had become something new, the Irish American.

The Parallel Society: 1900–1950

The half century between 1900 and 1950 was both a period of triumph for the Vermont Irish and a time of great distress. Falling agricultural prices beginning in the 1920s and continuing through the Depression severely impacted Irish farmers who eked out a living on hardscrabble land. Many rural Irish communities disappeared. At the same time, Vermont's major cities, particularly Burlington and Rutland—though they too suffered through hard economic times—saw their populations increase substantially: Burlington went from a little less than 19,000 residents in 1900 to over 33,000 in 1950, while Rutland went from over 11,000 to over 17,000. In both cities Irish Americans created their own society, one that paralleled the dominant Yankee culture. The Irish had their own physicians, their own hospitals, their own schools and colleges, their own churches, and their own social hierarchy. In the sense of community, if not wealth, it was a golden age for Vermont's Irish Americans. Everywhere were signs of success. Nowhere was this truer than in the realm of politics.

An Emigrant Elite

In 1915 Henry Bailey, later to become the first mayor of Winooski when it was incorporated as a city in 1921, noted that an influx of new immigrants had changed the ethnic complexion of his community. Where once there had been only Yankees, French Canadians, and Irish, now the tenements of the mill town swarmed with newcomers from Italy, Poland, Finland, Russia, and the Austro-Hungarian and Ottoman empires (Armenians and Lebanese from the latter). This transformation from just a few ethnic groups to many took place in every industrial center in Vermont and dramatically affected the role of the Irish in the Green Mountains.[1]

As the newer groups moved in to poorer working-class neighborhoods, the Irish, who were moving up the socioeconomic ladder, moved out. In Rutland, the Irish southwestern part of the city once known as "Nebraska" was quickly inundated with eastern and southern Europeans, primarily Poles and Italians, and eventually came to be known as "the Gut." The more-affluent Irish moved east of Main Street into Christ the King Parish. Winooski's "Cork Alley," which in the nineteenth century was an Irish neighborhood, also gave way to the newcomers. Burlington's Ward Three, while still an Irish stronghold, lost numbers as successful first- and second-generation Irish Americans moved "up the hill" or to expanding neighborhoods with more gracious homes in the northern and southern ends of the city.

While the old Irish neighborhoods were diluted with newer arrivals, the Irish found themselves in an unaccustomed role—that of an ethnic upper class. Yankee Vermonters might still look down on the Irish, but to the recently landed Pole or Italian, the Irishman, who spoke English, worked as a tradesman, a policeman, a physician or lawyer, who owned his own home, was an American, to be emulated and even deferred to. As late as the 1940s, Reg Godin, a young man of French Canadian descent in the railroad center of St. Albans, thought of the Irish as the city's elite.[2]

To say that the newcomers identified with the Irish is probably an overstatement. There was much that separated them—language, customs, and histories—but still they had much in common. They all shared the trauma of emigration, knew the hardship of working at laboring jobs, and frequently adhered to the same Catholic religion. And, like the Irish, the newcomers tended to vote Democratic. As the recent arrivals augmented the swelling ethnic populations in Vermont's urban centers, the Irish found themselves in a position of political leadership. As one observer in the 1930s commented about the Vermont Irish, they "look upon themselves as the champions of the newer elements."[3]

This newfound power resulted in a number of stunning political victories for the Irish in the opening decade of the twentieth century. In Rutland city in 1900, lawyer John Spellman—the Democratic stalwart who had tried unsuccessfully in 1886 to sway the Knights of Labor from nominating their own candidate for state representative—was elected mayor. Two years later William Powers, a railroad ticket agent, became mayor of St. Albans. In Montpelier, the state capital, residents in 1903 elected granite-quarry owner and banker Frank McMahon Corry—whose immigrant parents had made their living trucking produce to town from their farm in nearby Middlesex—to the city's highest office. In the same year residents of Burlington elected James Edmund Burke the first Irish Catholic mayor of the Queen City. In 1907, voters in the pulp mill town of Bellows Falls made lawyer Thomas O'Brien president of the village corporation, and a year later marble workers in Proctor elected Patrick Joyce president of the village trustees. In a speech in Montpelier, the head of one of Vermont's largest employers, the National Life Insurance Company, noted that "the great shift in the character of city populations" had created "changes in recent political conditions." Under the leadership of Irish American politicians, the "newer elements" in Vermont were wresting control of the state's cities from the once-ironclad grip of the Yankee Republican old guard.[4]

The story of James Burke's ascension to political power in Burlington exemplified the growth of Irish influence in urban Vermont. The Burkes were the prototypical Irish immigrant family. Burke's parents, James and Anna O'Neill Burke, had left Ireland in the 1840s and settled in Williston, a farming community just east of Burlington. There James plied his trade as a blacksmith and raised nine children—five girls and four boys. James Edmund, the second oldest, was born in 1849. Along with a brother, John, he took up his father's trade as a blacksmith. Two of the girls, in typical Irish American fashion, became schoolteachers.[5]

In 1872, shortly after marrying a neighbor girl, "Jim" Burke moved to Burlington and opened a blacksmith shop on Cherry Street in the center of town. Burlington then was a small city—it had only 11,365 residents in 1880—but it was growing rapidly; by 1900 it had added another 7,000 inhabitants. Cherry Street was in Ward Four, a neighborhood that contained the city's busy commercial center, Church Street, and small dwellings and tenement houses that housed working-class families—Irish, French Canadian, Italian, and Yankee. Ward Four, along with adjacent Ward Three and parts of Ward Two, contained the city's ethnic neighborhoods.

Jim Burke was an imposing figure. He was tall, handsome, and lean and muscular from years of blacksmithing. Even after giving up his blacksmith shop in 1914, he kept in shape with evening walks around the city. In demeanor he was serious and intense, and unlike some other Irish "pols" around the country he was scrupulously honest. No one ever questioned Jim Burke's integrity. Early in life an episode earned him a reputation for honesty. In 1880 a customer dropped a wallet containing seventy dollars in Burke's shop. When the young blacksmith discovered it, he immediately returned it to its owner. Learning of the incident, the *Burlington Free Press* dubbed Burke the "Honest Blacksmith." The nickname stuck.[6]

Like most of his fellow Irish Catholics, Burke was a Democrat. He believed that one of government's principal functions was protecting the poor and destitute. But he was also fiscally and socially conservative: the word "efficiency" was constantly on his lips. As mayor he ran a tight ship. Those city employees he deemed inefficient received harsh criticism. His social values reflected the conservative nature of his Catholic upbringing. He once prohibited the anarchist Emma Goldman from speaking in the city, and in the 1930s he banned women from wearing shorts in the city's downtown. He had old-fashioned values but believed that workingmen had to be protected from uncaring employers. His philosophy was that of the Progressive movement, and he once described himself as a "[Teddy] Roosevelt Democrat."[7]

In 1893, at age forty-four, Burke ran for one of the two aldermanic seats from Ward Four. As a Democrat he was up against history: Burlington had been continuously controlled by the Republicans since incorporation in 1865. Only twice before the turn of the century did Burlingtonians elect a Democratic mayor—neither from an Irish background—and never in that time did the Democrats win more than two or three of the ten seats on the board of aldermen. Irish Democrats, however, had slowly been gaining power. In 1875 a New York–born man of Irish parentage, Edmund O'Neill, from heavily Irish Ward Three, had been the first Irish Catholic elected to the board of aldermen. From then on a steady stream of Irishmen represented that ward in city hall.

Burke campaigned in an unusual way. Every day, usually in the evening, the tall, long-legged blacksmith ambled Ward Four streets. He greeted neighbors, heard the latest gossip, talked politics, and asked for their votes. And in 1893 his neighbors elected him to the board of aldermen. He campaigned in this personal, one-on-one way the rest of his life.[8]

Also elected that year was the Burlingtonian who came closest to being a ward boss in the style of the big-city machines: John Shea. A tailor by trade, Shea controlled the vote in Ward Three. From his headquarters in the firehouse of the Barnes Engine Company, where he had served as foreman for many years, Shea made sure the local people voted the "right way." Of him the *Burlington Free Press* pronounced: "Shea holds the Democratic party of the third ward in the hollow of his hand." Like Burke, Shea stood for the common man. His political philosophy he once summed up in the Benthamite slogan "the greatest good for the greatest number of people." The common people must have heard him, for beginning in 1893 Ward Three returned him at every election until his death in 1904.[9]

In 1900, with the help of John Shea, Burke made a run for the mayor's office but was unsuccessful. He tried again in 1902, but again victory eluded him. Each time he carried only Shea's Ward Three, losing handily in the other four wards. Then came 1903. This was a momentous year in Vermont politics, for the state legislature had just passed a law, known popularly as "local option," whereby each town would vote to be either "dry" or "wet." A town that voted to be "dry" would continue the "Maine law" that had been in effect in Vermont for fifty years, while a "wet" vote meant that a town could license establishments to sell alcohol. Local option was an issue sure to bring out large numbers of voters on town meeting day in 1903, particularly ethnic voters—Irish, Italians, and French Canadians—who never had subscribed to the lingering Protestant antipathy to alcohol.[10]

Attitudes toward local option followed ethnicity and geography: in the main, rural Vermonters stood for continued prohibition, while city dwellers desired the freedom to drink openly. Indeed, they had been doing so almost since the day the Maine law had first been introduced in the 1850s. Rare was the town or city hotel that did not have a backroom saloon. These illegal bars were big business to enterprising hoteliers. A record of beer and alcohol shipments received by James Sheehey, who ran the bar at the Weldon House Hotel in St. Albans in the late 1870s through the 1890s, mentions carloads of beer, lager, and St. Croix rum. Sheehey, a first-generation Irish American, did well enough in this trade that he owned a home in St. Albans, a weekend place in the country, and was able to send his two daughters to convent school in Quebec. One of his sons, John, later became president of Green Mountain Power, one of Vermont's largest utilities.[11]

The existence of saloons like Sheehey's was generally known and accepted. Vermont writer Rowland Robinson observed in the 1890s that "prohibition does not prohibit, and presents the anomaly of an apparently popular law feebly and perfunctorily enforced." Only occasionally, when a crusading minister or a diehard member of the Women's Christian Temperance Union raised a fuss, did the police make a token raid.[12]

Recognizing the unique opportunity created by the local-option issue, Burke again threw his hat into the ring. Opposing him was incumbent Donly Hawley, a physician and president of Burlington's exclusive Ethan Allen Club. It was Irish newcomer versus Yankee establishment. Burke proved a tireless campaigner. Utilizing his daily walks, he campaigned everywhere, going door to door in the neighborhoods, buttonholing passersby, and attending meetings of civic organizations. While Shea drummed up support among Burlington's Irish community, Burke courted other ethnics, including a growing number of Lithuanian Jews in the city's "Little Jerusalem." Relentlessly Burke hammered upon two themes: the expansion of the city budget under the Hawley administration, and the need for the city to acquire dock space on the waterfront for public use. As the election approached, the pro-Republican *Burlington Clipper* warned that Burke had a chance of winning and added "It must also be admitted that Mr. Burke is a fighter."[13]

On election day, March 3, 1903, a large crowd gathered at city hall to await the results. As the returns came in, the lead seesawed, with first Burke ahead, then Hawley, and then Burke again. Late in the evening the final count put Hawley ahead, 1,565 to 1,562. The election board declared the incumbent the winner. Burke immediately charged that there "are many men who voted today for me and whose ballots were thrown out. We propose to have them counted." Apparently the election officials nullified some ballots because they had been incorrectly marked. Hawley was duly sworn in as mayor, but his term was short-lived. Burke and the Democrats took their case to the state supreme court, and in May the court ruled that 168 discarded ballots should go to Burke. The court told Dr. Hawley to vacate City Hall. For the first time in its history, the Queen City had an Irish Catholic mayor. This was the beginning of a new era for Burlington: over the next half-century, Irish Catholics held the mayor's office a total of twenty-eight years.[14]

Along with Burke, local option proved to be a winner. Though rural towns voted against licensure, every major city in the state, with the exception of St. Johnsbury, returned a yes vote. The political victory of Burke in Burlington and the urban acceptance of local option clearly signaled that Vermont was in the midst of social and political change.

Burke's victory in 1903 inaugurated one of the most distinguished political careers in Vermont history. Seven times he was elected mayor, the last time in 1933 at age eighty-four, when the voters asked him to lead the city through the darkest days of the Depression. Four times he served as Burlington's representative to the Vermont legislature, and in 1908 he was the unsuccessful Democratic candidate for governor.

As mayor, Burke was known for his frugality, his conviction that utilities should be publicly owned, and for his toughness. During his years in office he established a municipal electric company, improved the facilities of the water department, created a paid police force, supported the creation of a regional airport (and took his first flight from it with Amelia Earhart), had the city purchase land on the waterfront, and supported the construction of a Carnegie library and a new railroad station in the city. Burke made Burlington one of the most progressive cities in the nation. One local newspaper called him "a city builder."[15]

To accomplish so much required thick skin, and Burke had it in abundance. He also had a temper. When a delegation from the local Masonic lodge, angered that the city was about to rescind the tax-exempt status of their Church Street property, opened their plea before the board of aldermen by caustically noting that the mayor was not a Mason, Burke erupted in indignation at the slight, admonishing the delegation for their ungentlemanly conduct. There were times too when his opponents on the board of aldermen, in desiring to thwart initiatives he supported, refrained from attending board meetings to deny them a quorum. Burke had a simple answer to that tactic: he called out the police and had them round up the wayward aldermen. Burke gave as good as he got.[16]

Mayor James Edmund Burke hosted Amelia Earhart at the opening of the Burlington Airport in 1934. (Courtesy of Special Collections, University of Vermont.)

His popularity was such that when he died in 1943 at the age of ninety-four, representatives from Burlington's French Canadian, Jewish, Italian, German, and Irish communities attended his funeral, along with the city's sitting mayor, Irishman John J. Burns. Even his erstwhile Republican opponents came to appreciate all that the tough Irishman had done for Burlington. In its editorial eulogy at Burke's passing, the conservative *Burlington Daily News* described the former mayor as one of Vermont's "Grand Old Men."[17]

La Petite Église

One Vermont ethnic group that early in the twentieth century still hesitated to join the Democratic fold was the French Canadians. This stemmed in part from a natural rivalry between them and the Irish—the state's two largest ethnic groups— but also from labor tensions between the two groups that went back to the "Great Turnout" of the 1860s and continued into the 1920s. In a tense strike action in 1922, employers in the Barre-area granite works brought in scabs from Quebec and broke the strike. While most granite workers came from Italian and Scottish backgrounds, there was a smattering of Irishmen, and they, like all those on strike, greatly resented the intrusion of the Canadians. In the midst of that strike, the French Canadian parish priest at St. Sylvester in Graniteville, adjacent to East Barre, complained to Bishop Rice that his Irish parishioners viewed him with hostility, suspicious that he had been responsible for bringing in French Canadian workers in response to the strike.[18]

The hostility between Irish and French Canadian workers lasted down to the Depression. Then the common plight of all workingmen, regardless of ethnic background, lowered the barriers between them. As one Irish American granite worker said in the late 1930s,

> We've tried to forget about '22. There are Frenchmen working beside me.
> We never talk about it. They don't want to and we don't want to. It had
> to happen, it's over with and finished now. There's no use opening an old
> sore. We have to work together, we might as well be friends.[19]

By the end of World War II, the intense feelings between the Irish and French Canadians were a thing of the past, remembered more in bantering jokes between the two groups than in any real animosity. Only in the continuing tradition of having an "Irish" church and a "French" church in the same town—and often an Irish section and a French section in the local Catholic cemetery—did the two communities remain separate. As one man who grew up in Winooski remembered, it was not until he was in high school "that I realized I was going to a Catholic church. They [French Canadians] called it the Irish church. I thought it was just like Anglican or Congregational."[20]

But a common Catholic faith led to friendships and frequently marriage. Today there are many Vermont Pomerleaus, Niquettes, Sorels, and other well-known French Canadian families with Irish mothers, just as there are many O'Briens, O'Connors, and Burkes with French Canadian mothers. Perhaps the story of John O'Brien and Yvonne Provost was typical of these "mixt" marriages. O'Brien, born in 1892 of Irish immigrant parents, went to work as a teenager in the Winooski woolen mills to support his mother, brother, and sisters after the early death of his father. Bright and ambitious, O'Brien took night courses in business and textiles, working his way up from bookkeeper to a position as foreman. In the mills he met an attractive young French Canadian girl, Yvonne Provost. According to family lore, O'Brien knew little French and Yvonne had little English, but love found a way. The two became husband and wife in 1917. John went on to an ever more successful career in the mills, rising to the top position in the 1940s.[21]

Love, however, did not always find a way to bridge the gap between the two groups. In the early years of the twentieth century, the simmering tension between Irish Americans and Americans of French Canadian descent led to a struggle within the Catholic Diocese of Burlington that came to be called, in ref-

John and Yvonne O'Brien, ca. 1950. John O'Brien was the resident manager of the American Woolen Mills in Winooski in the late 1940s and early 1950s. (Courtesy of the O'Brien family.)

erence to the aggrieved group, *La Petite Église*. The origins of the dispute went back to attitudes that had evolved among the French Canadian clergy beginning in the late 1800s. By then it was clear that the Catholic Church in New England was in the hands of an Irish hierarchy that was less interested in cultural separateness than in assimilation. French Canadian priests, on the other hand, represented a proud people who had been conquered by France's English foe, and they were intensely protective of French culture. For Canadian priests serving in Vermont's Anglo-dominated society, a primary goal was *survivance*, the maintaining of French customs, mores, and, most important, language. Some priests believed that if French Canadians lost their native language, they would lose their faith. Thus they strongly advocated national churches and French-language schools. Lay adherents of *survivance* expressed the importance of language in the slogan, "In business, English, in the home, French." *Survivance* hardly lent itself to the Irish Americans' goal of assimilation.[22]

In Vermont the issue of *survivance* cropped up in the early 1890s. In 1890 the aging Bishop de Goesbriand celebrated the golden jubilee of his ordination to the priesthood and at the same time asked Rome to appoint an auxiliary bishop to help him in his duties. For the jubilee festivities, priests and prelates traveled from across New England to Burlington. But not everyone was pleased with the celebration. Rev. Jean Audet, the Canadian pastor of St. Francis Xavier, the French church in Winooski, expressed the frustration of many of his fellow priests when he later wrote that although there were 35,000 Canadians in the diocese, they were totally forgotten in the occasion. It was, he said, "an Irish Affair." To keep the Burlington diocese from being dominated by an English-speaking, Irish-directed hierarchy, it was imperative to the advocates of *survivance* that the next bishop of Burlington be a French speaker.

In the end the Canadian priests were disappointed. Rome named Rev. John Stephen Michaud, the Irish priest with the French name, coadjutor bishop with the right of succession. Michaud was a solid choice. Since his ordination in the early 1870s, he had proved himself a devout priest and an able administrator. As a young priest he had established a number of parishes in northern Vermont and later had responsibility for building the large St. Joseph's Orphanage in Burlington and the impressive St. Francis de Sales church in Bennington. De Goesbriand—possibly because he was a Frenchman rather than a French Canadian—did not share the defensive beliefs of his Canadian priests and applauded Michaud's appointment; indeed, the Irishman had been the aging prelate's nominee for coadjutor bishop.[23]

But the Irishman's selection rankled the more extreme supporters of *survivance*. Michaud had little sympathy for the advocates of French-language churches. He once said that America was an English-speaking country and that except in a

*John Stephen Michaud—the
Irish bishop with the French name.
(Courtesy of the Roman Catholic
Diocese of Burlington.)*

few places like Winooski and St. Johnsbury, with their large French Canadian populations, the French language
would eventually die out in Vermont.
Hardly a sentiment to please Franco-
phones. Even before Rome officially
announced Michaud's appointment, a
group of French Canadian priests organized to lobby against his selection, and
then continued to meet even after the
Vatican named the coadjutor bishop.
Because of Michaud's French name,
but ignoring his Irish American upbringing, the group considered the bishop a
"traitor" to his French roots. This cabal of priests came to be known as *La Petite
Église*—the little church—after the many recalcitrant French priests who refused
to accept Napoleon's Concordat with Rome in 1801.[24]

La Petite Église must be kept in perspective. It had only a handful of adherents in Vermont—and they were Canadian-born priests, as opposed to American-
born priests from a French Canadian background—and they never contemplated
a serious breach with their church. Rather they wanted to influence the cultural
directions taken by the Irish-dominated, English-speaking hierarchy in New England. On a workaday basis, French Canadian and Irish American priests in Vermont got along well. Many of them had been friends or acquaintances since their
days together as seminarians in Montreal. But elsewhere in New England, *survivance* was a more serious problem. Oftentimes at clerical convocations in Massachusetts, Irish and French Canadian priests sat on opposite sides of the room, with
little interaction between them. In 1901, when French-speaking priests in Maine
lobbied for one of their own to be named bishop of Portland, Rome considered the
infighting to be so volatile that it appointed an outsider, William O'Connell of Massachusetts, to the see. In Woonsocket, Rhode Island, in the 1920s, Canadian Catholics brought suit against their Irish bishop for what they believed were attempts
to anglicize and assimilate national parishes. In retaliation the bishop excommu-
nicated the leaders of the protest. Priestly advocates of *survivance* in the Green

Mountains limited their activities to promoting the French language in schools and to influencing the selection of church prelates.[25]

The question of who would lead the church in Vermont came to the fore again in 1908. Early that year Michaud, who had become bishop in his own right on the death of de Goesbriand in 1899, was diagnosed with Bright's disease, an inflammation of the kidneys. Medical authorities gave him only months to live. Given Michaud's illness, Boston thought it best to name a coadjutor bishop. Over the next several months numerous discussions between the chancery in Boston and priests in Vermont took place. On at least one occasion Archbishop William O'Connell of Boston—the former bishop of Portland—traveled to Vermont to assess the situation. La Petite Église backed the candidacy of Quebec-born Rev. Norbert Proulx, pastor of Sacred Heart of Mary, the French church in Rutland, and a strong advocate for the French language. Others mentioned in the discussions were Rev. James Shannon, the Enosburg native and longtime pastor of the church in Middlebury, and Rev. Daniel O'Sullivan, native of Winooski and pastor of St. Mary in St. Albans. While he still lived, Michaud himself supported the candidacy of Rev. Shannon. But for the opposition of La Petite Église, Shannon probably would have succeeded Michaud.[26]

The matter of a coadjutor bishop was still unresolved when Michaud died in December 1908. La Petite Église took the unprecedented step of making a plea directly to the Vatican, bypassing the archdiocesan chancery in Boston. In a letter sent to Rome in January 1909 under the signature of Rev. Napoleon Dorion of Richford, La Petite Église enumerated the qualities required in the next bishop. Besides a strong spirituality and sense of charity, Dorion listed command of French and English, obedience to church authority, and the ability to get along with both French Canadian and Irish priests as essential characteristics in the next bishop. But surprisingly, instead of naming Father Proulx as the candidate best meeting those criteria, Dorion put forward the name of Irishman Daniel O'Sullivan.[27]

What had happened? The most logical explanation is that in the long negotiations in the previous year over the attempt to name a coadjutor bishop, the priests of La Petite Église concluded that Boston would never name a French Canadian bishop in Vermont. So they went to a backup position, advancing the name of someone who they believed was both acceptable to Boston and who also empathized with the goals of La Petite Église. O'Sullivan seemed to be that man.

Why O'Sullivan? In a way, he was the reverse of Michaud. He had an Irish name and an Irish family background, but he was also steeped in French culture and was fluent in the *patois* of Quebec. Though born in Winooski, he grew up in Quebec. In 1865 at age twelve, when he expressed an interest in becoming a priest, Bishop de Goesbriand sent him to seminary in Montreal. There under the watchful

Father Daniel O'Sullivan, whose driving ambition was to become bishop of Burlington. (Photo courtesy of the Roman Catholic Diocese of Burlington.)

eye of the Sulpicians—an order of French priests specifically tasked with the training of candidates for the priesthood—the young man from Vermont spent eleven years preparing himself for holy orders. At the time of his ordination in 1876 he had lived almost half his life in Quebec and had built a large network of friends among the French Canadian clergy.

Once back in Vermont, O'Sullivan served for a number of years in parishes across the state. The high point of his early clerical life probably came in 1883 when he was instrumental in calming tensions among Irish rioters in the Ely "war." The next notable step in his career occurred in 1884 when de Goesbriand named him president of St. Joseph College, the just-opened Catholic boys' high school housed in an old inn on the University of Vermont's college green (later the site of the de Goesbriand Hospital and currently that of the Given Medical Center). His selection was apparently based on his reputation as a scholar. When St. Joseph closed its doors after a brief seven-year existence, the bishop assigned O'Sullivan to be pastor of St. Mary in St. Albans—a position he would keep longer than expected. Both in St. Albans and across the diocese, O'Sullivan was a popular priest. Gregarious and outgoing, he had an Irishman's quick wit and facility at storytelling. Parishioners affectionately referred to him as "Father Dan." Even non-Catholics succumbed to his personal charm. Edward Curtis Smith, longtime president of the Central Vermont Railroad and a Republican governor of Vermont (1898–1900), frequently invited O'Sullivan to dinner at Seven Acres, his St. Albans estate. His French Canadian fellow priests got along well with him and often invited him to their parishes to give sermons in French. He once gave a series of Lenten homilies in Montreal.

Indeed it was O'Sullivan's skill as a speaker that set him apart from his contemporaries. Those who heard him in the pulpit or at the lectern frequently commented on his oratorical talents. Some of his admirers referred to him as "the silver-tongued orator of Vermont," and one who knew him later said, "His gestures, graceful and effortless, could have done ample justice to fabled actors who portrayed Hamlet in the heyday of their careers. He was at home giving a sermon at church or on the public rostrum." One nun remembered him as the priest "who was always sure of a full church of eager worshippers anxious to hear his message that came to them in the silver-tongued eloquence of the scholar and the saint." His reputation as an orator led to speaking engagements at Catholic and non-Catholic institutions alike.[28]

His eloquence and his personal popularity may have influenced him to enter politics, for O'Sullivan was intensely ambitious. Whether in church affairs or in the secular world, he was determined to make a name for himself. To this end, with Bishop Michaud's permission, in 1902 he entered the race for state representative from St. Albans. By a narrow majority he won and reportedly became the first Catholic priest to sit in a state legislature in the United States. He served two terms in Montpelier, with much of his energies—not surprisingly, given his urban, ethnic constituency—aimed at pushing through "local option."

But O'Sullivan's ambitions went beyond the Vermont House of Representatives. Since at least the early 1890s he had his heart set on becoming bishop of the Diocese of Burlington. As Bishop Michaud's health failed, O'Sullivan mounted an intensive campaign to be named his successor. In late 1907 he visited Rome and lobbied on his own behalf. Confident that the Vatican favored his candidacy, O'Sullivan was rumored to have returned to Vermont with a bishop's miter in his trunk. His brother Thomas, a Tammany Hall judge, a former member of the New York legislature, and a papal knight, also visited Rome to advance Father Dan's cause. With the priests of La Petite Église moving to support him, O'Sullivan might well have thought he would soon be the diocese's next bishop.[29]

There was, however, one obstacle: Bishop Michaud. While the old bishop lived, he did everything in his power to derail O'Sullivan's candidacy. He knew what few of O'Sullivan's many admirers knew: that the loquacious and amiable priest, so fond of the limelight, was an inept administrator, unable to keep his parish in the black. Complaints from creditors were endless. At times he even failed to pay the meager amount of money required to support the nuns at his parish school. On March 16, 1900, an angry Sister St. Sabine wrote Bishop Michaud: "Our convent in St. Albans has been approaching its ruin, especially as the pastor, Father O'Sullivan, finds it impossible to meet his obligations to our sisters." In an evaluation he made at this time—and which may have been sent to the archdiocesan chancery in Boston—Michaud wrote that O'Sullivan "does not trouble much about paying debts" and "is not what the canons of the Church require in the head of a diocese, when as such head, he should be the chief director of its finances."[30]

With Michaud's poor evaluation, and little agreement among Irish and French Canadian priests over an alternative candidate, Boston did what it had done in the case of Maine a few years before: it went with an outsider. On January 4, 1910, the chancery in Boston dashed the hopes of La Petite Église when it announced that a little-known priest, Joseph J. Rice, a Massachusetts Irishman, would be named the next bishop of Burlington. At age thirty-eight he would be the youngest bishop in the United States. What O'Sullivan thought of the announcement can only be guessed.

Rice, bishop from 1910 until his death in 1938, was an odd character. Scholarly, reserved, often in poor health, as bishop he lived a semi-reclusive existence. Boston apparently had selected him because he was a protégé of Archbishop (later Cardinal) O'Connell and could be expected to take a strong hand against the recalcitrant French Canadian clergy in Vermont. As Rice saw it, his job was to ensure that the clergy be held to the strictest accountability. He was not, as priests would say, a "priest's bishop." On the rare occasions when he left his residence to inspect parishes in the diocese, the pastors trembled in anticipation of the criticisms sure to follow. Father McMahon, the Fairfield priest well known as a collar-and-elbow wrestler, remembered that on one occasion in the 1920s he spent days getting his church and rectory all "spic and span" in anticipation of Rice's visit, only to be told by the bishop that the garage was a mess. In the oral history passed on by members of the Vermont clergy, Rice is spoken of as being "vindictive" and a "tyrant."

Rice's vindictiveness, if such it was, came down particularly hard on the priests of La Petite Église. Once installed as bishop, Rice learned of their attachment to *survivance*—and thus their implicit opposition to his appointment—and shunned them. Some he assigned to remote parishes and left them there. One of the saddest cases was that of Rev. Joseph Coté. Coté, who knew little English, was a strong advocate of *survivance* and was a friend of Father O'Sullivan. In 1904 Bishop Michaud assigned him to St. Isadore, a remote mountain parish in Montgomery along the Quebec border. It was the boondocks: nothing there but a tiny village, a few farms, scattered logging operations, and a small butter-box manufactory. Under

The appointment of Joseph John Rice as bishop of Burlington collapsed the hopes of those who wanted a French-speaker to lead the church in Vermont. (Photo courtesy of the Roman Catholic Diocese of Burlington.)

normal circumstances Coté could expect to spend a few years at St. Isadore and then be reassigned to a less-difficult posting. This did not happen. Rice left him there for the remainder of the priest's life. He died there in 1931.[31]

Rice's antipathy to La Petite Église led to a minor crisis. As the Canadian priests felt Rice's hostility, they conspired to resist his authority. When the bishop summoned the priests of the diocese to attend an annual convocation in Burlington, the priests of La Petite Église refused to attend and instead met at the rectory of St. Patrick Church in Fairfield, where one of their number, Rev. Napoleon Lachance, was pastor. In an attic room they socialized, talked of their hopes for *survivance*, and decorated their meeting place by painting their initials and fleurs-de-lis on the walls—their efforts are still visible today. This protest went on for a number of years, until Rice issued an ultimatum: either attend the annual convocation or lose their priestly faculties in the diocese—in short, submit or be fired. The priests, loyal servants of the church, chose to submit.

La Petite Église slowly withered away, for a variety of reasons. The French Canadian priests who constituted the movement all had died by the 1930s, and the Vermont-born priests who replaced them did not share the old emphasis on *surviv-*

ance. Then, too, Rice's successor, Bishop Matthew Brady, a Connecticut Irishman but a man more sympathetic than his predecessor to the needs of his French-speaking flock, decreed that any priest ordained for his diocese must be bilingual. And, as Bishop Michaud had always believed, with each passing generation there was less French spoken in Vermont.[32]

Although Rice was a stern taskmaster—or perhaps because of it—the church thrived during his tenure as bishop. When he became bishop there were approximately 50,000 Catholics in the state, and when he died in 1938 there were 100,000—about a third of the state's population. In addition, Rice put much emphasis on education. He founded Catholic high schools in Burlington, Brattleboro, St. Albans, and Montpelier. In Rutland he transformed a Catholic girl's school into coeducational Mount St. Joseph's Academy. To make sure that nuns and lay teachers were adequately prepared to serve in these schools, he supported the Sisters of Mercy in establishing Trinity College for women in Burlington in 1925. For his school-building efforts he was known as "the education bishop." When Cathedral High School, the institution he built in Burlington in 1917, expanded and moved into new quarters in South Burlington in 1959, the diocese renamed it Rice Memorial High School in his honor.[33]

Before leaving the subject of Irish influence in the Vermont Catholic Church, mention must be made of the unusual contribution of the town of Proctor. Home of Redfield Proctor's Vermont Marble Company, the town had had a significant Irish population since the early 1860s, although beginning in the 1880s large numbers of Swedes, Finns, French Canadians, Hungarians, and Italians had also moved in. But Proctor was never a big place: at its peak in 1910 it had only 2,871 residents. As elsewhere in Vermont, the Irish tended to concentrate in their own neighborhood. In Proctor the Irish section was around West Street. From 1920 to 1960, the West Street Irish families produced twenty-one priests and nuns. Two of the priests became bishops: Bernard Flanagan in Norwich, Connecticut, and Robert "Pat" Joyce in Vermont. Bishop Joyce, incidentally, was the son of the Patrick Joyce who had been elected president of Proctor's village trustees in the early 1900s. So striking was the number of priests and nuns who came from the West Street neighborhood that Catholics jokingly referred to it as Pope's Row.[34]

In at least one sense the priests of La Petite Église proved to have had a legitimate grievance: from Michaud's elevation to leader of the Diocese of Burlington until the early 1990s, every bishop of the Vermont church claimed Irish ancestry. As for Rev. Daniel O'Sullivan, he never achieved his dream of becoming a prelate of the church. After Bishop Rice's appointment, O'Sullivan stayed on at St. Mary's in St. Albans and died there in December 1918, a victim of the Spanish influenza epidemic that swept the country and the world at the end of World War I.

Out-Migration

Despite the advances made by the Vermont Irish, by the early 1900s many of their rural communities began to disappear, a result of better opportunities elsewhere, the hardships of living in backcountry Vermont, and finally, the impact of the Great Depression. The Green Mountain State was never an easy place to make a living. Too much of the land was rocky and steep and could provide little more than a subsistence existence. And, too, Vermont with its limited industrial base offered little in the way of nonagricultural employment. Thus, ironically, Vermont for much of its history was, like Ireland, an exporter of people.

Statistics tell the tale. Between 1850 and 1950 Vermont's population increased by only 63,627 residents—from 314,120 to 377,747, an increase of little more than 20 percent in a hundred years. Perhaps even more telling was the fact that in 1870, some 42 percent of native-born Vermonters lived outside the state. In the decade from 1910 to 1920 and again in the 1930s, when falling agricultural prices severely cut into farming income, Vermont's population actually decreased. In the most recent assessment of this time in Vermont, a team of historians concluded that "by 1930, the isolated backwoods and hilltop farms, where poverty ran deepest, and where the economic base remained a combination of subsistence, barter, and scarce cash, had almost vanished from the landscape."[35]

And it was on the "hilltop farms" that many of the rural Irish lived, content back in the 1850s and 1860s to own even the roughest patch of land. But the Depression did them in. Farmers threw up their hands and sought work wherever they could. The story of "Little Ireland" in the town of Starksboro was typical of what happened to many rural Irish communities in Vermont at this time.

Starksboro, a mountainous township, lies twenty miles south of Burlington. Beginning in the late 1840s, a number of famine Irish families settled in a high valley that runs west out of the mountains along Lewis Creek. With poor, rocky soil, the valley was sparsely settled and covered in trees. The former Yankee owners, who considered the land of little value, happily sold it to the land-hungry Irish. By the end of the 1850s a dozen small Irish farms with about a hundred inhabitants clung to the dirt track that snaked along Lewis Creek. Eventually the community of Hannans, Conways, Caseys, Dillons, Butlers, and others grew so large that the town erected a school in the valley. For a long time visiting priests traveled by sleigh or team through snow and muddy roads to celebrate Mass in the schoolhouse. If the roads were impassable and the priest could not get through, Irish families would gather at the schoolhouse on Sundays and recite the rosary. Unsurprisingly, the valley became known as Little Ireland.

Initially, the Irish made their living in the valley by logging. They cut down trees in the winter, stacked them by Lewis Creek, and let the high waters of spring carry them to a sawmill below. Some logs they squared off and used to build the cabins that were their first homes. When they cleared enough land, they kept milk cows and sold the milk to a local creamery. They supplemented their dairy income by making maple syrup. Expenses were kept low: firewood provided free heat in potbellied stoves, and frugal farmwives canned fruit and vegetables while the men provided venison for the table. As mentioned earlier, entertainment took the form of "kitchen tonks," while homemade hard cider and sap beer made gatherings more sociable. The valley was so remote that electricity reached it only in the 1960s.

It was such a hard existence, particularly in the 1920s and 1930s, that young people drifted away. William Conway and Gerald Heffernan were typical of this mini-exodus. Conway, whose grandfather was one of the first Irish to settle in the valley, left the family farm to join the Marines in World War II and never came back. Instead, he went underground as a miner in Moriah, New York, where, he once said, it was always warmer than working the farm in snow-covered Vermont. Heffernan too left Starksboro following service in the war. After attending St. Michael's College in Colchester on the GI Bill, he became a teacher and moved to Connecticut. By 1944 there were so few children in the Little Ireland school that the town shuttered its doors. In time only the sign announcing the Little Ireland Road remained as a testament to the high valley's earlier history.[36]

The Starksboro experience was repeated again and again in Vermont. The old Irish community in Underhill that dated to before the famine shrank in size. Dr. W. Scott Nay, a physician who practiced in Underhill, remarked in his memoirs written in the 1930s that "nearly all the young [Irish] people left town," and "the farms the older ones occupied have been vacated and very few of the first families remain." On the Irish Settlement Road that once echoed with the voices of Irish children, only a few houses and a small cemetery remained, with stones marking the final resting place of Barretts, Doons, Flynns, Marlowes, and others.[37]

One episode of loss that ended on a happy note had to do with the Collins family of West Berkshire near the Canadian border. In 1840 three young immigrant brothers from County Sligo, Tim, Pat, and Roger Collins, pooled their resources and bought fifty acres of good farmland in West Berkshire. Over the years through hard work and frugal planning they eventually owned a thousand acres. As time passed and generations moved on, the land was broken up, some going to other members of the family and some sold outright. By the early 1930s Roger Collins, a son of one of the three brothers, and his wife, Mary, occupied the original homestead with 137 acres. But they were up in years, and as the Depression wore on, they found themselves increasingly in debt. Eventually their bank foreclosed, and

Some things never change. William Howrigan (at right) and his son Robert dig potatoes, ca. 1945. The large Howrigan family estimated they had to put by 350 bushels of potatoes each year to get them through the tough times of the 1930s and '40s. (Courtesy of Harold and Anne Howrigan.)

in 1935 they lost the farm that had been in their family for over a hundred years. It then passed to other owners. This might have been the end of the story of the Collins farm, except that in 2004 Tim Collins, a successful New York lawyer and great-grandson of Roger, purchased the property, with plans to retire there.[38]

One of the few rural places that retained its strong Irish flavor through the Depression and World War II was Fairfield in Franklin County. Across its low, rolling hills dozens of families—Howrigans, Ryans, Branons, Brennans, Connors, and others—traced their roots back to the immigrants of the 1830s and 1840s. Why it survived when so many other rural Irish communities disappeared might be related to sheer size. Even with significant out-migration, the community was so large that many descendants of the old Irish families stayed on to work the land. Moreover, unlike the more mountainous terrain of Moretown and Underhill, the gently rolling hills of Fairfield were more conducive to agriculture. Finally, many cash-strapped Yankee property holders sold their land to loggers in the 1940s, who, once it was logged off, often resold it at bargain prices to the remaining farmers, many of whom were Irish. The Fairfield Irish may have simply outlasted many of their neighbors.[39]

Today there are hundreds of roads and places in Vermont whose names are reminders of earlier Irish inhabitants: places like Bolger Road in Fair Haven, Kelly Road in Brattleboro, Daley Brook in Dorset, and Kelly Bay in Alburg. Other names are evidence of whole Irish communities now gone: Irish Hill in Shelburne, Irish Settlement Road in Underhill, Paddy Hill Road in Moretown, Irish Hill in Berlin, and Little Ireland in Starksboro. Only the names remain as fading evidence of earlier farm communities.

Sometimes even the memory is lost. There is a road in East Fairfield called Shenang. The initial *sh* sound in Shenang—so common in Irish—suggests it probably is a corrupt form of an Irish word introduced by Fairfield's first Irish settlers. Today no one in Fairfield knows what it means: lost like so much of Vermont's Irish past.[40]

Before leaving the subject of out-migration, it is worth noting the connection that two individuals who achieved some fame outside Vermont had with the Green Mountain Irish: John Kelly and Francis Hassett.

John "Jack" Kelly was the son of John Henry Kelly and Mary Kelly, originally from Newport, County Mayo. John Henry and Mary emigrated from Ireland in the 1870s and went to Rutland, where Mary, who was a Costello, had many relatives. How long they remained in Rutland is unclear, but by the 1880s they had moved to Philadelphia, where Kelly found work as a mason. There in 1889 their eldest son, John, who was always known as "Jack," was born. Handsome, athletic, and bright, Jack went to work as a bricklayer, then started his own company, and eventually became one of Philadelphia's wealthiest contractors.

A road sign is the only visible reminder of the once-large Irish community in Moretown.

Besides business, Kelly's other passion was athletics. He was a superb sculler, spending hours on the Schuylkill River as a member of Philadelphia's famed Vespers Rowing Club and rising to the top of his sport. In the 1920 and 1924 Olympics his Rutland Costello relatives beamed with pride as he won gold medals in both the single and double sculling events. They could also point out that in the doubles events in the Olympic Games his partner was his cousin Paul Costello. But for fans of the silver screen, Jack Kelly is probably best remembered not for his athletic prowess but as the father of Grace Kelly, the elegant leading lady in Hollywood films of the 1940s and 1950s and later the wife of Prince Rainier of Monaco.

Another notable Irish American with roots in Vermont was William Hassett, secretary to Presidents Franklin D. Roosevelt and Harry S. Truman. Hassett was born and raised in Northfield, the railroad and textile town where the Hassetts had been one of the first Irish families to settle. In Northfield, Hassett's father worked for the Central Vermont Railroad, while William received an education in the local public schools. A good student, he attended Clark University in Worcester, Massachusetts, but for financial reasons was forced to drop out in 1904 after only two years. Having earlier shown a talent for writing, he went into journalism, his first job being a stint as a reporter for the *Burlington Free Press*. After a number of years learning his trade in the Queen City, he moved to Washington, D.C., where he held positions with the *Washington Post* and the Associated Press.

In 1933 Hassett went to work for the National Recovery Administration. His duties there brought him to the attention of Roosevelt, and in 1935 the president invited him to join the White House staff as assistant secretary to the president. As Hassett wrote speeches and "ghosted" letters for the president, the two became friends. FDR appreciated the Vermonter's calm demeanor and his skills at storytelling. One of Roosevelt's biographers wrote that the tall, white-haired Hassett was "a good, quiet companion for Roosevelt when he wanted to get away from the hurly-burly of Washington." Pundits in the capital called Hassett "the bishop" for his courtly demeanor and Catholic beliefs. In 1944 Roosevelt promoted him to the position of secretary to the president, and it was Hassett, traveling with the president in Georgia in April 1945, who announced to the world Roosevelt's passing.[41]

Hassett continued in the same capacity for President Truman until the latter left office in 1952. Then, at age seventy-two, with almost forty years spent in the nation's capital, the old Vermonter retired, returning to live in the family home in Northfield. He died there in 1965.

Acceptance and Assimilation

One of Truman's biographers referred to Hassett as a "New Englander." That this devout Catholic whose peasant grandparents left Ireland only a hundred years before should be described by a term that typically connotes Puritan ancestry, white-steepled Congregational churches, and emotional reserve suggests that by the mid-twentieth century the Irish in Vermont—and everywhere in New England—were no longer viewed as an alien people but simply as Americans. Hadn't the *Burlington Daily News* on the occasion of James Edmund Burke's death in 1943 described him as one of Vermont's "Grand Old Men"?

There is other evidence of Vermonters' acceptance of the Irish. Consuelo Northrop Bailey, who in 1953 was the first woman Speaker of the Vermont House of Representatives and later the state's first female lieutenant governor, came from one of the original Yankee families that settled Fairfield in the 1790s. When she was growing up in the years before World War I, many of her Fairfield neighbors were Irish. In her memoirs written in the 1970s, she relates that her closest neighbors were the Irish Mackins and Hales and that there was no sense at all of prejudice against them. Nor was there much prejudice the other way. Bailey recounted how Nellie Mackin, daughter of an Irishman from Cork, baked pies for all church suppers, Catholic and Protestant, and Nellie's husband, according to Bailey, often remarked that he "calculate[d] heaven is big enough for all kinds." Perhaps something in rural life, the shared hardships of farming, the familiarity of one family with another, checked the nurturing of negative stereotypes.[42]

There were other episodes of extraordinary friendship between Yankees and Irish. The experience of Tim James O'Connor in Brattleboro in the 1920s may not have been common, but it was also not all that unusual. Tim James was born in 1907 to Irish-speaking immigrants from Kerry. He was orphaned by age fifteen and, along with his two older sisters, was raised by Irish neighbors. To help out with expenses, while he was in high school he held a part-time job with Edward Barrows, a local coal dealer. Barrows thought so much of the young man that when Tim James finished high school Barrows supported him in a two-year course at Bentley Business School, now Bentley College, in Waltham, Massachusetts. After graduation Tim James returned to work for Barrows and remained with his company for forty years. In the early 1980s Tim James's son, also a Tim, was Speaker of the Vermont House of Representatives. Thus through the help of a Yankee family did one Irishman, despite a rocky start in life, achieve great success.[43]

Still, despite much evidence of acceptance, prejudice remained. Even Consuelo Northrop Bailey's claim that there was no ill-feeling against Irish Catholics in Fairfield on the eve of World War I implies that she knew this was unusual. At times prejudice broke out in violence. Amid the antiforeign sentiment that swept the United States in the years following World War I, there were a number of ugly incidents in Vermont involving the Ku Klux Klan.

In 1922 Klan activists from outside the state began organizing in Vermont. Since there were few Jews and blacks in the Green Mountain State, the Klansmen targeted the foreign-born, with the slogan "America for Americans"; and as many of the immigrants were Catholics, the church was a primary target of Klan hostility. On the night of August 9, 1924, three Klansmen broke into Burlington's cathedral and stole a number of religious objects. The police quickly apprehended the trio and recovered the stolen items. A court eventually sentenced them to a few months in jail. This slap on the wrist, however, did not deter the Klan. In late 1925 they burned a cross on the steps leading to the vestibule of St. Augustine's in Montpelier; the burn mark is still visible today. After this episode, the Klan began to decline both regionally and nationally, rent by factionalism and financial scandals. In Vermont it never did number more than a few thousand members, and in general Vermonters strongly opposed its secrecy and its objectives.[44]

How much Klan hostility was directed at the state's Irish population as opposed to the newer immigrants—mainly Poles and Italians—is an open question. By the 1920s the Irish had been established so long in Vermont that many citizens of the Green Mountains considered them as Yankee as the Yankees. But there were still pockets of prejudice. One Vermonter in the 1930s commented that "to be an Irishman—a Papist and a Democrat—is a red flag to a bull to many a Puritan Yankee." Down to the mid-twentieth century, certain banks in the state declined to promote Catholics to executive positions. And as late as 1949, faculty in the University of Vermont's Political Science Department bragged that while they hired Jews, they had never hired a Catholic.[45]

The narrow-mindedness of the Political Science Department, however, does not seem to have permeated the entire university, for in the 1940s and 1950s the dean of the College of Agriculture—a key division in a state heavily dependent on dairy farming—was Joseph Carrigan, a second-generation Irish American Catholic whose family were dairy farmers in Pittsford. After Carrigan's retirement, the dairy-science building at UVM in 1965 was named for him. Perhaps academics who had come from a liberal arts background, where suspicion of the church of Rome lingered, harbored a hostility toward Catholicism not shared by individuals involved in the practical matter of farming.

Burlington's Irish World

The Irish American world of the early twentieth century, as it existed in Vermont's largest city, was vibrant, confident, successful, entrenched, and, in its own way, insular. Though no one knew it at the time, that Irish American world was also passing. Those years were a high point in terms of community identity and cohesiveness. While relations with their non-Irish neighbors, whether French Canadian or Yankee, were friendly, the Irish felt most comfortable among their own. What was their world like?

First of all, it was large. Speaking at a St. Patrick's Day dinner in 1904, a beaming Alderman John Shea, who had just helped Jim Burke to his mayoral victory, boasted that according to the 1900 U.S. census, 60 percent of Burlington's residents claimed Irish ancestry. Shea certainly exaggerated. While there are no exact figures for the Irish, a rough estimate by the priests at the cathedral in the 1930s put the number of their Irish parishioners at around 5,000, or about 20 percent of the city's population.[46]

But in the sense of impact, Shea was correct. Irish residents who remembered that era have commented that each of the three realms of urban life—the political, mercantile, and financial—was controlled by a different group: the Irish dominated city hall, the Jews operated the retail establishments, and the Yankees held a firm grip on the banks. There were exceptions, of course. Patrick McAuliffe, the son of an Irish shoemaker, worked his way up from bookstore salesman to the ownership in 1912 of a successful stationery and book business on Burlington's main commercial avenue, Church Street, while another Irish American, Thomas Wright, whose immigrant father had once worked in Burlington's waterfront lumberyards, was co-owner of Abernathy's, one of the city's leading department stores. In the 1930s Wright's assistant in running the store was J. Edward Moran, who would be Burlington's mayor in the 1950s. Even in banking, where the Yankees held sway, the Irish made inroads. Patrick McSweeney, the physician who supported so many of his siblings and relatives through medical school, spearheaded a group of Irish investors who in 1906 established the Champlain Trust Company in Winooski. John J. Flynn, while not a card-carrying member of the Catholic Irish community, founded the Chittenden Trust Company.[47]

Two of the most important Burlington-area businessmen in that era were also Irish Americans: contractor Eugene Cashman and mill manager John O'Brien. O'Brien has already been mentioned in connection with his marriage to Yvonne Provost, but in the 1940s the hardworking and religiously devout O'Brien was one of the most important men in the state. As resident manager of the American Woolen Mills in Winooski, he was in charge of the largest private employer in the state. During World War II more than 3,000 men and women went to work in the mills each day, producing thousands of yards of "fighting cloth" to make blankets, overcoats, and uniforms.[48]

In construction Eugene Cashman was involved in almost every major project undertaken in the Burlington area in the first three decades of the twentieth century. Among the most notable are three buildings that still stand and are part of Burlington's architectural heritage: City Hall, Memorial Auditorium, and the McAuliffe Block on the corner of Church and College streets. Cashman had come to Burlington in 1900 as a twenty-eight-year-old after having learned his craft working nine years with his immigrant father in his native Quincy, Massachusetts. Eugene quickly established a reputation as a master builder of large, complex projects when he successfully completed the reconstruction of the breakwater at Burlington bay and built the submarine sewage pipe system that extended out into Lake Champlain. By the late 1920s his reputation was such that the once exclusively Yankee Ethan Allen Club welcomed him as a member.[49]

But in the main, it was in the realm of politics that the Burlington Irish established their niche. In the half century from 1900 through 1950, Burlington's city hall had a distinctly Irish air. As already noted, a succession of Irish Americans beginning with Jim Burke held the mayoral seat; but there were also numerous city clerks who claimed Irish ancestry, including Edward Corley, a successful real estate investor and grocer on Church Street, and businessman Michael Devitt McMahon, who owned a shop selling fine china and advertised himself as "the china man," and who was married to a niece of Civil War hero John Lonergan. Over at the police station, three Irishmen—Patrick Russell, Patrick Cosgrove, and Donald Russell (Patrick's son)—led the force for nearly fifty years. Even the city's postmaster during the 1920s and 1930s, Patrick Mahoney, was Irish. He had formerly held the same position in Poultney among the slate-working Irish but had moved to Burlington to better support his children while they attended the University of Vermont.[50]

Burlington's Irish community also made inroads in the Vermont legislature. In 1933, as city residents wrestled with Depression woes, they elected one of the first three Irish Catholic Democrats ever to sit in the Vermont Senate—Thomas Magner. Magner had an interesting background. He was born in Limerick, Ireland, in 1860 and as a young man studied to be a physician; but he ran afoul of the law for his political activities, and "his departure from Ireland was made advisable." Settling in the United States, he went to work for the Metropolitan Life Insurance Company, first in Massachusetts and then in New Hampshire. In 1900 he relocated to Burlington when the company made him manager of its Vermont operations. Almost unique for an Irishman of the time, as a prominent business executive he resided on North Prospect Street in Ward One, the city's exclusive "hill section." Despite his corporate success, however, Magner remained a Democrat and was closely tied to the city's Irish community: his daughter Patricia married Joseph McNamara, a graduate of the College of the Holy Cross and Harvard Law School, one of Burlington's leading attorneys, and later U.S. attorney for the district of Vermont. Magner's unique background and social connections made him a winning candidate for the Vermont Senate.[51]

What held the Vermont Irish together as a distinct community were churches and schools. In Burlington, French Canadians attended St. Joseph Church and its school near the center of the city and St. Anthony near the cotton textile mills in the south end, while Irish Catholics claimed the cathedral as their own. Grammar school children of Irish ancestry attended Cathedral Grammar School, opened in 1917 by Bishop Rice, or Mount St. Mary's, operated by the Sisters of Mercy since 1886, primarily as a girls' school, admitting boys only up to the third grade. Later, in 1939 Christ the King School opened on the city's south side to serve the overflow of English-speaking students—mainly Irish—that swamped Cathedral Grammar School's facilities. Only when it came time to attend secondary school at Cathedral High did French Canadian and Irish young people come together in the classroom.[52]

While over time religion and schooling increasingly brought the Irish and French Canadians together, just the opposite was the case with the Catholic Irish and the city's Protestants. Separate schools created two separate social worlds, and this meant little intermarriage between the groups. Moreover, Irish Catholic families frowned on intermarriage. And up until the 1940s, the Catholic Church even prohibited young Catholics from joining the YMCA, YWCA, or the Boy Scouts out of fear of the possible proselytizing efforts of these "Protestant" organizations.[53]

The separate primary and secondary school systems often extended into university education. While many young Irish Vermonters with professional aspirations attended the University of Vermont, perhaps an equal number of them matriculated at St. Michael's College in Colchester. A few, either with broader horizons or more financial resources, traveled to Worcester, Massachusetts, to study at the Jesuit-operated College of the Holy Cross.

This separate collegiate experience continued in the business sphere. Protestant businessmen in Burlington and in general throughout the state almost universally belonged to the Masonic Order. Besides the order's commitment to doing good works, it also functioned as a business network. But because of the traditional hostility between Freemasonry and the Catholic Church, Irish businessmen declined to join—and probably would have been rejected had they wished to do so. They looked elsewhere for social and business connections. Almost to a man they belonged to the Knights of Columbus, a Catholic benevolent organization, and almost as frequently to the Benevolent and Protective Order of Elks (BPOE). Catholics joined the Elks because, unlike the Masonic Order, it did not have a history of anti-Catholicism, and it gave Catholic businessmen contacts beyond their own ethnic community.[54]

Ironically, Irish America's largest fraternal organization, the Ancient Order of Hibernians (AOH), failed to put down strong roots in Vermont. Irishmen in the slate and marble regions of Rutland, led by Poultney postmaster Patrick Mahoney (before he relocated to Burlington) and West Rutland insurance agent James Burke (no relation to Mayor Burke), established a state chapter in 1900. In 1903 Burlington merchant Thomas Wright organized the Irish in the Queen City, and by 1904 there were ten branches of the AOH in the state, with an estimated 700 members. For the next fifteen years the Vermont AOH supported various Irish charities, fought anti-Irish discrimination, and called for Ireland's independence from England.[55]

But the Vermont AOH failed to survive World War I. As one Irish Burlingtonian said, in explaining its demise in the Green Mountains, "There was no time then [during World War I] to root just for the Irish." Then, after the war, the leaders of the Vermont Irish—men like Rutland's Thomas Moloney, Burlington's Patrick McAuliffe, Thomas Wright, Thomas Magner, and Patrick Mahoney, and St. Albans's Maurice Walsh and Michael Magiff—shifted focus again, directing their attention to alleviating distress in Ireland caused by the Anglo-Irish War of Independence. Their energies went into fund-raising for the Irish White Cross, a relief organization. Once Ireland achieved its independence in 1922, little enthusiasm remained for reviving the AOH. In Vermont it drifted out of existence.[56]

Perhaps the fact that the AOH was short-lived in Vermont said something about the Green Mountain Irish. Monsignor John McSweeney, who grew up in Burlington in the 1930s and 1940s and was a grandson of Dr. Patrick McSweeney, maintained that his family never wore their ethnicity on their sleeves: they celebrated their Irishness at church suppers and entertainments on St. Patrick's Day, but that was it. The rest of the year they were simply Americans. Perhaps because they were secure in their own social world—their own parallel society— they did not consciously think of themselves as a people apart. As one Irish American woman, who seems to have equated "society" with assimilation, said in the 1930s:

Like everybody else in town, I used to think it would be nice to be a
member of Burlington's hill society, but after I had been made welcome

in the finest homes on the hill I discovered that I preferred my relatives and the friends I had known since childhood, and, as I got older, to watch their children come along. Being a member of Society has ceased to have any meaning to me.[57]

For her, and probably for many like her, it was enough to be with her own.

Epilogue

For more than a hundred years, the Vermont Irish had lived close together. They attended the same churches and schools, belonged to the same social and business organizations, and intermarried almost exclusively with their Catholic coreligionists. By the latter half of the twentieth century, however, that old ethnic world had largely passed away. A number of factors account for this change. One was the increased educational opportunities provided by the GI Bill after World War II. Greater education led to better job opportunities, which led to more mobility. Some of the Irish who once lived in Bennington, Rutland, Burlington, and St. Albans moved to the emerging suburbs or out of the state entirely, although many remained, still interconnected by marriage and schooling.

Then, too, as the Irish became better educated, a growing secularism often replaced their once-staunch adherence to the Catholic Church. Increasingly, parents were less inclined than their own parents had been to send their children to parochial schools. This trend was reinforced after 1961, when a Vermont court ruled as unconstitutional the longtime practice of towns without their own high schools to pay tuition to send their youngsters to nearby high schools, including Catholic schools. This ruling undermined the finances of many Catholic high schools, requiring higher tuition bills for the parents of the affected students. Many Catholic families could no longer afford Catholic education. In 1959 Catholic school enrollment in Vermont reached its peak and then began a long decline. High schools closed: Mount St. Mary Academy in Burlington, St. Michael in Montpelier, Central Catholic in St. Albans, Bennington Catholic, and St. Michael in Brattleboro. And this decline paralleled a drop in the numbers of young men and women entering the religious life. Thus the very institutions that had for generations formed the foundations of Irish communal life in Vermont found themselves eroding.

Another factor lessening the cohesiveness of Vermont's old Irish communities was the unexpected influx of outsiders into the Green Mountains. Reversing the stagnating trend of the previous hundred years, beginning shortly after World War II Vermont's population began to grow substantially, attracting people from the East's major cities seeking a more rural, simple existence. Between 1950 and 2000 Vermont's population increased by more than 60 percent, going from 377,747 to 608,827. The newcomers frequently had no connection to Vermont's older communities and little to no knowledge of Vermont's ethnic past. Significantly, in the 1980s, when Burlington native Brian Burns ran for mayor—the office once held for many years by his uncle John J. Burns—he lost resoundingly, later lamenting that he was a stranger in his own hometown. Not only had Vermont's Irish Catholic community changed, but Vermont too had changed.

Ironically, it was in this time of diminishing communal awareness that individual Irish Americans achieved some of their greatest successes in Vermont. In

U.S. Senator Patrick Leahy cutting the ribbon officially opening the Vermont History Center in Barre, 2002. (Courtesy of the Vermont Historical Society.)

*Poster for Burlington's first
Irish Heritage Festival, 1996.*

1972 Thomas Salmon, Ohio-born and Massachusetts-raised, became the first Irish Catholic governor of Vermont and later the first Irish Catholic president of the University of Vermont. Patrick Leahy, the grandson of an immigrant who died of black lung disease from working in the Barre granite industry, in 1974 became not only the first Irish Catholic, but also the first Democrat, ever elected from Vermont to the U.S. Senate. As of this writing he continues to serve in the Senate, the chair of its important Judiciary Committee. Currently, Vermont's lone congressman, Peter Welch, is a transplanted Irishman from Massachusetts and a graduate of College of the Holy Cross. Two Irishmen, the already mentioned Tim O'Connor of Brattleboro and Ralph Wright of Bennington, held the powerful position of Speaker of the Vermont House of Representatives. Also belonging in this influential group of Irish Vermonters is Elizabeth Candon, a member of the Sisters of Mercy and a niece of the late Dean Carrigan of UVM. Sister Elizabeth, as she is affectionately known, grew up on a dairy farm in Pittsford and rose to become Secretary of the Agency of Human Services in the administration of Governor Richard Snelling in the 1980s, the first woman and the first nun to hold a major administrative position in Vermont. These outstanding public servants are so much a part of mainstream Vermont life that their ethnic backgrounds are rarely noted.

But if the strong communal life that once existed in Irish Vermont is less strong today than it was fifty years ago, there seems to be no diminution of interest in Irish heritage. Irish Americans like to joke that "nostalgia isn't what it used to be," but they are still a nostalgic people, tied in barely conscious ways to the land and culture of their ancestors. As the days of anti-Irish prejudice increasingly fade into the remote past, there has been an uptick of interest in all things Irish—from music, to dance, to literature, to movies. In Vermont this interest has manifested

*The "Four Fenians"
singing at Fairfield's
annual St. Patrick's Day
festivities: from left to
right, Chris Branagan,
Chuck Thomas, John
Schreindorfer, and
Harold Howrigan.
(Courtesy of Mary
Howrigan Schreindorfer.)*

itself in a number of ways, from the offering of Irish history and literature courses at the state university, to the creation of an Irish heritage festival in Burlington in the mid-1990s, to the popularity of Green Mountain folk groups emphasizing traditional Irish music.

In a show of continuity perhaps unique in Vermont, the state's oldest rural Catholic Irish settlement, Fairfield, has for the past two generations held an annual St. Patrick's Day dinner in the social hall of St. Patrick Church on the Sunday prior to March 17. On this day, while Vermont is still covered with mounds of snow, farm families bring platters of baked hams, roasted turkeys, an array of salads and vegetables, and vanilla ice cream topped with maple syrup and set the dishes out on long buffet tables. Scores of people attend, although the numbers can sometimes dip a bit if the sap is running and some of the men have to stay at their sugarhouses to tend to the boiling. Once the meal is over, nervous performers take to the stage and entertain their neighbors with Irish songs, instrumentals, and storytelling. Perhaps it is fitting that we end our story with these farm people, many of whose Irish ancestors settled here in the 1820s, some of whom had relatives who fought in the Civil War, and still others with great-great-grandparents who might have sheltered dispirited Fenians. It is even more fitting that the day's entertainment ends with the hall resounding first to the words of "The Soldier's Song," Ireland's national anthem, and, finally, to "The Star-Spangled Banner."

Notes

Chapter 1

1. *New York Times*, November 13, 1960.

2. See Michael J. O'Brien, *A Hidden Phase in American History: Ireland's Part in America's Struggle for Liberty* (New York: Dodd, Mead, 1920) and his "Remarks at the Annual Meeting," *Journal of the American Irish Historical Society* (1919): 85–90. A complete listing of O'Brien's numerous writings can be found in Seamus P. Metress's *The Irish American Experience: A Guide to the Literature* (Washington, DC: University Press of America, 1981).

3. See Michael J. O'Brien, "Stray Historical Items from the Green Mountain State," *Journal of the American Irish Historical Society* 18 (1919): 182–86, and "Early Irish Settlers in the Champlain Valley," *Recorder* 4 (1927): 1–4.

4. Information on McMeecham is found in Kenneth Scott, *British Aliens in the United States during the War of 1812* (Baltimore: Genealogical Publishing Co., 1979), 10. The Obrion-Allen deed, dated June 27, 1785, is in the Allen Family Papers, Bailey/Howe Library, University of Vermont, Burlington, box 7, folder 67. For Thomas O'Brien see Abby Maria Hemenway, ed., *The Vermont Historical Gazetteer,* 5 vols. (Burlington, VT: A. M. Hemenway, 1868), 3:779. Reference to John Murray is in W. S. Rann and H. P. Smith, eds., *History of Rutland County* (1886; Bowie, MD: Heritage Books; 1993), 307.

5. Melvin Watts and Jessie I. Beckley, *History of Londonderry* 2 (Londonderry: Town of Londonderry, 1975).

6. On satellite communities of Londonderry, New Hampshire, see Edward Lutwyche Parker, *The History of Londonderry* (Boston: Perkins and Whipple, 1851), 180. On the introduction of the potato see Addison Edward Cudworth, *The History of Londonderry with Genealogical Sketches* (Montpelier: Vermont Historical Society, 1936), 13; and Hemenway, *Gazetteer*, 5:16.

7. Burr Morse of East Montpelier, grandson of Senator Aiken, confirmed the senator's Scots-Irish ancestry with the author in a telephone conversation, February 2, 2008. For Londonderry census, see U.S. Census, Manuscript Schedule, *First Census*, 1790. See also Cudworth, *History of Londonderry*, 16, 17.

8. Lewis Cass Aldrich, ed., *The History of Franklin and Grand Isle Counties, Vermont* (Syracuse, NY: D. Mason and Co., 1891), 790.

9. Martha Bigelow Wardenbury, "Will Gilliland, Pioneer of the Valley of Lake Champlain," *Proceedings of the Vermont Historical Society* 9 (September 1941): 186–97. Gilliland's regiment went through many name changes: Originally known as the Earl of Donegal's Regiment, it was designated the Thirty-fifth Regiment of Foot in 1747, then four years later it became the Prince of Orange's Own Regiment, and in 1782 it was renamed the Thirty-fifth Regiment of Foot. In 1881 the Thirty-fifth merged with the 107th

Regiment of Foot to become the Royal Sussex Regiment.

10. Winslow C. Watson, *Pioneer History of the Champlain Valley* (Albany, NY: J. Munsell, 1863), 194–95. Watson listed those from whom Gilliland bought grants, and they included individuals with the following Irish surnames: John Williamson, Daniel Moriarity, Christopher Dongan, Cornelius Hays, Peter Sullivan, John McKarty, John Sullivan, John Welsh, John Jameson, Anthony Garret, Michael Kiough, Patrick McMullen.

11. *Belfast Newsletter*, June 3, 1766. See Stephen A. Royle and Caitríona Ní Laoire, "'Dare the boist'rous main': The role of the *Belfast Newsletter* in the process of emigration from Ulster to North America, 1760–1800," *The Canadian Geographer* 50 (March 2006): 56–73.

12. Watson, *Pioneer History*, 41–48.

13. Wardenbury, "Will Gilliland," 186–97.

14. Information on Bell can be found in Allen L. Stratton, *History of the Town of Alburgh, Vermont*, 2 vols. (North Hero, VT: A. L. Stratton, 1986–2000) 2:35–36. See also U.S. Census, Manuscript Schedule, *First Census*, 1790. For Peter Carrigan see Stratton, *Town of Alburgh*, 2:78. In many of the original documents Carrigan is spelled "Carygan."

15. Stratton, *Town of Alburgh*, 1:1–30.

16. *Northern Sentinel*, March 31, 1815; May 5, 1815; and July 21, 1815. For deserters in Canada see Elinor K. Senior, "The Provincial Cavalry in Lower Canada, 1837–1850," *Canadian Historical Review* 57 (1976): 13–14.

17. Lewis Cass Aldrich and Frank Holmes, eds., *History of Windsor County, Vermont* (Syracuse, NY: D. Mason and Co., 1891), 945. In correspondence, descendants of Michael Madden now living in Gorham, New Hampshire, informed this writer that in the family's oral tradition Michael came from Galway, not Cork, was impressed there, and made his escape in Boston rather than in a Canadian port (letter from Anne Ansley, March 15, 2007). I have used the version from the Windsor County book because it was published in 1891 and I suspect the authors were much closer to the truth, as Madden's children were then still alive. In either case the main story line of Madden's arrival in America remains the same.

18. O'Brien, "Stray Historical Items," 183.

19. John J. Duffy, ed., *Ethan Allen and His Kin: Correspondence, 1771–1819*, 2 vols. (Hanover, NH: University Press of New England, 1998), 2:167. Ira Allen is quoted in James Wilbur, *Ira Allen, Founder of Vermont*, 2 vols. (Boston: Houghton Mifflin, 1928), 2:86. On Kelly's background see "The Burghers of New Amsterdam and the Freemen of New York, 1675–1866," *Collections of the New York Historical Society for the Year 1885* (New York: 1886), 97.

20. An account of Brush's life can be found in John J. Duffy and Eugene A. Coyle, "Crean Brush vs. Ethan Allen: A Winner's Tale," *Vermont History* 70 (2002): 103–110.

21. Richard B. Morris quote is from the introduction to Alein Austin's *Matthew Lyon: New Man of the Democratic Revolution* (University Park: Pennsylvania State University Press, 1981), ix. The discussion of Lyon's career is also from Austin.

22. Michael J. O'Brien, *Pioneer Irish of New England* (1937; reprint, Baltimore: Genealogical Publishing Co., 1998), 191–92.

23. Andrew N. Adams, *A History of Fair Haven, Vermont* (Fair Haven: Leonard and Phelps, Printers, 1870), 98, 361–62. See also U.S. Census, Manuscript Schedule, *First Census*, 1790. It lists the following individuals with Irish surnames or possible Irish surnames, plus the number of individuals in their households: Charles Boyle (3), Cornelius Doghasty (7), Jeremiah Darrar (7), Matthew Lyon (16), James McCarter (5), Alex McCarter (3), James McLuiry (5), Charles McCarthy (8), and Dan McCarthy (9).

24. Quoted in Austin, *Matthew Lyon*, 3.

25. For a complete discussion of this incident see Brian T. Neff, "Fracas in Congress: The Battle of Honor between Matthew Lyon and Roger Griswold," *Essays in History* 41 (Department of History, University of Virginia, 1999).

26. Section IX of Vermont's 1777 Constitution can be found in William Doyle, *The Vermont Political Tradition* (Barre, VT: William Doyle, 1984), 239–49. On the execution of Ann Glover see Vincent A. Lapomarda, "Ann Glover," *The Encyclopedia of the Irish in America*, ed. Michael Glazier (Notre Dame, IN: University of Notre Dame Press, 1999), 364–65. On religion in early Vermont see T. D. Seymour Bassett, *The Gods of the Hills: Piety and Society in Nineteenth Century Vermont* (Montpelier: Vermont Historical Society, 2000). According to Bassett, in 1791 there were fewer than a hundred organized churches in the state: sixty Congregational, thirty Baptist, two or three Episcopal, two Quaker monthly meetings, and one Presbyterian—and, of course, no Catholic.

27. Town of Bethel, *Town Records*, vols. 1, 2.

28. Clarence Winthrop Bowen, *History of Woodstock, Connecticut*, 8 vols. (Norwood, MA: Plimpton Press, 1926), 5:50; 5:616; 1:108. When a breakaway group in the 1750s attempted to establish a second church in town, Richard Jr. was one of those who vigorously opposed such a fracturing of the community.

29. Carleton E. Fisher and Sue Gray Fisher, *Soldiers, Sailors, and Patriots of the Revolutionary War, Vermont* (Camden, ME: Picton Press, 1992), 191.

30. Aldrich and Holmes, *Windsor County*, 569.

31. Ibid., 849–53.

32. Heman Powers, letter to Nathaniel Powers, April 25, 1856, Powers Family MSS, Miscellaneous File, Vermont Historical Society Library, Barre. See also Joann Powers, *The Powers Family and the Descendants of the Twin Sons of Thomas Powers and Olive Harvey* (Decorah, IA: Annundsen Publishing Co., 1992).

33. See Aldrich and Holmes, *Windsor County*, 849–53, and Henry Swan Dana, *History of Woodstock, Vermont* (Boston: Houghton Mifflin, 1889), 348.

34. American Council of Learned Societies, "Annual Report of the American Historical Association for the Year 1931," *Proceedings* 1 (1931): 107–452.

35. *New York Times*, November 13, 1960.

36. Historian Donald Harman Akenson has roundly criticized the 1931 report. He points out the pitfalls of relying on surnames, but far more seriously he notes that the researchers did not count every name in the census but only took a sampling. See his

Being Had: Historians, Evidence, and the Irish in North America (Ontario: P. D. Meany Co., 1985), 13–36.

37. Kerby Miller, *Emigrants and Exiles: Ireland and the Irish Exodus to North America* (New York: Oxford University Press, 1985), 137.

Chapter 2

1. Anonymous [Nathaniel Hawthorne], "The Inland Port," *The New-England Magazine* 9 (December 1835): 398–409.

2. Bernard Brewin, letter to his parents, January 18, 1837, in possession of John Leddy, Burlington, VT. In Ireland the name Brewin is usually spelled "Bruen" or "Bruin." Encouraging letters quoted in Kerby Miller, *Emigrants and Exiles*, 203.

3. D. Aidan McQuillan, "Beaurivage: The Development of an Irish Identity in Rural Quebec, 1820–1860," online posting, http://members.tripod.com/gail25/que4.htm, October 25, 2004. Information on tariffs from Miller, *Emigrants and Exiles*, 194.

4. Quoted in James O'Beirne, "Early Irish in Vermont," *Vermont History* 28 (1960): 66.

5. *Burlington Sentinel*, August 19, 1836. The newspaper changed its name from the *Northern Sentinel* in the early 1830s. Englishman's report quoted in T. D. Seymour Bassett, "Irish Migration to Vermont before the Famine," *Chittenden County Historical Society Bulletin* 4 (1966): n.p. Irishwoman giving birth on deck is found in Gideon Lathrop, "Diary of Gideon Lathrop, 1823–1839," TS, Vermont Historical Society, Barre. Report on "unusual number of Irish" arriving found in *Northern Sentinel*, August 2, 1822.

6. Lathrop, "Diary."

7. Evelyn M. Wood Lovejoy, *History of Royalton, Vermont, with Family Genealogies, 1769–1911* (Burlington, VT: Free Press Printing Co., 1911), 957, 958.

8. C. H. Willey, "Some Historical Facts about the O'Hara Family," TS, 1893, Vermont Historical Society, Barre.

9. The family name changed over the years. Originally spelled "Donaghy," and sometimes "Donoghue," by the end of the nineteenth century it was spelled "Donoway." Poultney Donaghys found in Hemenway, *Gazetteer*, 3:997. Middlebury Donaghys in Samuel Swift, *History of the Town of Middlebury in the County of Addison, Vermont* (1859; reprint, Rutland, VT: C. E. Tuttle Co., 1971), 178.

10. Peter or Thomas Donaghy to Michael Donaghy, August 4, 1840, Donoway Family Papers, Sheldon Museum, Middlebury, VT, box 56, folder 8.

11. "Chain migration" characterized Irish settlement patterns everywhere in North America and in the antipodes. For a fuller discussion of this phenomenon see Donald Harman Akenson, *The Irish Diaspora: A Primer* (Toronto: P. D. Meany Co., 1996).

12. The O'Gradys came from County Laois, formerly Queens County, Ireland, and settled in Shelburne about 1800. They are mentioned as operating an inn there in 1808. See Marie Harding and Charlotte Tracy, *The History of Shelburne* (Burlington, VT: Queen City Printers, 1989), 14. One son, John O'Grady, became a well-known steamboat captain on Lake Champlain in the 1840s, and another son or grandson, William, born in Shelburne in 1823 and graduated UVM in 1848, was the first superintendent of schools in San Francisco in 1856.

13. U.S. Census, Manuscript Schedule, *Fourth Census*, 1820, and *Fifth Census*, 1830.

14. From a list of business advertisers in *Walton's Register and Farmer's Almanac for 1842* (Montpelier, VT: E. P. Walton and Sons, n.d.). Population figure is from Brian Walsh's study of the Burlington Irish, in which he counted the number of individuals with Irish surnames in the Manuscript Schedule of the 1840 census. As already mentioned, counting surnames has certain problems, but a far bigger danger in the pre-1850 census numbers is underreporting, because only the name of "head of household" is listed, followed by the number of individuals living in that household. If a young, single Irishman boarded in a home where the owner had an English surname, the presence of an Irishman would not show up in the count. In calculating the numbers of Irish in Fairfield, Underhill, Moretown, Castleton, and Middlebury, I have used the same method as Walsh. I believe, however, that those numbers, if they err, do so on the conservative side, and that in fact there were significantly more Irish people in the towns mentioned than those reported in this chapter.

15. U.S. Census, Manuscript Schedule, *Third Census*, 1810, and *Fourth Census*, 1820.

16. See Mary Lee Dunn, *Ballykilcline Rising: From Famine Ireland to Immigrant America* (Amherst: University of Massachusetts Press, 2008), 71–95. Hanley story in Charles Morrissey, "The Case for Oral History," *Vermont History* 31 (July 1963): 153.

17. Rev. James E. Horan, "History of St. Patrick's Parish, Fairfield, Vermont," TS, Special Collections, Bailey/Howe Library, University of Vermont, Burlington, 3. Of all the early pre-famine Irish residents of Fairfield, we know the counties of origin of only a few. That information comes from inscriptions on gravestones and from work done by Thomas Howrigan, M.D., of Fairfield, who reviewed applications for citizenship in Franklin County for the nineteenth century. What that information showed was an unusually high number of immigrants from County Louth. Early Fairfield-area families with County Louth connections: Duffy, King, Sharkey, McEnany, Kirk, Killin, Brady, Clark, Kane, Ryan (James), Clinton, Conlin, and Deniver. From nearby Counties Cavan and Meath: Sheridan and Crosby.

18. Horan, "St. Patrick's Parish," 4. Mignault in northwestern Vermont in Rev. James Fitton, *Sketches of the Establishment of the Church in New England* (Boston: Patrick Donahoe, 1872), 242.

19. Thomas, Robert, and Harold Howrigan, interview with the author, Fairfield, VT, June 22, 2003. McMahon purchase in Town of Fairfield, *Land Records*, vol. 10, deed dated April 20, 1840, 482. Connolly purchase, ibid., vol. 9, deed dated October 5, 1830, 393.

20. U.S. Census, Manuscript Schedule, *Seventh Census*, 1850. The Fairfield Houstons seem to have been Catholics, for the family is buried in Fairfield's Catholic cemetery. However, most Houstons associated with Vermont were of Ulster Scots Presbyterian background, coming from County Derry in the eighteenth century. In Vermont they were prominent in the Londonderry and Walden areas. It is possible, of course, that the Fairfield Houstons were originally Protestants but converted to the church of their Irish Catholic neighbors. Information on the profitability of maple syrup from the Howrigan interview. Irish purchasing farms from the Fairfield *Land Records*, vols. 8–10. Population figures from the U.S. Census, Manuscript Schedule, *Sixth Census*, 1840.

21. Town of Fairfield, *Town Meeting Records*, March 7, 1836.

22. Neil Bartlett, *From the West Side of Mount Mansfield* (Tucson, AZ: W. N. Bartlett, printed by Alphagraphics, 2000). Sheep count is from Loraine Dwyer, *The History of Underhill, Vermont* (Underhill, VT: Underhill Historical Society, 1976), 8.

23. U.S. Census, Manuscript Schedule, *Sixth Census*, 1840. Information on the Doons comes from an interview conducted in 1990 by Underhill schoolchildren with Mrs. Thelma Stone, descendant of Felix Doon and Margaret Malone. Typescript of the interview in the author's possession.

24. Stone interview.

25. Mary Reagan, *A Brief History of Moretown, Vermont, for the Celebration of Moretown's Heritage and St. Patrick's Church Centennial* (Moretown, VT, 1982). The post-famine Northfield Irish have been well documented in Gene Sessions, "Years of Struggle: The Irish in the Village of Northfield, 1845–1900," *Vermont History* 55 (spring 1987): 69–95. Names and population estimate from U.S. Census, Manuscript Schedule, *Sixth Census*, 1840.

26. Gwilym R. Roberts, *New Lives in the Valley: Slate Quarries and Quarry Villages in North Wales, New York, and Vermont, 1850–1920* (Somersworth, NH: New Hampshire Printers, 1998), 336. Information on the McKeans was provided by Peter Patten, interview with the author, Fair Haven, Vermont, January 24, 2005. Patten is a native of Fair Haven and an amateur historian whose Irish-American ancestors settled in the Castleton–Fair Haven area in the 1840s. Brian, Michael, and James McKean all appear in the 1840 census. Population figures are from the U.S. Census, Manuscript Schedule, *Sixth Census*, 1840. This figure of approximately fifty or sixty Irish Catholics in the area is confirmed in Claire Burditt and Sylvia Sullivan, eds., *Castleton Looking Back: The First 100 Years* (Castleton, VT: Castleton Historical Society, 1998), 28.

27. U.S. Census, Manuscript Schedule, *Sixth Census*, 1840.

28. There is an interesting side story to the life of James Daugherty. In a lecture given in 1940 in Sherbrooke, Quebec, Rev. T. J. Walsh, SJ, of Loyola College, Montreal, noted that one of the judges of the superior court, Marcus Doherty, who had been born in Dungiven, County Derry, Ireland, in 1820, had been sent by his mother to a paternal uncle, Rev. James Doherty of Vermont, in 1832. Marcus attended the University of Vermont but apparently moved to Quebec's Eastern Townships about 1842. There he married and raised a family. His son, Charles Doherty, was minister of justice in Canada's Borden government, 1911–20. The uncle could have been no other than the James Daugherty mentioned here, and it is interesting to note that Father Walsh omitted to mention that Rev. Doherty was a Protestant minister, not a priest. The complete lecture is contained in T. J. Walsh, SJ, "Pioneer English Catholics in the Eastern Townships: Paper Read at Annual Meeting of the Canadian Catholic Historical Association," Sherbrooke, Quebec, October 1, 1940, TS in the author's possession. Information on James Daugherty's life can be found in Committee of the Associated Alumni, University of Vermont Obituary Record No. 1 (Burlington, VT: 1895), 49.

29. Fitton, *Sketches*, 244.

30. Rev. Jeremiah O'Callaghan, *Usury, Funds and Banks; also Forestalling Traffick and Monopoly; likewise pew rent and grave tax, together with Burking and Dissecting: as well as the Gallican Liberties.* . . . (Burlington, VT: Printed for the author, 1834), 4–64. For O'Callaghan on the number of Catholics, see Rev. Frederick R. Wilson, "A History of Catholicism in Vermont," *Vermont History* 21 (July 1953): 212. O'Callaghan quoted on need for a priest in Vermont in Howard Coffin, *An Inland See* (Burlington, VT: Roman Catholic Diocese of Burlington, 2001), 6, 7. For O'Callaghan's dismissal from Cork diocese see O'Beirne, "Early Irish in Vermont," 69. Account of O'Callaghan's early life in his *Usury, Funds and Banks*, 4–64.

31. Hemenway, *Gazetteer*, 1:626.

32. Rev. Vincent Maloney, "St. Teresa's Parish, Morrisville," 1.

33. Emily Flynn, *History of the Town of Underhill* (Underhill, VT, 1941), 32.

34. The church-building group there was led by James and Henry McNally. The 1840 census lists a James MacNawley, Charles O'Kane, James Birney, and Frederick Arnault. Mass was first said in Swanton in 1828 in the home of James McNally. See Ledoux's *History of Swanton*.

35. Quoted by Professor Thomas Moriarty in a lecture, "From the Cork Gaeltacht to Holyoke, Massachusetts: The Turbulent Career of Reverend Jeremiah O'Callaghan," Fletcher Free Library, Burlington, VT, March 12, 1996.

36. Rev. Jeremiah O'Callaghan, *Creation and Offspring of the Protestant Church and the Vagaries and Heresies of John Henry Hopkins, Protestant bishop.* . . . (Burlington, VT: Jeremiah O'Callaghan, 1837), iii, 2.

37. John Henry Hopkins, *Primitive Church* (Burlington, VT: John Henry Hopkins, 1835), and *Primitive Creed* (Burlington, VT: John Henry Hopkins, 1834).

38. O'Callaghan, *Creation and Offspring*, 122. O'Callaghan's letter on his forthcoming book, *Burlington Sentinel*, February 10, 1837.

39. O'Callaghan, *Usury, Funds and Banks*, 4–64. "Shatter-brained" quote from *Burlington Free Press*, October 13, 1837.

40. Quoted in John G. Shea, *History of the Catholic Church in the United States*, 4 vols. (New York: J. G. Shea, 1886–92), 3:488. "More than they thought prudent" quoted in *Metropolitan Catholic Almanac, and Laity's Directory for 1839* (Baltimore: Fielding Lucas Jr., 1839), 116. "Work of an arsonist," *Burlington Free Press*, May 11, 1838.

41. *Northern Sentinel*, July 5, 1822, and June 17, 1825.

42. Quoted in O'Beirne, "Early Irish in Vermont," 65.

43. *Burlington Free Press*, July 6, 1843.

44. Hope Nash, *Royalton, Vermont* (Royalton: Town of Royalton, 1975), 23.

"Reward," *Northern Sentinel*, March 27, 1829. Steamer *Phoenix* incident in Ralph Nading Hill, *Lake Champlain: Key to Liberty* (Woodstock, VT: Countryman Press, 1987), 200.

45. *Burlington Free Press*, April 14, 1843. "Superstitious Paddy," *Northern Sentinel*, January 1, 1830.

46. Rev. John S. Michaud, "The Diocese of Burlington," *History of the Catholic Church in the New England States*, ed. William Byrne (Boston: 1899), 131. "Blind and unqualifiedly submissive," *Burlington Free Press*, July 31, 1835.

47. Teresa Viele, *Following the Drum: A Glimpse of the Frontier Life* (New York: Rudd and Carleton, 1858), 30. "They have at Castleton" quoted in Roberts, *New Lives in the Valley*, 337.

48. O'Beirne, "Early Irish in Vermont," 70. "Green Mountain boys ever seemed," Fitton, *Sketches*, 244. "Where liberality permitted," ibid., 243.

Chapter 3

1. Donoway Papers, Sheldon Museum, box 56, folder 8. The letter is unsigned, but internal evidence in this and other letters suggests it was written by Thomas Donaghy.

2. Miller, *Emigrants and Exiles*, 281, 291–92.

3. Donald Harman Akenson in *The Irish Diaspora* argues that the decision to emigrate is always a choice, that the act of emigrating is itself evidence that one had the wherewithal to be able to afford to leave and thus could have stayed. I'm not convinced that emigration is evidence that one had some means, other than in the very short term. One might have had a few pence to survive for another few months, but one's long-term prospects were not good if one remained in Ireland.

4. Marianna O'Gallagher, *Grosse Ile: Gateway to Canada, 1832–1937* (Ste-Foy, Quebec: Lives Carraig Books, 1984), 51.

5. *Vermont Chronicle*, July 21, 1847. Also see J. Kevin Graffagnino, Samuel B. Hand, and Gene Session, eds., *Vermont Voices, 1609 through the 1990s* (Montpelier: Vermont Historical Society, 1999), 159; and *Burlington Free Press*, March 10, 1848.

6. Quoted by Professor Thomas Moriarty in a lecture, "From the Cork Gaeltacht to Holyoke, Massachusetts: The Turbulent Career of Reverend Jeremiah O'Callaghan," Fletcher Free Library, Burlington, VT, March 12, 1996.

7. *Vermont Chronicle*, July 21, 1847. Poor Farm relief report from Burlington, VT, Town/City Records, box 8, folder 46, Special Collections, Bailey/Howe Library, University of Vermont.

8. *Burlington Free Press*, July 24, 1849.

9. Terry Coleman, *Passage to America* (Harmondsworth, UK: Penguin Books, 1974), 82–83. "Passage Certificates" quote from *Burlington Free Press*, April 3, 1848.

10. Sister Agnes McElroy, "The Interesting Life of John McElroy," TS in the possession of Margaret Ryan, Fairfield, VT.

11. A Finnegan family from Newtown Hamilton came to Vermont in the summer of

1847 following the same route as the McElroys and settled in Hyde Park. They would have been related to the McElroys and the Finnegans of Fairfield. An account of this Finnegan family's journey to Vermont can be found in Dorothy Cable, *Three Summers with Pop* (New York: Pyramid Press, 1939), 56–57.

12. John T. Leddy, letter to the author, March 7, 2002. Patrick Sheridan and his family appear in the 1840 census residing in Underhill, and they were most certainly relatives of Margaret Sheridan Leddy. See U.S. Census, Manuscript Schedule, *Sixth Census*, 1840.

13. Joan Rowley Harley and Anne Rowley Howrigan, eds., *Collection of Letters of the Rowley Family, 1867–1956* (St. Albans, VT: L. G. Printing, 2004), 1.

14. Mary Lee Dunn, *Ballykilcline Rising: From Famine Ireland to Immigrant America* (Amherst: University of Massachusetts Press, 2008), 73. For a detailed account of the rent strike in Ballykilcline see Robert James Scally, *The End of Hidden Ireland: Rebellion, Famine, and Emigration* (New York: Oxford University Press, 1995).

15. Harold Meeks, *Time and Change in Vermont: A Human Geography* (Chester, CT: Globe Pequot Press, 1986) 106–139, 178.

16. Katherine F. Duclos, *The History of Braintree, Vermont* (Montpelier, VT: Capital City Press, 1976), 89. In the railroad gangs that worked in Georgia, Vermont, in 1850 and were reported in the census of that year, the workers were almost exclusively Irish males in their twenties; rarely did the census show any accompanying numbers of Irish females. U.S. Census, Manuscript Schedule, *Seventh Census*, 1850. For provenance of Irish famine arrivals, see Gene Sessions, "Years of Struggle: The Irish in the Village of Northfield, 1845–1900," *Vermont History* 55 (spring 1987): 71. In the many "Irish" cemeteries in Vermont visited by this writer, where place of birth is recorded on the tombstone, County Cork predominates.

17. Peter Patten, interview with the author, March 1, 2007.

18. www.borntoexplore.org/familyhistory/harringtons.htm.

19. U.S. Census, Manuscript Schedule, *Seventh Census*, 1850. Figures cited represent only immigrants and first-generation Irish Americans and do not include those who might have been second- and even third-generation Irish Americans.

20. U.S. Census, Manuscript Schedule, *Seventh Census*, 1850, and Brian Walsh, "Dreams Realized? Irish-Americans and Progress, Burlington, Vermont, 1830–1930" (master's thesis, University of Vermont, 1993), 18–19. "All Irish and Yankee" quote from *Burlington Free Press*, February 21, 1949.

21. Timothy O'Connor, interview with the author, October 16, 2007.

22. U.S. Census, Manuscript Schedule, *Seventh Census*, 1850.

23. *Seventh Census of the United States, Bureau of the Census, Nativity by State: Foreign Born, 1850* (Washington, DC: Robert Armstrong, Public Printer, 1853).

24. Horan, "Saint Patrick's Parish," 9. See also Jimmy Arkinson, interview with the author, March 14, 2004, and *Burlington Free Press*, December 12, 1879.

25. Nicholson wrote of her experiences in Ireland. See Asenath Hatch Nicholson, *Annals of the Famine in Ireland*, ed. Maureen Murphy (Dublin: Lilliput Press, 1998). For Timothy Follet and Barnet man quote, see *Burlington Free Press*, February 22, 1847, and

April 30, 1847. Rachel Robinson letter to George Robinson in Robinson Letters, Sheldon Museum, Middlebury, VT, box 3, file 6.

26. "The Yankee Priest Says Mass in Brattleboro: Joseph Coolidge Shaw Describes His Visit in 1848," *Vermont History* 44 (fall 1976): 201. Anecdote about Irishmen's camp quoted in Duclos, *History of Braintree*, 89. Paymaster's remarks quoted in Daniel L. Wells, letter to Henry L. Sheldon, January 19, 1848, Sheldon MSS, Sheldon Museum, Middlebury, VT. Remarks of East Braintree woman quoted in Allen F. Davis, "The Girl He Left Behind: The Letters of Harriet Hutchinson Salisbury," *Vermont History* 33 (January 1965): 281.

27. Quoted in Evelyn M. Wood Lovejoy, *History of Royalton, Vermont, with Family Genealogies, 1769–1911* (Burlington, VT: Free Press Printing Co., 1911), 579.

28. *Burlington Free Press*, August 25, 1853, November 14, 1853, February 12, 1855, and May 8, 1855.

29. Ibid., August 11, 1849.

30. Ibid., January 11, 1872. Quote about seeing the governor in *Rutland Herald*, April 7, 1859.

31. Samuel B. Hand, *The Star That Set: The Vermont Republican Party, 1854–1974* (Lanham, MD: Lexington Books, 2002) 7–8.

32. *Burlington Free Press*, May 3, 1855. Postmaster Cain was born on the Isle of Man, which lies halfway between England and Ireland, and thus he was a Manxman. However, it is fairly certain his background was Irish, and he always identified with the Irish community in Rutland. "Hand against everyman" quote from Edward Lowe Temple, *Old Rutland* (Rutland: by the author, 1923), 24.

33. Hand, *Star That Set*, 7–8.

34. See Dorothy Hemenway Ashton, *Sheldon, Vermont* (St. Albans, VT: Regal Art Press, 1979); and Richard J. Purcell, "Vermont Schools and Early Irish Teachers," *Catholic Educational Review* 33 (May 1935): 279–81. For John McCuen, see *Burlington Free Press*, October 10, 1888

35. Howard Coffin, *An Inland See: A Brief History of the Roman Catholic Diocese of Burlington* (Barre, VT: L. Brown and Sons, 2001), 14–15.

36. Lance Harlow, *Vermont's First Catholic Bishop: The Life of Bishop Louis De Goesbriand, 1816–1899* (Barre, VT: L. Brown and Sons, 2001), 60, 75.

37. Patrick C. Hannon, "A History of St. Bridget Parish," TS, Special Collections, Bailey/Howe Library, University of Vermont, 10.

38. Information on the "Highgate Affair" comes from Ronald C. Murphy and Jeffrey Potash, "The 'Highgate Affair': An Episode in Establishing the Authority of the Roman Catholic Diocese of Burlington," *Vermont History* 52 (winter 1984): 33–43, and from Harlow, *Vermont's First Catholic Bishop*, 70–71. The 1850 census shows a total population of 2,563 for Highgate, with 130 people born in Ireland and their children numbering 91. With a total of 221 immigrant and first-generation Irish Americans, they accounted for 8.4 percent of Highgate's population. U.S. Census, Manuscript Schedule, *Seventh Census*, 1850.

39. David Blow, "A Cathedral for Burlington," *Vermont History* 36 (summer 1968): 109–125.

40. Frank E. Hartwell, "Bolton in the Mountains," *Vermont History* 23 (October 1955): 307, and T. D. Seymour Bassett, "500 Miles of Trouble and Excitement: Vermont Railroads, 1848–1861," *Vermont History* 49 (summer 1981). *Burlington Free Press*, July 10, 1846.

41. For "Irish Brigade," see T. D. Seymour Bassett, "Irish Migration to Vermont Before the Famine," *Chittenden County Historical Society Bulletin* 4 (March 17, 1996): n.p. See also Barry Salussolia, "The City of Burlington and Municipal Incorporation in Vermont," *Vermont History* 54 (winter 1986): 5–19.

42. Salussolia, "City of Burlington," 13.

43. Fairfield Town Records, vol. 1A, 285.

Chapter 4

1. William White, letter to Jacob Weed, January 14, 1863, Vermont Historical Society, Barre, Misc. File 0249.

2. John J. Duffy, Samuel B. Hand, and Ralph H. Orth, *The Vermont Encyclopedia* (Hanover, NH: University Press of New England, 2003), 161.

3. Conclusions here are based on a study of a number of Vermont towns that had considerable Irish populations in 1860. Burlington, for example, which was about 38 percent Irish (Walsh's figure) in a population of 7,716, sent an estimated 894 men off to war, of which only 166 (18.5 percent) had Irish surnames. Underhill, with its long-established Irish community, had a population of 1,637 in 1860, of which 545 (33 percent) were Irish, and sent 161 men to war, but only 18 (11 percent) had Irish surnames. The same was true in Castleton, with its large Irish population. That slate town had a population of 2,852 in 1860, with 770 (27 percent) of them Irish. It sent 252 men to war, but only 33 (13 percent) had Irish surnames. Information on enlistments from various Vermont towns comes from Thomas Ledoux, "Roster of Enlistments by Town," online posting, http://vermontcivilwar.net, accessed September 1, 2008. Ledoux points out that Vermonters sometimes enlisted in places other than their hometowns, and this would skew the above percentages. Nationwide assessment is from James M. McPherson, *Battle Cry of Freedom* (New York: Oxford University Press, 1988), 606.

4. Kenneth Moore, "Frederick Holbrook," *Vermont History* 32 (April 1964): 76. Report of Capt. C. R. Crane, provost marshal, First District of Vermont, to Brig. Gen. T. G. Pitcher, acting assistant provost-marshal-general, Rutland, June 18, 1863, in Fred C. Ainsworth and Joseph W. Kirkley, eds., *The War of the Rebellion: A Compilation of the Official Records of the Union and Confederate Armies* (Washington, DC: Government Printing Office, 1899) series 3, 3:384–85. Information from New York draft riots in McPherson, *Battle Cry*, 105.

5. Ainsworth and Kirkley, *War of the Rebellion*, 384–85.

6. Jeffrey D. Marshall, ed., *A War of the People: Vermont Civil War Letters* (Hanover,

NH: University Press of New England, 1999), 9. Stones thrown at recruits, *Burlington Free Press*, September 29, 1863.

7. Information on Irish casualties comes from Ledoux, "Roster of Enlistments" online posting. See note 3 above.

8. Ralph Orson Sturtevant, *Pictorial History, Thirteenth Regiment, Vermont Volunteers, War of 1861–1865* (N.p., 1910), 427.

9. Ibid. Reports on disbanding of Lonergan's unit in *Burlington Free Press*, June 18, 1861, and *Rutland Herald*, June 19, 1861.

10. Interestingly, the third-in-command of the Second Regiment was English-born Maj. Charles Joyce of Northfield. In the 1850s he was one of the most outspoken leaders of the Know-Nothing Party in Vermont. It's also worth pointing out that of all the officers in the Second Regiment, Lonergan was the sole Irishman. Could it be that as an Irishman Lonergan was simply treated more harshly than his colleagues and that his unit was singled out to be made an example of?

11. Sturtevant, *Thirteenth Regiment*, 425–29.

12. Ibid. On request for a Catholic chaplain see Coffin, *Inland See*, 20.

13. G. G. Benedict, *Vermont in the Civil War: A History of the Part Taken by the Vermont Soldiers and Sailors in the War for the Union, 1861–1865.* 2 vols. (Burlington, VT: Free Press Association, 1888), 2:456–69. Lonergan received his Medal of Honor in 1893, just before the guidelines for its issuance were tightened.

14. *Burlington Free Press*, November 19, 1864. Savage's Station was fought on June 29, 1862, in Virginia as part of the Seven Days' Battle. Fisher quote in Dorothy Canfield Fisher, *Vermont Tradition: The Biography of an Outlook on Life* (Boston: Little, Brown, 1953), 305. Henchey deaths found online at http://VermontCivilWar.org/research/myplace.php?input=bakersfield, accessed April 8, 2009.

15. Edward A. Daniel, "The Life and Times of Thomas B. Kennedy," TS, Vermont Historical Society Library, Barre.

16. Cecil Woodham-Smith, *The Great Hunger* (New York: Harper & Row, 1962), 412.

17. For newspaper reports on Fenian activity, see *Burlington Daily Free Press*, March 17–18, 1864; December 30, 1864; April 22, 1864; October 6, 1864.

18. On the overall strategy of the Fenian movement see Brian Jenkins, *Fenians and Anglo-American Relations during Reconstruction* (Ithaca, NY: Cornell University Press, 1969), and Mabel Gregory Walker, *The Fenian Movement* (Colorado Springs, CO: R. Myles, 1969).

19. *Vermont Journal*, January 27, 1866. This imagery of the blood sacrifice on the altar is an interesting precursor to the idea of blood sacrifice that was integral to the thinking of Padraig Pearse in preparing for the Easter Rising of 1916. Lonergan was described in the *Burlington Daily Free Press*, March 19, 1866, as the leader of the Fenian movement in Vermont.

20. Irish American criticisms of planned attack on Canada, *Burlington Daily Free Press*, March 19, 1866. Opposition of the Catholic Church to Canadian invasion, *Burl-*

ington Free Press, March 15, 1866. Numbers in Fenian circles, *Rutland Herald*, March 22, 1866. Fenian circles in Vermont, Homer Calkin, "St. Albans in Reverse: The Fenian Raid of 1866," *Vermont History* 35 (January 1967): 22.

21. *Burlington Daily Times*, March 19, 1866.

22. Sean Cronin, "The Fenians and Clan Na Gael," *Encyclopedia of the Irish*, ed. Michael Glazier, 317–18.

23. Quoted in Edward Adams Sowles, *History of Fenianism and Fenian Raids in Vermont* (Rutland, VT: Tuttle and Co., 1880), 11, 12. Had "the drill of a soldier," *St. Albans Messenger*, June 8, 1866.

24. Calkin, "St. Albans in Reverse," 28.

25. E-mail from Ed Daniel, March 17, 2005, about Fenian who fell ill and died in Fairfield. Irish Vermonters welcome Fenians, *Burlington Daily Times*, June 8, 1866.

26. *Burlington Daily Times*, June 2, 4, 7, 1866.

27. *Burlington Free Press*, June 6, 1866.

28. Aldrich, *Franklin and Grand Isle Counties*, 213; and Calkin, "St. Albans in Reverse," 31.

29. *Watchman and State Journal*, June 22, 1866.

30. Hugh Short, "The Irish in Rutland in 1880," *Rutland Historical Society Quarterly* (winter 1984): 3–5, and *Rutland Herald*, May 28 and June 3, 1866.

31. *Burlington Free Press*, March 15, 19, 1867.

32. "America is the Irishman's wife," *Burlington Free Press*, March 17, 1870. Fenians stockpile arms, *Rutland Herald*, May 25, 1870.

Chapter 5

1. *Poultney Journal*, June 13, 1879.

2. Patrick Blessing, "Irish in America," *Encyclopedia of the Irish*, ed. Glazier, 461. Numbers of Irish-born living in Vermont, U.S. Census, Manuscript Schedule, *Ninth Census*, 1870.

3. Michael Austin, "Carving Out a Sense of Place: The Making of the Marble Valley and the Marble City of Vermont" (PhD diss., University of New Hampshire, 2002). "Young Ireland" quote from Aldrich, *Franklin and Grand Isle Counties*, 84. Howrigan family information from U.S. Census, Manuscript Schedule, *Seventh Census*, 1850. By the 1860s over a third of all Irish emigrants were between the ages of twenty and twenty-four. See David Fitzpatrick, "Emigration: 1801–1921," *Encyclopedia of the Irish*, ed. Glazier, 257.

4. The figure of 21,120 was arrived at by a detailed study of the Manuscript Schedule of the U.S. census for eight Vermont towns in 1870. The towns were St. Albans, Rutland, Brattleboro, Vershire, Dorset, Fair Haven, Poultney, and Burlington. Because place of birth was listed, one could ascertain the number of people born in Ireland. Then because the listings appeared in family groups, one could count the children born of at least one Irish parent in the United States or Canada. In the eight towns studied there were 4,474 individuals born in Ireland, and they had a total of 6,642 children born in North America and still living at home. This gave a ratio of just under 1.5 individuals born in North America for every Irish-born person. Even this ratio represents an under-reported figure, because individuals born in North America of Irish parents but not living with those parents would not have been included.

5. *Ninth Census of the United States* (Washington, DC: Government Printing Office, 1872).

6. In the 1870 census Poultney lists 270 Irish-born, and their children amounted to another 358, for a total of 628, or 22.2 percent of the total town population. Those born in Wales amounted to 131, and their children born in U.S. 54, or 4.6 percent. Among the Welsh there were many single men, and this may suggest that they had not been in the U.S. long enough to marry and begin families and thus add to their numbers. For Rutland County figures: The *Ninth Census of the United States* shows that the number of Irish-born living in Rutland County was 3,738. Multiply this by 1.5 for the second generation and one gets 5,607. The two figures together give an estimated total of 9,345 Irish people and their children, or about 23 percent of the total population of Rutland County. In 1870 Rutland town's total population was 9,841, with 1,575 born in Ireland. Multiplying the latter figure by the 1.5 ratio discussed in note 4 results in 2,363 second-generation Irish Americans. The two figures together are 3,938, or 40 percent of the total. By actual count of children of Irish parents in the Manuscript Schedule of the 1870 census, this writer came up with 1,803 individuals. This method produced 3,378 first- and second-generation Irish Americans, or 34.4 percent of Rutland's total population.

7. U.S. Census, Manuscript Schedule, *Ninth Census*, 1870. The census shows 326 Irish-born and 396 born of at least one Irish parent.

8. As late as the 1970s, the "Cork Alley Bar" stood at the corner of West Allen Street and Mallets Bay Avenue in Winooski, although the neighborhood had long since ceased to be inhabited by Irish Americans. Colchester in 1870 had a population of 3,911, including 228 born in Ireland. Using the 1.5 multiplier, there were an estimated 342 first-generation Irish American residents. Total Irish would then be 570, or 14.5 percent. Again, given the underreporting in the census figures, this total was probably closer to 20 percent. Percentage of Burlington residents in 1870 from Irish backgrounds is taken from Walsh, "Dreams Realized?" 38.

9. David A. Wilson, *United Irishmen, United States* (Ithaca, NY: Cornell University Press, 1998), 60.

10. In 1870 Bennington had a population of 5,760. Of that number, 624 were born in Ireland and another 673 were the children of at least one Irish-born parent. U.S. Census, Manuscript Schedule, *Ninth Census*, 1870.

11. *Statistics of the Population of the United States at the Tenth Census, June 1, 1880* (Washington, DC: Government Printing Office, 1883), 849.

12. Hunger for land in Ireland has been documented in Conrad Arensberg's *The Irish Countryman* (Garden City, NY: American Museum Science Books, 1968) and is the central theme in J. B. Keane's play *The Field*.

13. Thomas, Robert, and Harold Howrigan interview, June 20, 2003. Ryan family holdings in Edward A. Daniel, "The Life and Times of Capt. Thomas Kennedy," TS, Vermont Historical Society, Barre.

14. Hiram Carleton, *Genealogical and Family History of the State of Vermont*, 2 vols. (New York: Lewis Publishing Co., 1903), 1:559. Hart's information in Rann and Smith, *Rutland County*, 938, 939.

15. *Burlington Free Press*, March 10, 2003.

16. Ibid., June 25, 1869.

17. Jan Albers, Hands on the Land: *A History of the Vermont Landscape* (Cambridge, MA: MIT Press, 2000), 230.

18. See entry for "Slate Valley and Slate" in *Vermont Encyclopedia*, Duffy, Hand, and Orth, 270. The entry makes no mention of the Irish, only that "immigrants from Wales came in steady numbers to work in the industry." Jan Albers in her *Hands on the Land* also omits any mention of the Irish in the slate quarries but notes "the skilled workers came from Wales."

19. The number of Irish and Welsh includes both immigrants and their American-born children. See U.S. Census, Manuscript Schedule, *Seventh Census*, 1850, *Eighth Census*, 1860, and *Ninth Census*, 1870.

20. Poultney and Castleton figures from *Ninth Census*.

21. *Rutland Herald*, July 21, 1854.

22. Icy slate slag incident in Albers, *Hands on the Land*, 232. General information on slate work from Paul R. Hancock, "The Labor Movement in the Vermont–New York Slate Industry," *North American Journal of Welsh Studies* 1 (summer 2001): 9193, 228.

23. Albers, *Hands on the Land*, 228.

24. Michael Sherman, Gene Sessions, and P. Jeffrey Potash, eds., *Freedom and Unity: A History of Vermont* (Barre: Vermont Historical Society, 2004), 293; and Leon Fink, *Workingmen's Democracy: The Knights of Labor and American Politics* (Urbana and Chicago: University of Illinois Press, 1985), 72.

25. H. E. Clark, M.D., "Observations on Dr. Pratt's Essay on the Origin of Fever," *Canada Medical and Surgical Journal* 1 (1872–73 July–June): 257–63.

26. Number of Catholics in Rutland town in Patrick C. Hannon, "A History of St. Bridget Parish," TS, Special Collections, Bailey/Howe Library, University of Vermont, 11. Population figure is from U.S. Census, Manuscript Schedule, *Twelfth Census*, 1900. Total population for West Rutland was 2,914. Irish immigrants and their children amounted to 886. Source for "Stonepegger" appellation is Fink, *Workingmen's Democracy*, 73. James Gorman of Burlington told this author on March 13, 2009, that the legendary Burlington High School coach Buck Hard told Gorman's grandfather when he was a schoolboy in the 1920s not to throw a brushback pitch when playing against the West Rutlanders, for they would retaliate by throwing stones at the Burlington team.

27. Hannon, "St. Bridget Parish," 8–12.

28. Joseph E. Doran, ed., *Slate Quarries in West Castleton, Vermont* (N.p., 1998), 7, and Hannon, "St. Bridget Parish," 8–12.

29. Patten interview, October 3, 2007.

30. *Rutland Daily Herald*, March 2, 3, 4, 1880.

31. Hannon, "St. Bridget Parish," 14.

32. Account of five deaths in Hannon, "St. Bridget Parish," 79. Earlier accidents reported in *Rutland Daily Herald*, March 10, 1868, and May 1, 1868.

33. Hannon, "St. Bridget Parish," 4.

34. Ruth Rasey Simpson, *Hand Hewn in Old Vermont* (North Bennington, VT: Poly Two Press, 1979), 195.

35. The Erie Canal figures are for 1870. See U.S. Department of Commerce, Bureau of the Census, *Historical Statistics of the United States, Colonial Times to 1970* (White Plains, NY: Kraus International Publications, 1970), Series D, 718–21.

36. Fink, *Workingmen's Democracy*, 82.

37. Hannon, "St. Bridget Parish," 74.

38. Ibid., 72–73, and *Rutland Daily Herald*, May 26, 1868.

39. Hancock, "Labor Movement," 93, and *Fair Haven Journal*, June 4, 1870.

40. Duffy, Hand, and Orth, *Vermont Encyclopedia*, 308.

41. *Burlington Free Press*, July 9, 1883. Henry's description quoted in Ruth Henry Hubbard, "Pills, Pukes and Poultices and a Doctor's Account of the Ely Copper Riots," *Vermont History* 52 (spring 1984): 77–88.

42. U.S. Census, Manuscript Schedule, *Tenth Census*, 1880. Out of 851 copper miners, 190 were Irish and 116 English/Cornish. Interestingly, in the Allihies copper mining district in West Cork in the nineteenth century, owners often brought in Cornish workers to replace Irish miners, much to the latter's anger.

43. *Burlington Free Press*, June 30, 1883.

44. Among the dozen ringleaders later arrested for promoting the strike were Irishmen Pat Haley, Tom Ford, Jerry McCormick, Fred Thornton, Martin Scully, and John and William McVetey. See Collamer Abbott, *Green Mountain Copper: The Story of Vermont's Red Metal* (Randolph, VT: Herald Printers, 1973), 24.

45. On March 12, 2007, this writer met a woman named Foley who had moved to Vermont from Montana. While doing genealogical research she had been surprised to learn that an ancestor of hers had lived at one time in Vershire. Vermont census figures by town at www.ancestry.com/~vermontgenealogy resources/A-Ltownp. Accessed May 5, 2008. Contemporary accounts of the work stoppage can be found in *Burlington Free Press*, June 30, 1883, July 7, 9, 11, 1883.

46. Hasia Diner, *Erin's Daughters in America: Irish Immigrant Women in the Nineteenth Century* (Baltimore: Johns Hopkins University Press, 1983), 30–31.

47. Mrs. Percival Clement, letter to Charles Clement, September 30, 1886, Clement Family Papers, Rutland (VT) Public Library. Figures for female workers in Rutland town in U.S. Census, Manuscript Schedule, *Ninth Census*, 1870.

48. Diner, *Erin's Daughters*, 90.

49. U.S. Census, Manuscript Schedule, *Ninth Census*, 1870.

50. Albers, *Hands on the Land*, 158. Figures on textile workers in Ludlow and Winooski from U.S. Census, Manuscript Schedule, *Ninth Census*, 1870.

51. Winooski teachers listed in the *Burlington Free Press*, June 11, 1917. Dorset, Underhill, and Fairfield teachers counted in the U.S. Census, Manuscript Schedule, *Twelfth Census*, 1900. Hannon, in "St. Bridget Parish," names the teachers in School No. 7 in 1869, 9. Irish American female teachers as stereotypical civil servants in Timothy Walch, "Parochial Education," in *Encyclopedia of the Irish*, ed. Glazier, 242.

52. Foren and Hassett show up as teachers in the U.S. Census, Manuscript Schedule, *Tenth Census*, 1880. Wages of schoolteachers in Sherman, Sessions, and Potash, *Freedom and Unity*, 318.

53. Mary Anne Duffy Godin, Patrick Duffy, Joann Ryan Duffy, and Reg Godin, interview with the author, July 23, 2007.

54. Hannon, "St. Bridget Parish." On Northfield's opposition to hiring a Catholic teacher see Sessions, "Years of Struggle," 79, 113.

55. Winfield Scott Nay, *The Old Country Doctor* (Rutland, VT: Tuttle Publishing Co., 1937), 44. *Burlington Free Press*, June 25, 1869.

56. Sessions, "Years of Struggle," 84.

57. U.S. Census, Manuscript Schedule, *Ninth Census*, 1870.

58. Walsh, "Dreams Realized?" Appendix B, 126–38.

59. Comments on O'Keefe in Harry Barry et al., *Before Our Time: A Pictorial Memoir of Brattleboro, Vermont, from 1830 to 1930* (Brattleboro: Stephen Greene Press, 1974), 134. Department chiefs around Vermont: Fire Chief William P. Hogan in Bennington; Police Chief John F. Mahoney in St. Albans; Police Chief Jeremiah Donahue in Northfield. In 1896 a court found Patrick McGreevey guilty of possessing five barrels of beer and a jug of whiskey. He was convicted again in 1901 for a similar offense; see *Burlington Free Press*, February 8, 1896, and November 1, 1901. Not much is known about Noble Flanagan. Clearly Flanagan is an Irish name, and there was an Irish family named Noble living in the Bolton/Richmond area east of Burlington in the mid-nineteenth century. As Flanagan was born in Hinesburg, not far from Bolton and Richmond, it is probable that he was of Irish ancestry. However, it is likely that he was Protestant; it is hard to imagine a Catholic holding the positions he did in the 1860s. On percentage of Irish policemen in Burlington in 1890 see Walsh, "Dreams Realized?" 63.

60. *Book of Biographies: Rutland County, Vermont* (Buffalo, NY: Biographical Publishing Co., 1899), 141–42.

61. *Burlington Free Press*, September 12, 1940.

62. Robert B. Michaud, *Salute to Burlington, Vermont* (Montpelier, VT: Capital City Press, 1991), 28, and *Burlington Free Press*, September 12, 1940.

63. *Burlington Free Press*, December 11, 1922.

64. Ibid., September 13–19, 1940. The city of Burlington declined to accept the property Flynn bequeathed it on the grounds it did not have the money to either create another park or to operate an aged-men's home.

65. Figures for Burlington physicians from Elin Anderson, *We Americans: A Study of Cleavage in an American City* (Cambridge, MA: Harvard University Press, 1937), 35. The earliest known number of physicians practicing in the state, and their names, was found in a handwritten booklet titled "Record of Medical Examinations." It begins with the year 1905, when all physicians practicing in the state, or who desired to practice in the state, had to qualify by examination for licensure. Previously no examination had been required, and this was an attempt to certify the qualifications of all physicians, even those who had been practicing medicine for years. This record is kept at the Board of Health, which is a part of the Vermont Department of Health in Burlington. For a listing of medical school graduates from 1860 to 1900 see *The General Catalogue of the University of Vermont and the State Agricultural College* (Burlington: Free Press Association, 1901).

66. Harley and Howrigan, *Letters of the Rowley Family*.

67. *Burlington Free Press*, May 14, 1904.

68. Msgr. John McSweeney, telephone interview with the author, February 1, 2007. Patrick's two brothers who became doctors were Jeremiah and Dennis; the two cousins were Roland "Michael" McSweeney and Jeremiah Sheehan.

69. Quoted in "Dr. John Hanrahan," *The Rutland Historical Society Quarterly* 4, no. 1 (winter 1974): 8.

70. *Book of Biographies*, 334–35.

71. Quoted in Stuart Murray, *Rudyard Kipling in Vermont: Birthplace of the Jungle Books* (Bennington, VT: Images from the Past, 1997), 49.

72. Mary Cabot, *Annals of Brattleboro, 1681–1895*, 2 vols. (Brattleboro, VT: Hildreth and Co., 1922), 2:949. See Murray, *Kipling in Vermont*, 96.

Chapter 6

1. *Burlington Free Press*, August 9, 1902.

2. Hamilton Child, *Gazetteer and Business Directory of Chittenden County, Vermont for 1882–1883* (Syracuse, NY: Printed at the Journal Office, 1882), 191; and Aldrich, *Franklin and Grand Isle Counties*, 763–64.

3. Joan Sheehey Pfeiffer, interview with the author, September 2, 2008.

4. Katherine Ryan, "The Ryan Family," TS in the possession of Margaret Ryan, Fairfield, VT.

5. John Rowley, letter to his parents, December 19, 1867, in Harley and Howrigan, "Letters of the Rowley Family."

6. *Burlington Daily Free Press*, March 18, 1865. Catherine Rogan Michaud's bootlegging activity in Coffin, *Inland See*, 32. On January 20, 1858, the *Burlington Free Press* reported that a Catherine Ragan was fined $2,000 and sentenced to three months' hard labor for violating the liquor law. The name is so close to Mrs. Michaud's maiden name that it is hard to escape the conclusion that this was Stephen Michaud's mother.

7. Bishop de Goesbriand in his diary recorded the names of the priests in the diocese: in 1861 there were five from an Irish background and nine of French or French

Canadian; in 1865 he recorded twenty priests in the diocese, nine with Irish surnames and eleven, including his own, with French; at an 1882 retreat he recorded thirty-six priests present, nineteen with Irish surnames and seventeen with French. See Louis de Goesbriand, *Diary*, Special Collections, Bailey/Howe Library, University of Vermont, 17, 33, 123. Information on O'Sullivan family in Arthur F. Stone, *The Vermont of Today*, 4 vols. (New York: Lewis Historical Publishing Co., 1929), 4:700.

8. David Blow, "The Catholic Parochial Schools of Burlington, 1853–1918," *Vermont History* 54 (summer 1986): 149–63, and Vincent Alden, "Many Burlingtonians Took Pride in Fact They Were Educated Here Under Michael Mulqueen," *Burlington Free Press*, November 11, 1941.

9. Marion Duquette, *The Sisters of Mercy of Vermont: 1872–1991* [Burlington, VT], 1991.

10. U.S. Census, Manuscript Schedule, *Ninth Census*, 1870. That year Brattleboro's population stood at 4,933.

11. John W. Rowell, *Vermont Reports*, Ferriter v. Tyler, vol. 4 (N.p, 1876), 445–77.

12. Mary Cabot, *Annals of Brattleboro, 1681–1895*, 2 vols. (Brattleboro, VT: Hildreth and Co., 1922), 2:649–50.

13. Information on the school conflict in Brattleboro is drawn from Rowell, *Vermont Reports*, 445–77; the St. Michael, Brattleboro, file in the archives of the Diocese of Burlington; and David Blow, "The Brattleboro School Affair," *Vermont Catholic Tribune*, February 16, 1979. Stories of Rev. Lane's physical prowess from Patten interview, October 3, 2007.

14. *Vermont Phoenix*, July 15, 1874.

15. Rowell, *Vermont Reports*, 445–77.

16. Patrick Hannon, "Chronology of Brattleboro School Issue," TS, St. Michael file, Diocese of Burlington Archives, Burlington, VT.

17. *Vermont Phoenix*, December 18, 1874.

18. Veronica Maloney Ryan, interview with the author, January 28, 2004.

19. Basil S. Douros, *Roots of the Blackthorne Tree* (Rancho Murieta, CA: Five and Dot Corp., 2002), 124–26.

20. E. Estyn Evans, *Irish Folk Ways* (London: Routledge & Keegan Paul, 1957), 286.

21. For a discussion of Irish words in American English see Daniel Cassidy, *How the Irish Invented Slang* (Petrolia, CA: CounterPunch, 2007). Bridget Wall smoking her pipe in Neil Bartlett, *From the West Side of Mount Mansfield* (Tucson, AZ: W. N. Bartlett, 2000).

22. Veronica Maloney Ryan recounted story of Bessie Ryan in interview. *Pocha* mentioned in [John McNab Currier], *The Violet Book of Neshobe: being a complete collection of the songs of Jimmy Carney* [Albany, NY: Munsell], 1883, 8, 9. Tim O'Connor, interview with the author, November 10, 2007. Frank Patten's use of Irish from Patten interview, October 3, 2007.

23. Elaine G. Purdy, ed., "The Final Civil War Diary of Charles B. Mead of Company

F, First Vermont Sharpshooters," *Rutland Historical Society Quarterly* 32 (2002): 9.

24. Letter from Thomas Howrigan, March 17, 2007.

25. Patten interview, October 3, 2007.

26. Gerald Heffernan, telephone interview with the author, December 12, 2007.

27. Ryan, "The Ryan Family."

28. *Violet Book of Neshobe.*

29. Edward McLysaght, *Irish Life in the Seventeenth Century,* 2nd ed. (Dublin: Irish Academic Press, 1979), 152. *The Táin: From the Irish Epic Táin Bó Cuailnge,* trans. Thomas Kinsella (Oxford: Oxford University Press, 1969), 82.

30. Emily Flynn, *History of the Town of Underhill* (Underhill, VT: n.p., 1941), 66. In the late 1800s there were two Francis Cahills in Underhill, father and son, but it is not clear which one was the famous strongman. Reference to St. Johnsbury men in *Burlington Free Press*, January 24, 1855.

31. Charles Morrow Wilson, *The Magnificent Scufflers* (Brattleboro, VT: Stephen Greene Press, 1959), 7.

32. John Ennis, "How Kildare Exiles Carried the Game Abroad," *Leinster Leader* (County Kildare, Ireland), March 16, 1907; that early Irish priests brought the sport to the Green Mountains is found in Wilson, *Magnificent Scufflers*, 7–49.

33. Ralph Orson Sturtevant, *Pictorial History, Thirteenth Regiment, Vermont Volunteers, War of 1861–1865* [n.p., 1910], 621.

34. *Burlington Free Press*, November 26, 1878. Account of the 1873 match in the *Burlington Free Press*, June 2, 1873.

35. Wilson, *Magnificent Scufflers*, 40–49.

36. Rev. Philip Branon, interview with the author, January 8, 1993. "Mick" Brennan feats from Thomas Howrigan interview with the author, June 20, 2003.

37. Jerrold Casway, "Baseball: The Early Years," in *Encyclopedia of the Irish*, ed. Glazier, 43–44. On the "Emerald Age" of baseball see Ralph Wilcox, "Irish Americans in Sports: The Nineteenth Century," in *Making the Irish American*, eds. J. J. Lee and Marion Casey (New York: New York University Press, 2006), 447.

38. *Rutland Daily Herald*, April 23, 1868; *Burlington Free Press*, June 2, 1877; and *Rutland Herald*, August 11, 1879.

39. Tom Simon, "Father of the Forkball," *Green Mountain Boys of Summer: Vermonters in the Major Leagues, 1882–1993*, ed. Tom Simon (Shelburne, VT: New England Press, 2000), 109–11.

40. Seamus Kearney and Tom Simon, "Ed Doheny: His Mind Was Thought to be Deranged," in *Green Mountain Boys of Summer*, ed. Simon, 34–36.

41. For a list of Vermont legislators in the nineteenth century see John M. Comstock, ed., *A List of the Principal Officers of Vermont from 1777–1918* (St. Albans, VT: St. Albans Messenger, 1918).

42. For many years McQueeney, a devout Catholic, rang the church bell at St. Patrick to announce the Angelus, Mass, or the death of a parishioner. See Horan's "St. Patrick's Church," 8.

43. Edward A. Daniel, "The Life and Times of Capt. Thomas Kennedy," TS, Vermont Historical Society Library, Barre.

44. Hand, *Star That Set*, 80. Those who served in the Civil War were John Rooney, Woodford; Michael Quinlan, Shelburne; and John Conway, Norton. All three names show up on lists of Civil War veterans from Vermont, but it is possible that these were not the same individuals elected to the Vermont House of Representatives. House membership from Charles W. Porter, secretary of state, *Vermont Legislative Directory: Biennial Session, 1888* (Rutland: Tuttle Co., 1888).

45. The first alderman identified as Irish Catholic was New York–born Edmund O'Neill, elected from the third ward in 1875.

46. Sutherland Falls later became Proctor. Figures from 1887 put Rutland village's population at 10,300, West Rutland's at 4,000, and Proctor's at 1,700. See *Charter and Ordinances of the City of Rutland* (Rutland, VT: Carruthers and Thomas Printers, 1894).

47. Quoted in Kendall Ward, "The Howe Scale Company: Its Time and Its People," *Rutland Historical Society Quarterly* 30, no. 4 (2000): 3–15.

48. *Rutland Weekly Herald*, January 29, 1886. The organizer was J. J. Largan. While nothing is known about him, the fact that he came from Boston and had an Irish name suggests he was of Irish background.

49. Hannon, "St. Bridget Parish," 124.

50. *Rutland Daily Herald*, February 11, 12, 1886.

51. Ibid., February 22, 1886.

52. Patten interview, October 3, 2007.

53. Gillespie's ethnic background appears to have been Irish, but the records are confusing. The 1900 U.S. census says he was born in Ireland, but the 1910 census says he was born in Scotland of an Irish mother and a Scottish-born father. As Gillespie is a name common to both Scotland and the north of Ireland, it is also possible that his father's family were earlier Irish emigrants to Scotland. In any case James Gillespie always identified with Rutland's Irish Catholic community, living in an Irish neighborhood and marrying an Irish American woman. On the Knights' organizing success see Fink, *Workingmen's Democracy*, 72.

54. *Rutland Weekly Herald*, May 25, 1886.

55. Fink, *Workingmen's Democracy*, 80–81.

56. *Rutland Weekly Herald*, September 3, 1886.

57. Ibid., September 9, 1886. Comments about keeping saloons closed in Fink, *Workingmen's Democracy*, 82.

58. *Burlington Free Press*, November 20, 1886.

59. Fink, *Workingmen's Democracy*, 83–84.

60. For example, in 1900, of the eleven city aldermen, five came from Irish Catholic backgrounds: James Creed, Ward One; Michael Gilrain, Ward Two; Thomas E. Toohey, Ward Three; Hugh Duffy, Ward Seven; and Frank Mangan, Ward Eight. John D. Spellman was mayor.

Chapter 7

1. Henry A. Bailey, "The Administration of the Village of Winooski" (master's diss., University of Vermont, 1915).

2. Reg Godin, interview with the author, July 23, 2007.

3. Quoted in Anderson, *We Americans*, 212.

4. Quoted in Sherman, Sessions, and Potash, *Freedom and Unity*, 351.

5. According to family genealogist James Burke, James Edmund Burke was born in Ellensburg, Clinton County, New York. See James Burke, *The Ancestors of James Bourke, Co. Clare and Anne O'Neill, Co. Limerick, Ireland* (Syracuse, NY: n.p., 2007).

6. *Burlington Free Press*, November 23, 1880.

7. Greg Guma, *Burlington's Progressive Past: The Age of Burke* (Burlington, VT: Maverick Media, 1984), n.p.

8. *Burlington Daily News*, April 24, 1943.

9. *Burlington Free Press*, February 12, 1904. Shea's political power, ibid., February 16, 1903. Fire company service, ibid., November 24, 1880.

10. Sherman, Sessions, and Potash, *Freedom and Unity*, 329.

11. Diary of James Sheehey, in the possession of Joann Sheehey Pfeiffer, Marshfield, VT.

12. Rowland E. Robinson, *Vermont: A Study of Independence* (Rutland, VT: Charles E. Tuttle Co., 1975), 323.

13. *Burlington Clipper*, February 21, 1903. Burke was a friend to the city's Jewish community. When the state formally chartered the Hebrew Democratic Club of Burlington in 1904, Mayor Burke was the keynote speaker at its celebration. See the *Burlington Free Press*, March 7, 1904.

14. Burke served as mayor 1903–7, 1909–11, 1913–15, and 1933–35; John J. Burns served 1939–48; and John Edward Moran held the office 1948–57. On Burke's demand for recount see *Burlington Free Press*, March 4, 1903.

15. *Burlington Daily News*, April 26, 1943. Burke's accomplishments, ibid., April 24, 1943.

16. *Burlington Free Press*, December 22, 1933. Burke's reprimand to Freemasons in Guma, *Burlington's Progressive Past*.

17. *Burlington Daily News*, April 26, 1943. Representing the various ethnic communities at Burke's funeral were Rabbi Herman, George Agel, and Alex Colodny, Jewish; Frank Merola, Italian; Alfred Heininger, German; and Mayor John Burns, Patrick Mahoney, and Bernard Leddy, Irish.

18. *History of St. Sylvester Church, Graniteville, Vermont, 1895–1995* (Graniteville, VT: Perez, Lithography, 1996), 32.

19. WPA interview with an Irish American granite worker in Barre in the late 1930s. Script of interview at Vermonthistory.org/freedom_and_unity/create_image/unrest, February 19, 2009.

20. Quoted in Coffin, *Inland See*, 116.

21. J. William O'Brien, interview with the author, January 29, 2001, and Robert O'Brien, interview with the author, December 16, 1998.

22. Rev. John Ledoux, interview with the author, December 12, 1996.

23. Coffin, *Inland See*, 30–33. Michaud's comment on "Irish Affair," ibid., 31.

24. Ledoux interview. On language loss, see Coffin, *Inland See*, 45.

25. Gerald J. Brault, *The French-Canadian Heritage of New England* (Hanover, NH: University Press of New England, 1986), 88. On Portland, Maine, see James M. O'Toole, *Militant and Triumphant: William Henry O'Connell and the Catholic Church in Boston, 1859–1944* (Notre Dame, IN: University of Notre Dame Press, 1992), 37. On Irish and French Canadian priests in Massachusetts, Branon interview, January 11, 1993.

26. Coffin, *Inland See*, 46.

27. Rev. Napoleon Dorion, letter to Cardinal R. Merry del Val, January 8, 1909, Archives, Roman Catholic Diocese, Burlington, VT.

28. Comments of Sister Catherine, TS, St. Mary's File, Archives of the Roman Catholic Diocese, Burlington, VT. Comment on his eloquence from John M. Lynch, "Father Dan," TS, St. Mary's File, Archives of the Roman Catholic Diocese, Burlington, VT. His homilies in French, ibid.

29. Coffin, *Inland See*, 48. A miter in his trunk, David Blow, interview with the author, November 5, 1996.

30. Draft of Bishop Michaud's evaluation is in the Archives of the Roman Catholic Diocese, Burlington, VT. Sister St. Sabine, letter to Bishop Michaud, March 16, 1900, St. Mary's File, Archives of the Roman Catholic Diocese, Burlington.

31. Ledoux interview, December 12, 1996. Rev. Thomas McMahon's comments on Rice visit in letter to Msgr. Bernard Flanagan, July 29, 1948, St. Patrick's File, Archives of the Roman Catholic Diocese, Burlington, VT.

32. Branon interview, January 11, 1993.

33. Coffin, *Inland See*, 66.

34. Sister Miriam Ward, RSM, telephone conversation with the author, February 24, 2007.

35. Sherman, Sessions, and Potash, *Freedom and Unity*, 408. Decrease in Vermont's population, ibid., 433. Number of Vermonters living out of state, Hand, *Star That Set*, 34.

36. Bertha B. Hanson, *Bertha's Book: A View of Starksboro's History—1917–1994* (Starksboro, VT: Starksboro Village Meeting House Society, 1998), 35. William Conway, from interview with Gerald Heffernan, July 15, 2003, TS, in possession of the Starksboro Historical Society. Also, Gerald Heffernan, interview with the author, December 12, 2007. Also on Starksboro, Edward and Hanna Hannan, "A History of St. Ambrose Parish," TS, in possession of the author.

37. Nay, *Old Country Doctor*, 45.

38. Tim Collins, "The Collins Family—175 Years," TS, in possession of the author.

39. Eleanor Wheeler Ballway, ed., *Fairfield, VT: Reminiscences* (Essex, VT: Essex

Publishing Co., 1977), 40.

40. Don Connor, whose family has been in Fairfield for generations, said he thought Shenang might mean a rough, rocky hill, but was unsure of this. Don Connor, interview with the author, June 20, 2003.

41. Robert H. Ferrell, *Harry S. Truman: A Life* (Columbia: Missouri University Press, 1996), 188. Comment on friendship with FDR quoted in Sherman, Sessions, and Potash, *Freedom and Unity*, 475.

42. Consuelo Northrop Bailey, *Leaves Before the Wind* (Burlington, VT: George Little Press, 1976), 94, 95.

43. O'Connor interview.

44. Maudean Neill, *Fiery Crosses in the Green Mountains: The Story of the Ku Klux Klan in Vermont* (Randolph Center, VT: Greenhill Books, 1989), 12–89.

45. *Burlington Free Press*, May 14, 2007. On bank bias against Catholics, Patrick Robins, interview with the author, March 8, 2009. "Red flag to a bull" quote in Anderson, *We Americans*, 25.

46. Anderson, *We Americans*, 18–19. Shea's claim reported in *Burlington Free Press*, March 18, 1904. Brian Walsh, in his study of Burlington's Irish community, estimated that approximately 20 percent were Irish; see Walsh, "Dreams Realized?" 77.

47. Other investors in the Champlain Trust Company included Burlington merchant Michael Devitt McMahon and Winooski lawyer and politician Henry Conlin. McMahon was the china shop owner married to the former Martha Lonergan, niece of Civil War hero John Lonergan. Mention of Moran working for Thomas Wright in Robert B. Michaud, *Salute to Burlington, Vermont* (Montpelier, VT: Capital City Press, 1991), 101–4. Spheres of influence controlled by different ethnic groups in Burlington from the Robins interview.

48. Vincent Feeney, *The Great Falls on Onion River: A History of Winooski, Vermont* (Winooski, VT: Winooski Historical Society, 2002), 141.

49. Stone, *Vermont of Today*, 3:284.

50. Patrick Mahoney (grandson), interview with the author, September 23, 2008.

51. Information on Magner's background from Stone, *Vermont of Today*, 3:257. The other two Irish Catholics elected to the Vermont Senate at this time were Patrick J. Farrell of Swanton and Maurice Walsh of St. Albans.

52. For further information on Burlington's Catholic schools see David Blow, *Historic Guide to Burlington Neighborhoods*, vol. 2 (Burlington, VT: Chittenden County Historical Society, 1997), 65–66.

53. Anderson noted that among first- and second-generation Irish Americans there was little intermarriage outside one's ethnic group, although this shifted significantly with the third generation. Anderson, *We Americans*, 189. On Catholic attitudes against the YMCA , YWCA, and the Boy Scouts, see Michaud, *Salute to Burlington*, 84.

54. For a discussion of the long history of hostility between the Catholic Church and the Masonic Order see Jasper Ridley, *The Freemasons: A History of the World's Most Powerful Secret Society* (New York: Arcade Publishing, 2001).

55. *Burlington Free Press*, February 1, 1904; September 15, 1904; August 26, 1908.

56. In the 1990s there was an effort in the Rutland area to reestablish the AOH in Vermont, but it lasted for only a few years. For Vermonters involved with the Irish White Cross see W. J. Williams, *Report of the Irish White Cross to 31st August, 1922* (Dublin: Martin Lester, 1922), 17–21. Quote about apathy in Vermont toward the AOH during World War I from Anderson, *We Americans*, 158.

57. Quoted in Anderson, *We Americans*, 157. McSweeney interview, on attitude toward celebrating Irishness.

Bibliography

Interviews and Correspondence

Ansley, Anne
Arkinson, Jimmy
Blow, David
Branon, Rev. Philip
Collins, Mary
Costello, Paul
Costello, Thomas
Duffy, Joann Ryan
Duffy, John
Duffy, Patrick
Fitzgerald, John "Dick"
Godin, Mary Anne Duffy
Godin, Reg
Goss, Evelyn
Heffernan, Gerald
Howrigan, Anne Rowley
Howrigan, Harold
Howrigan, Robert
Howrigan, Thomas
Leddy, John
Ledoux, Rev. John
Mahoney, Patrick
McSweeney, Rt. Rev. Msgr. John
O'Brien, J. William
O'Brien, Robert
O'Connor, Timothy
Patten, Peter
Pfeiffer, Joann Sheehey
Robins, Patrick
Ryan, Margaret
Ryan, Veronica
Ward, Sister Miriam, RSM

Primary Sources

Ainsworth, Fred C., and Joseph W. Kirkley, eds. *The War of the Rebellion: A Compilation of the Official Records of the Union and Confederate Armies.* Series 3, vol. 3. Washington, DC: Government Printing Office, 1899.

Allen Family Papers. Special Collections, Bailey/Howe Library, University of Vermont.

Bailey, Consuelo Northrop. *Leaves Before the Wind.* Burlington, VT: George Little Press, 1976.

Bailey, Henry A. "The Administration of the Village of Winooski." Master's diss., University of Vermont, 1915.

Cable, Dorothy F. *Three Summers with Pop.* New York: Pyramid Press, 1939.

Charter and Ordinances of the City of Rutland. Rutland, VT: Carruthers and Thomas Printers, 1894.

Committee of the Associated Alumni. University of Vermont Obituary Record. No. 1. Burlington, VT, 1895.

Comstock, John, ed. *Deming's Vermont Officers and Gazetteer.* St. Albans, VT: St. Albans Messenger Co., 1918.

[Currier, John McNab], *The Violet Book of Neshobe: being a complete collection of the songs of Jimmy Carney.* [Albany, NY: Munsell], 1883.

Duffy, John J., ed. *Ethan Allen and His Kin: Correspondence, 1772–1819.* 2 vols. Hanover, NH, and London: University Press of New England, 1998.

Fisher, Dorothy Canfield. *Vermont Tradition: The Biography of an Outlook on Life.* Boston: Little, Brown, 1953.

Fitton, Rev. James. *Sketches of the Establishment of the Church in New England.* Boston: Patrick Donahoe, 1872.

General Catalogue of the University of Vermont and State Agricultural College. Burlington: Free Press Association, 1901.

Goesbriand, Louis de. Diary. Copy of MS. Special Collections, Bailey/Howe Library, University of Vermont.

Graffagnino, Kevin, Samuel B. Hand, and Gene Sessions, eds. *Vermont Voices, 1609 through the 1990s.* Montpelier: Vermont Historical Society, 1999.

Harley, Joan Rowley, and Anne Rowley Howrigan, eds. *Collection of Letters of the Rowley Family, 1867–1956.* St. Albans, VT: L. G. Printing, 2004.

[Hawthorne, Nathaniel]. "The Inland Port." *New England Magazine* 9 (December 1835): 398–409.

Hopkins, John Henry. *The Church of Rome in her Primitive State, Compared with the Church of Rome at the Present Day: Being a Candid Examination of Her Claims to Universal Dominion.* Burlington, VT: Vernon Harrington, 1837.

Lathrop, Gideon. "The Diary of Gideon Lathrop, 1823–1839." TS. Vermont Historical Society, Barre.

Metropolitan Catholic Almanac, and Laity's Directory for 1839. Baltimore: Fielding Lucas Jr., 1839.

Michaud, Rev. John S. "The Diocese of Burlington." *History of the Catholic Church in the New England States*. Edited by William Byrne. Boston, 1899.

Michaud, Robert B. *Salute to Burlington, Vermont*. Lyndonville, VT: Lyndon State College, 1991.

Nay, W. Scott. *The Old Country Doctor*. Rutland, VT: Tuttle Co., 1937.

Nicholson, Asenath Hatch. *Annals of the Famine in Ireland*. Edited by Maureen Murphy. Dublin: Lilliput Press, 1998.

Ninth Census of the United States. Washington, DC: Government Printing Office, 1872.

O'Callaghan, Jeremiah. *Creation and offspring of the Protestant church: also the vagaries and heresies of John Henry Hopkins, protestant bishop. . . .* Burlington, VT: Printed for the author, 1837.

———. *Usury, Funds and Banking Monopoly, Forestallings, Traffick*. 5th ed. New York and Burlington, VT: Graves Anatomy, 1856.

———. *Usury, Funds and Banks; also Forestalling Traffick and Monopoly; likewise pew rent and grave tax, together with Burking and Dissecting: as well as the Gallican Liberties. . . .* Burlington, VT: Printed by the author, 1834.

———. *Usury: Or Lending at Interest*. 3rd ed., London, 1828.

Porter, Charles W., Secretary of State. *Vermont Legislative Directory: Biennial Session, 1888*. Rutland, VT: Tuttle Co., 1888.

Purdy, Elaine G., ed. "The Final Civil War Diary of Charles B. Mead of Company F, First U.S. Sharpshooters." *Rutland Historical Society Quarterly* 32 (2002): 3–27.

Robinson Family Letters. Sheldon Museum, Middlebury, VT.

Robinson, Rowland E. *Vermont: A Study of Independence*. Rutland, VT: Charles E. Tuttle Co., 1975.

Rowell, John W. *Vermont Reports*. Vol. IV. N.p., 1876.

Ryan, Katherine. "The Ryan Family." TS. In the possession of Margaret Ryan, Fairfield, VT.

Scott, Kenneth. *British Aliens in the United States during the War of 1812*. Baltimore: Genealogical Publishing Co., 1979.

Sheehey, James. Diary, 1880–1899. In the possession of Joann Sheehey Pfeiffer, Marshfield, VT.

Sheldon MSS. Sheldon Museum. Middlebury, VT.

Statistics of the Population of the United States at the Tenth Census, June 1, 1880. Washington, DC: Government Printing Office, 1883.

Stone, Thelma, interviewed by Underhill students, 1990. TS. In the possession of the author.

Town of Bethel. *Town Meeting Records*. Bethel, VT.

Town of Fairfield. *Land Records*. Fairfield, VT.

———. *Town Meeting Records*. Fairfield, VT.

Vermont Board of Health. Record of Medical Examinations, 1905. MS. Vermont Department of Health, Burlington.

Viele, Theresa. *Following the Drum: A Glimpse of Frontier Life*. N.p., 1858.

Bibliography

Walton's Vermont Register and Farmer's Almanac for 1842. Montpelier, VT: E. P. Walton and Sons, [1842].

Walton's Vermont Register and Farmer's Almanac for 1845. Montpelier, VT: E. P. Walton and Sons, [1845].

Walton's Vermont Register and Farmer's Almanac for 1849. Montpelier, VT: E. P. Walton and Sons, [1849].

White, William. William White Letters, Misc. File 0249. Vermont Historical Society, Barre.

Whyte, Robert. *1847 Famine Ship Diary*. Ed. James J. Mangan. Cork, Ireland: Mercier Press, 1994.

Wickman, Donald H., ed. *Letters to Vermont: From Her Civil War Correspondents to the Home Press*. Vol 1. Bennington, VT: Images from the Past, 1998.

Willey, C. H. "Some Historical Facts about the O'Hara Family." TS. O'Hara Family Papers. Vermont Historical Society, Barre.

Williams, W. J. *Report of the Irish White Cross to 31st August, 1922*. Dublin: Martin Lester, 1922.

Books

Abbott, Collamer. *Green Mountain Copper: The Story of Vermont's Red Metal*. Randolph, VT: Herald Printers, 1973.

Adams, Andrew N. *A History of the Town of Fair Haven, Vermont*. Fair Haven: Leonard and Phelps Printers, 1870.

Akenson, Donald Harman. *Being Had: Historians, Evidence, and the Irish in North America*. Port Credit, Ontario: P. D. Meany Co., 1985.

———. *The Irish Diaspora: A Primer*. Toronto: P. D. Meany Co., 1996.

Albers, Jan. *Hands on the Land: A History of the Vermont Landscape*. Cambridge, MA: MIT Press, 2000.

Aldrich, Lewis Cass, ed. *The History of Franklin and Grand Isle Counties, Vermont: With Illustrations and biographical sketches of some of the prominent men and pioneers*. Syracuse, NY: D. Mason and Co., 1891.

Aldrich, Lewis Cass, and Frank R. Holmes, eds. *The History of Windsor County, Vermont*. Syracuse, NY: D. Mason and Co., 1891.

Anderson, Elin. *We Americans: A Study of Cleavage in an American City*. Cambridge, MA: Harvard University Press, 1937.

Arensberg, Conrad. *The Irish Countryman*. Garden City, NY: American Museum Science Books, 1968.

Ashton, Dorothy Hemenway. *Sheldon, Vermont*. St. Albans, VT: Regal Art Press, 1979.

Austin, Aleine. *Matthew Lyon: "New Man" of the Democratic Revolution, 1749–1822*. University Park: Pennsylvania State University Press, 1981.

Ballway, Eleanor W., ed. *A Genealogical Study of Some Families Who Came to Fletcher,*

Vermont before 1850, and of a Few of Their Descendants. Burlington, VT: Vantage Press, 1981.

————, ed. *Fairfield, Vermont, Reminiscences.* Essex, VT: Essex Publishing Co., 1977.

Barry, Harold, et al. *Before Our Time: A Pictorial Memoir of Brattleboro, Vermont, from 1830–1930.* Brattleboro, VT: Stephen Greene Press, [1974].

Bartlett, Neil. *From the West Side of Mount Mansfield.* Tucson, AZ: Printed by Alpha-graphics, 2000.

Bassett, T. D. Seymour. *The Gods of the Hills: Piety and Society in Nineteenth-Century Vermont.* Montpelier: Vermont Historical Society, 2000.

Benedict, G. G. *Vermont in the Civil War: A History of the Part Taken by the Vermont Soldiers and Sailors in the War for the Union, 1861–1865.* 2 vols. Burlington, VT: Free Press Association, 1888.

Bicentennial Committee. *Fairfax, Vermont: Its Creation and Development.* N.p., [1976].

Book of Biographies: Rutland County, Vermont. Buffalo, NY: Biographical Publishing Co., 1899.

Bowen, Clarence Winthrop. *History of Woodstock, Connecticut.* Norwood, MA: Plimpton Press, 1926.

Brault, Gerald J. *The French Canadian History of New England.* Hanover, NH: University Press of New England, 1986.

Burdett, Claire, and Sylvia Sullivan, eds. *Castleton Looking Back: The First 100 Years.* Castleton, VT: Castleton Historical Society, 1998.

Burke, James. *The Ancestors of James Bourke, Co. Clare, and Anne O'Neill, Co. Limerick, Ireland.* Syracuse, NY, 2007.

Byrne, William, ed. *History of the Catholic Church in the New England States.* Boston: Hurd and Everts, 1899.

Cabot, Mary. *Annals of Brattleboro, 1681–1895.* 2 vols. Brattleboro, VT: Hildreth and Co., 1922.

Carleton, Hiram. *Genealogical and Family History of the State of Vermont.* New York: Lewis Publishing Co., 1903.

Cassidy, Daniel. *How the Irish Invented Slang.* Petrolia, CA: CounterPunch, 2007.

Child, Hamilton. *Gazetteer and Business Directory of Chittenden County, Vermont for 1882–1883.* Syracuse, NY: Printed at the Journal Office, 1882.

Coffin, Howard. *An Inland See: A Brief History of the Roman Catholic Diocese of Burlington.* Barre, VT: Roman Catholic Diocese of Burlington, 2001.

Coleman, Terry. *Passage to America.* Harmondsworth, UK: Penguin Books, 1974.

Cox, Fred G. *The Illustrated Historical Souvenier of Bethel, Vt.* Bethel, VT, 1895.

Crockett, Walter Hill. *Vermont: The Green Mountain State.* 5 vols. New York: Century History Co., 1921. Vol. 5 was published in 1923.

Cudworth, Addison Edward. *The History of Londonderry with Genealogical Sketches.* Montpelier: Vermont Historical Society, 1936.

Cushing, Irene, ed. *Bethel: The Early Years.* Bethel, VT: Bethel Historical Society, 1974.

Davidson, James A., et al., eds. *Rutland in Retrospect.* Rutland, VT: Rutland Historical

Society and Academy Books, 1978.

Diner, Hasia R. *Erin's Daughters in America: Irish Immigrant Women in the Nineteenth Century*. Baltimore: Johns Hopkins University Press, 1983.

Doran, Joseph M., ed. *Slate Quarries in West Castleton, Vermont*. N.p., 1998.

Douros, Basil. *Roots of the Blackthorn Tree*. Rancho Murieta, CA: Five and Dot Corp., 2002.

Duclose, Katharine F. *The History of Braintree, Vermont*. Montpelier, VT: Capital City Press, 1976.

Duffy, John J., Samuel B. Hand, and Ralph H. Orth, eds. *The Vermont Encyclopedia*. Hanover, NH: University Press of New England, 2003.

Dunn, Mary Lee. *Ballykilcline Rising: From Famine Ireland to Immigrant America*. Amherst: University of Massachusetts Press, 2008.

Duquette, Marion. *The Sisters of Mercy of Vermont: 1872–1991*. Burlington, VT, 1991.

Dwyer, Loraine. *The History of Underhill, Vermont*. Underhill, VT: Underhill Historical Society, 1976.

Eisenschiml, Otto, ed. *Vermont General: The Unusual War Experiences of Edward Hastings Ripley, 1862–1865*. New York: Devin Adair, 1960.

Evans, E. Estyn. *Irish Folkways*. London: Routledge and Kegan Paul, 1957.

Fanning, Charles, ed. *New Perspectives on the Irish Diaspora*. Carbondale: Southern Illinois University Press, 2000.

Feeney, Vincent E. *The Great Falls on Onion River: A History of Winooski, Vermont*. Winooski, VT: Winooski Historical Society, 2002.

Ferrell, Robert H. *Harry S. Truman: A Life*. Columbia: University of Missouri Press, 1996.

Fink, Leon. *Workingmen's Democracy: The Knights of Labor and American Politics*. Urbana: University of Illinois Press, 1983.

Fisher, Carleton E., and Sue Gray Fisher, eds. *Soldiers, Sailors, and Patriots of the Revolutionary War*. Camden, ME: Pictou Press, 1992.

Flynn, Emily. *History of the Town of Underhill*. Underhill, VT, 1941.

Gale, David C. *Proctor: The Story of a Marble Town*. Brattleboro: Vermont Printing Co., 1922.

Guma, Greg. *Burlington's Progressive Past: The Age of Burke*. Burlington, VT: Maverick Media, 1984.

Hance, Dawn D. *The History of Rutland, Vermont, 1761–1861*. Rutland, VT: Academy Books, 1991.

Hand, Samuel B. *The Star That Set: The Vermont Republican Party, 1854–1974*. Lanham, MD: Lexington Books, 2002.

Hansen, Bertha B. *Bertha's Book: A View of Starksboro's History*. Starksboro, VT: Village Meeting House Society, 1998.

Harding, Marie, and Charlotte Tracy. *The History of Shelburne*. Burlington, VT: Queen City Printers, 1989.

Harlow, Lance W. *Vermont's First Catholic Bishop: The Life of Bishop Louis De Goesbriand, 1816–1899*. Barre, VT: Lance W. Harlow, 2001.

Hayes, Lyman Simpson. *History of the Town of Rockingham, Vermont*. Bellows Falls, VT: Published by the town, 1907.

Hemenway, A. M., ed. *Vermont Historical Gazetteer*. 5 vols. Burlington, VT: Miss A. M. Hemenway, 1868.

Hill, Ralph Nading. *Lake Champlain: Key to Liberty*. Woodstock, VT: Countryman Press, 1987.

Historical Rutland. Rutland, VT: Phillip H. Brehmer, 1911.

History of St. Sylvester Church, Graniteville, Vermont, 1895–1995. Graniteville, VT: Perez, Lithography, 1996.

Hopkins, John Henry Jr. *The Life of the Late Right Reverend John Henry Hopkins, First Bishop of Vermont*. New York: F. J. Huntington and Co., 1873.

Jackson, Kathryn. *The Milton Story: 1763–1963*. Essex Junction, VT: Printed by the Essex Publishing Co., 1963.

Jenkins, Brian. *Fenians and Anglo-American Relations during Reconstruction*. Ithaca, NY: Cornell University Press, 1969.

Johnston, Henry P., ed. *The Record of Connecticut Men in the Military and Naval Service during the War of the Revolution, 1775–1783*. Hartford, CT, 1889.

Joslin, et al. *A History of the Town of Poultney, Vermont*. Poultney, VT: Journal Printing Office, 1875.

Kinsella, Thomas, trans. *The Táin: From the Irish Epic Táin Bó Cuailnge*. London: Oxford University Press, 1969.

Ledoux, Rodney R., ed. *The History of Swanton, Vermont*. Swanton, VT: Swanton Historical Society, 1988.

Lovejoy, Evelyn M. Wood. *History of Royalton, Vermont, with Family Genealogies, 1769–1911*. Burlington, VT: Free Press Printing Co., 1911.

MacDonald, Capt. John A. *Troublous Times in Canada: A History of the Fenian Raids of 1866 and 1870*. Toronto: W. S. Johnston and Co., 1910.

MacLysaght, Edward. *Irish Life in the Seventeenth Century*. 2nd ed. Dublin: Irish Academic Press, 1950.

Macy, Harry, ed. *Underhill Genealogy*. Baltimore: Gateway Press for the Underhill Society of America, n.d.

Marshall, Jeffrey D., ed. *A War of the People: Vermont Civil War Letters*. Hanover: New Hampshire University Press of New England, 1999.

McCormack, John William. *Recollections of a Vermont Boyhood, 1887–1909*. Bethel, VT: Bethel Historical Society, 1984.

McLaughlin, James. *Matthew Lyon: The Hampden of Congress*. New York: Wynkoop, Hallenbeck, Crawford Co., 1900.

McPherson, James M. *Battle Cry of Freedom*. New York: Oxford University Press, 1988.

Meeks, Harold. *Time and Change in Vermont: A Human Geography*. Chester, CT: Globe Pequot Press, 1986.

Miller, Kerby. *Emigrants and Exiles: Ireland and the Irish Exodus to North America*. New York: Oxford University Press, 1988.

Murray, Stuart. *Rudyard Kipling in Vermont: Birthplace of the Jungle Books*. Bennington, VT: Images from the Past, 1997.

Nash, Hope. *Royalton, Vermont*. Royalton, VT: Town of Royalton, 1975.

Neidhardt, W. S. *Fenianism in North America*. University Park: Pennsylvania State University Press, 1975.

O'Brien, Michael J. *Pioneer Irish in New England*. 1937. Baltimore: Genealogical Publishing Co., 1998.

O'Toole, James M. *Militant and Triumphant: William Henry O'Connell and the Catholic Church in Boston, 1859–1944*. Notre Dame, IN: University of Notre Dame Press, 1992.

Parker, Edward Lutwyche. *The History of Londonderry (N.H.)*. Boston: Perkins and Whipple, 1851.

Rann, W. S., and H. P. Smith, eds. *History of Rutland County, Vermont*. Syracuse, NY: D. Mason and Co., 1886.

Roberts, Gwilym R. *New Lives in the Valley: Slate Quarries and Quarry Villages in North Wales, New York, and Vermont, 1850–1920*. Somersworth, NH: New Hampshire Printers, 1998.

Richardson, Frederick W. *Nineteenth Century Springfield*. Springfield, VT: Springfield Printing Corp., 2000.

Richmond, George, et al. *Biographical Sketches of Leading Citizens of Rutland County, Vermont*. Buffalo, NY: Biographical Publishing Co., 1899.

Rutland Town: *A Collection of Stories Spanning Over 200 Years of Town History*. Rutland, VT: Historical Society of Rutland Town, 1991.

Senior, Hereward. *The Fenians and Canada*. Toronto: Macmillan Co., 1978.

Shaughnessy, Jim. *The Rutland Road*. Berkeley, CA: Howell-North Books, 1978.

Shea, John G. *History of the Catholic Church in the United States*. 4 vols. New York: J. G. Shea, 1886–92.

Sherman, Michael, Gene Sessions, and P. Jeffrey Potash. *Freedom and Unity: A History of Vermont*. Barre: Vermont Historical Society, 2004.

Simon, Tom, ed. *Green Mountain Boys of Summer: Vermonters in the Major Leagues, 1882–1993*. Shelburne, VT: New England Press, 2000.

Simpson, Ruth Rasey. *Hand Hewn in Old Vermont*. North Bennington, VT: Poly Two Press, 1979.

Sowles, Edward Adams. *History of Fenianism and Fenian Raids in Vermont*. Rutland, VT: Tuttle and Co., 1880.

Stone, Arthur F. *The Vermont of Today*. 4 vols. New York: Lewis Historical Publishing Co., 1929.

Stratton, Allen L. *History of the Town of Alburgh, Vermont*. North Hero, VT: A. L. Stratton, 1986–2000.

Sturtevant, Ralph Orson. *Pictorial History, Thirteenth Regiment, Vermont Volunteers, War of 1861–1865*. [N.p., 1910].

Swift, Samuel. *History of the Town of Middlebury in the County of Addison, Vermont*. Rutland, VT: C. E. Tuttle Co., [1971].

Ullery, Jacob G. *Men of Vermont*. Brattleboro, VT: Transcript Publishing Co.,1894. Part II, 265.

Walker, Mabel Gregory. *The Fenian Movement*. Colorado Springs, CO: Ralph Myles Publisher, 1969.

Watson, Winslow C. *Pioneer History of the Champlain Valley*. Albany, NY: J. Munsell, 1863.

Wells, Elsie C. Bakersfield, *Vermont: The Way It Was, the Way It Is*. Canaan, NH: Phoenix Publishing Co., 1976.

West, Robert Edward, ed. *Rutland in Retrospect*. Rutland, VT: Rutland Historical Society and Academy Books, 1978.

Willey, George F. *The History of Londonderry*. Vol. 2, ed. by Jessie I. Bickley and Melvin E. Watts. Londonderry, NH: Town of Londonderry, 1976. Reprint from 1895 original.

Wilson, Charles Morrow. *The Magnificent Scufflers: Revealing the Great Days When America Wrestled the World*. Brattleboro, VT: Stephen Greene Press, 1959.

Woodham-Smith, Cecil. *The Great Hunger: Ireland, 1845–1849*. New York: Harper and Row, 1962.

Wright, Mrs. F. C. *History of Milton, Vermont*. Special Collections, Bailey/Howe Library, University of Vermont, 1941.

Articles

Alden, Vincent. "Many Burlingtonians Took Pride in the Fact They Were Educated Under Michael Mulqueen." *Burlington Free Press*, November 11, 1941.

American Council of Learned Societies. "Annual Report of the American Historical Association for the Year 1931." *Proceedings* 1 (1931): 107–452.

Bassett, T. D. Seymour. "500 Miles of Trouble and Excitement: Vermont Railroads, 1848–1861." *Vermont History* 49 (summer 1981): 133–54.

———. "Irish Migration to Vermont before the Famine." *Chittenden County Historical Society Bulletin* 4 (March 17, 1966): no pagination.

———. "The Leading Villages in Vermont in 1840." *Vermont History* 26 (July 1958): 161–86.

Beattie, Betsy. "Opportunity across the Border: The Burlington Area Economy and the French Canadian Worker in 1850." *Vermont History* 55 (summer 1987): 133–52.

Blessing, Patrick. "Irish in America." The Encyclopedia of the Irish in America. Edited by Michael Glazier. Notre Dame, IN: Notre Dame University Press, 1999: 453–70.

Blow, David. "The Brattleboro School Affair." *Vermont Catholic Tribune*, February 16, 1979.

———. "A Cathedral for Burlington." *Vermont History* 36 (summer 1968): 109–25.

———. "The Catholic Parochial Schools of Burlington, 1853–1918." *Vermont History* 54 (summer 1986): 149–63.

Calkin, Homer. "St. Albans in Reverse: The Fenian Raid of 1866." *Vermont History* 35 (January 1967): 19–34.

Carter, Edward C. "Ragged Matt, the Democrat." *Vermont Historical Society Proceedings* (1965): 400–408.

Casway, Jerrold. "Baseball: The Early Years." *The Encyclopedia of the Irish in America.* Edited by Michael Glazier. Notre Dame, IN: Notre Dame University Press, 1999: 42–47.

Clark, H. D. "Observations on Dr. Pratt's Essay on the Origin of Fever." *Canada Medical and Surgical Journal* 1 (1872–73 July–June).

Cooke. "Mrs. Cooke's Civil War Diary for 1863–1864." *Vermont History* 25 (January 1957): 56–65.

Cronin, Sean. "The Fenians and Clan Na Gael." *The Encyclopedia of the Irish in America.* Edited by Michael Glazier. Notre Dame, IN: Notre Dame University Press, 1999: 317–21.

Davis, Allen F. "The Girl He Left Behind: The Letters of Harriet Hutchinson Salisbury." *Vermont History* 33 (January 1965): 274–82.

Delany, Rev. C. C. "The Catholic Church." *Vermont, the Green Mountain State.* vol. 5. Edited by Walter Hill Crockett. New York: Century History Co., 1925: 491–505.

Dijon, Harold. "Goody Glover an Irish Victim of the Witch Craze, Boston, Massachusetts, 1688." *Journal of the American Irish Historical Society* 5 (1905): 16–22.

Dowden, Albert Ricker. "John Gregory Smith." *Vermont History* 32 (April 1964): 79–97.

"Dr. John Hanrahan," *Rutland Historical Society Quarterly* 4, no. 1 (winter 1974): 8.

Duffy, John J., and Eugene A. Coyle. "Crean Brush vs. Ethan Allen: A Winner's Tale." *Vermont History* 70 (summer/fall 2002): 103–10.

Fitzpatrick, David. "Irish Emigration: 1801–1921." *The Encyclopedia of the Irish in America.* Edited by Michael Glazier. Notre Dame, IN: Notre Dame University Press, 1999: 254–62.

Hancock, Paul R. "The Labor Movement in the Vermont–New York Slate Industry." *North American Journal of Welsh Studies* 1 (summer 2001): 87–100.

Hartwell, Frank E. "Bolton in the Mountains." *Vermont History* 23 (October 1955): 303–11.

Hubbard, Ruth Henry. "Pills, Pukes and Poultices and a Doctor's Account of the Ely Copper Riots." Edited by Collamer Abbot. *Vermont History* 52 (spring 1984): 77–88.

Huden, John C. "Beginning of Catholic Schools in Vermont." *Vermont History* 11 (September 1943): 169–73.

Lucey, Rev. William J. "The Diocese of Burlington." *Record of the American Catholic Historical Society of America* 64 (September and December 1953).

Lutz, Paul V. "I Can Almost reach the Oranges, but I have no Charlotte to divide them with." *Vermont History* 34 (October 1966): 246–67.

Moore, Kenneth. "Frederick Holbrook." Vermont History 32 (April 1964): 65–77.

Morrissey, Charles T. "The Case for Oral History." *Vermont History* 31 (July 1963): 145–55.

Murphy, Ronald, and P. Jeffrey Potash. "The 'Highgate Affair': An Episode in Establishing the Authority of the Roman Catholic Diocese of Burlington." *Vermont History* 52 (winter 1984): 33–43.

Neff, Brian T. "Fracas in Congress: The Battle of Honor between Matthew Lyon and Roger Griswold." *Essays in History* 41. Department of History, University of Virginia, 1999.

New York Historical Society. "The Burghers of New Amsterdam and the Freemen of New York, 1675–1866," *Collections of the New York Historical Society 1885*. New York: 1886.

O'Beirne, James. "Some Early Irish in Vermont." *Vermont History* 28 (January 1960): 63–72.

O'Brien, Michael J. "Early Irish Settlers in the Champlain Valley." *Recorder* 4 (1927): 1–4.

———. "Stray Historical Items from the Green Mountain State." *The Journal of the American Irish Historical Society* 55 (1919): 182–86.

O'Connor, Thomas F. "Notes and Documents, II: The Catholic Church in Vermont, a Statistical Survey, 1832–1854." *Proceedings of the Vermont Historical Society* 11 (March 1943).

O'Gallagher, Marianna, and Rose Masson Dompierre. *Eyewitness: Grosse Isle, 1847*. Ste-Foy, Quebec: Lives Carraig Books, 1995.

Purcell, Richard J. "An Irish Crusader for American Democracy." *Studies: An Irish Quarterly Review of Letters, Philosophy, and Science* 25 (March 1936): 47–64.

———. "Vermont Schools and Early Irish Teachers." *Catholic Educational Review* 33 (May 1935): 277–81.

Royle, Stephen A., and Caitríona Ní Laoire. "'Dare the boist'rous main': The role of the Belfast Newsletter in the process of emigration from Ulster to North America, 1760–1800." *The Canadian Geographer* 50 (March 2006): 56–73.

Salussolia, Barry. "The City of Burlington and Municipal Incorporation in Vermont." *Vermont History* 54 (winter 1986): 5–19.

Senior, Elinor K. "The Provincial Cavalry in Lower Canada, 1837–1850." *Canadian Historical Review* 57 (1976).

Sessions, Gene. "Years of Struggle: The Irish in the Village of Northfield, 1845–1900." *Vermont History* 55 (spring 1987): 69–95.

Short, Hugh. "The Irish in Rutland in 1880." *Rutland Historical Society Quarterly* (winter 1984), 3–5.

Soules, Hon. Edward A. "History of Fenianism and Fenian Raids in Vermont." *Proceedings of the Vermont Historical Society* (October 19, 1880): 1–43.

Stillwell, Lewis B. "Migration from Vermont, 1776–1860." *Proceedings of the Vermont Historical Society*, New Series, 5 (June 1937): 63–246.

Walch, Timothy. "Parochial Education." *The Encyclopedia of the Irish in America*. Edited by Michael Glazier. Notre Dame, IN: Notre Dame University Press, 1999.

Ward, Kendall. "The Howe Scale Company: Its Time and Its People." *Rutland Historical*

Society Quarterly 30, no. 4 (2000): 3–15.

Wardenbury, Martha Bigelow. "Will Gilliland, Pioneer of the Valley of Lake Champlain." *Proceedings of the Vermont Historical Society* 9 (September 1941): 186–97.

Wilcox, Ralph. "Irish Americans in Sports: The Nineteenth Century." *Making the Irish American*. Edited by J. J. Lee and Marion Casey. New York: New York University Press, 2006.

Wilson, Rev. Frederick R. "A History of Catholicism in Vermont." *Vermont History* 21 (July 1953): 211–19.

"The Yankee Priest Says Mass in Brattleboro: Joseph Coolidge Shaw Describes His Visit in 1848." *Vermont History* 44 (fall 1976): 198–202.

Unpublished Materials

Cabot, Mary R. "Supplementary Notes to the Annals of Brattleboro." TS. Vermont Historical Society, Barre.

Catherine, Sister Mary. "Comments Concerning Fr. O'Sullivan." St. Mary Parish File, Archives of the Roman Catholic Diocese of Burlington, Burlington, VT.

Collins, Tim. "The Collins Family—175 Years." TS. In the author's possession.

Daniel, Edward A. "The Life and Times of Thomas B. Kennedy." TS. Vermont Historical Society, Barre.

Flynn, Emily A. "A History of the Town of Underhill." TS. Special Collections, Bailey/Howe Library, University of Vermont.

Hannan, Edward, and Hanna Hannan. "A History of St. Ambrose Parish." TS. In the author's possession.

Hannon, Patrick. "A History of St. Bridget Parish." TS. Special Collections, Bailey/Howe Library, University of Vermont.

———. "A Chronology of the Brattleboro School Issue." TS. Archives of the Roman Catholic Diocese of Burlington, Burlington, VT.

Horan, James E. "Saint Patrick's Parish, Fairfield, Vermont." Horan TS. Special Collections, Bailey/Howe Library, University of Vermont.

Howrigan, Joseph. "Chronology of the James A. Howrigan Family History." TS. In the author's possession.

Johnson, Otto T. "History of Proctor, Vermont." 2 vols. TS. Proctoriana Collection, Vermont Historical Society, Barre.

Lathrop, Gideon. "The Diary of Gideon Lathrop, 1823–1839." Lathrop MS. Vermont Historical Society, Barre.

Leach, Chester K. "Dear Wife: The Civil War Letters of Chester K. Leach." Compiled by Edward J. Feidner. Burlington, VT: the Center for Research on Vermont, University of Vermont, 2002.

Lynch, John M. "Father Dan." TS. St. Mary Parish File, Archives of the Roman Catholic Diocese of Burlington, Burlington, VT.

Maloney, Rev. Vincent. "History of St. Teresa Parish, Hyde Park, Vermont, and of Holy

Cross Mission, Morrisville, Vermont." TS. Special Collections, St. Michael's College Library, Colchester, VT.

McElroy, Sister Agnes. "The Interesting Life of John McElroy." TS. In the possession of Margaret Ryan, Fairfield, VT.

Moore, Walter. "Catholic Rutland." Moore MS. St. Michael's College Library, Colchester, VT.

Moriarty, Thomas. "From the Cork Gaeltacht to Holyoke, Massachusetts: The Turbulent Career of Reverend Jeremiah O'Callaghan, 1780–1861." TS. In the author's possession.

Pitkin, Fred E., and Ozias C. Pitkin. "History of Marshfield, Vermont." Pitkin TS. Marshfield Historical Society, Marshfield, VT.

Walsh, Rev. T. J. "Pioneering English [speaking] Catholics in the Eastern Townships: Paper Read at the Annual Meeting of the Canadian Catholic Historical Association" (Sherbrooke, Quebec, October 1, 1940). TS. In the author's possession.

Willey, C. H. "Some Historic Facts about the O'Hara Family." O'Hara TS. Vermont Historical Society, Barre.

Theses

Austin, Michael. "Carving Out a Sense of Place: The Making of the Marble Valley and the Marble City of Vermont." PhD diss., University of New Hampshire, 2002.

Bailey, Henry Albion. "The Administration of the Village of Winooski." Thesis, University of Vermont, 1915.

Bowie, Chester Winston. "Redfield Proctor: A Biography." PhD diss., University of Wisconsin, Madison, 1980.

Cooley, Roger. "Redfield Proctor: A Study in Leadership." PhD diss., University of Rochester, 1955.

Walsh, Brian J. "Dreams Realized? Irish-Americans and Progress, Burlington, Vermont, 1830–1910." Thesis, University of Vermont, 1993.

Pamphlets

Historical Sketch of the Catholic Church in Swanton, 1899. 1899. N.p., 1938.

Leonard, Rev. T. J. *The 100th Anniversary of the Establishment of the Parish: Assumption of the Blessed Virgin Mary, Middlebury, Vermont, 1837–1937.* 1937.

O'Callaghan, Jeremiah. *A Critical Review of Mr. J. K. Converse's Calvinistic Sermon.* 1834.

———. *The Creation and Offspring of the Protestant Church; also the vagaries and heresies of John Henry Hopkins, Protestant bishop, and of other false teachers.* Burlington: Printed for the author, 1837.

———. *The Hedge around the Vineyard.* 1844.

———. *Atheism of Brownson's Review.* 1852.

Reagan, Mary. *A Brief History of Moretown, Vermont, for the Celebration of Moretown's Heritage and St. Patrick's Church Centennial*. N.p., 1982.

Newspapers

Burlington Clipper
Burlington Daily Free Press
Burlington Daily News
Burlington Daily Times
Burlington Free Press
Burlington Sentinel
Fair Haven Journal
Leinster Leader
New York Times
Northern Sentinel
Poultney Journal
Rutland Herald
St. Albans Messenger
Vermont Catholic Tribune
Vermont Chronicle
Vermont Phoenix
Watchman and State Journal

Web Sites

http://members.tripod.com/gail25/que4htm

http://vermontcivilwar.net

http://vermontcivilwar.org/research/myplace.php?input=bakersfield

http://freepagesgenealogy.rootsweb.ancestry.com/~vermontgenealogy

Index

Index

Author Vincent E. Feeney, longtime adjunct professor of history at the University of Vermont, received his doctorate from the University of Washington, where he studied under the renowned Irish historian Giovanni Costigan. Feeney's historical articles have appeared in *Eire-Ireland*, *Vermont History*, *The Vermont Encyclopedia*, and *The Encyclopedia of the Irish in America*, the latter published by the University of Notre Dame Press. He is also the author of *The Great Falls on Onion River: A History of Winooski, Vermont*. Mr. Feeney resides in Marshfield, Vermont, with his wife, Carlen, and continues to research and write history.